TV Fem
and T

M000288273

TV Female Foursomes and Their Fans

Featuring *The Golden Girls,*
Designing Women, Living Single,
Sex and the City, Girlfriends,
Cashmere Mafia and *Hot in Cleveland*

WENDY A. BURNS-ARDOLINO

For Anne,
We are both stranger
than we think!

Hugs,
Wendy

McFarland & Company, Inc., Publishers
Jefferson, North Carolina

ISBN 978-0-7864-5852-3 (softcover : acid free paper) ∞
ISBN 978-1-4766-2232-3 (ebook)

LIBRARY OF CONGRESS CATALOGUING DATA ARE AVAILABLE

BRITISH LIBRARY CATALOGUING DATA ARE AVAILABLE

© 2016 Wendy A. Burns-Ardolino. All rights reserved

*No part of this book may be reproduced or transmitted in any form
or by any means, electronic or mechanical, including photocopying
or recording, or by any information storage and retrieval system,
without permission in writing from the publisher.*

Front cover image © Elena Mikhaylova/Thinkstock

Printed in the United States of America

*McFarland & Company, Inc., Publishers
Box 611, Jefferson, North Carolina 28640
www.mcfarlandpub.com*

For
Cinderella, CJ, Elle, Sara, Griff, Gabriele,
Ruth, Tracella, and the RWT sisters

Acknowledgments

An academic book project may seem in many ways to be a solitary venture, but is not. If it is done well, it requires dialogue with other scholars in the field, and the fields that border it. This means papers presented at conferences, late-night phone discussions with longtime writing partners, and impromptu consultations in hallways, doorways, offices, and coffee shops. I am fortunate be part of a longstanding community of interdisciplinary scholars who have supported and encouraged me on this journey. I am grateful to them for their thoughtful inquiries, for their probing questions, and for their unfailing interest in a project that sits just beyond the edges of their own areas of scholarly inquiry.

I have appreciated the opportunity to present pieces of this larger project to peers at conferences over the past seven years, and more importantly to have received formative feedback from conference attendees at the Southeastern Women's Studies Association, the National Women's Studies Association Conference, the Association of Graduate Liberal Studies Programs, the Cultural Studies Association, and the Popular Cultural Association. These professional organizations provide a sounding board for this new scholarship and members helped to shape the chapters of the larger project as well as provide a framework for conceptualizing the whole project. I would like to claim that I knew all along where the book project was going, but I did not. Instead, I relied on the primary research material, in this case the fan-based message boards, blogs and forums, the dialogue, plots, and narratives of the female foursome shows themselves coupled with historical and contemporary scholarship cutting across the disciplines of cultural studies, media studies, and women's studies. It is at the nexus of these disciplines that this project lives and breathes.

As a scholar-fan, I have come into contact with many other such

Acknowledgments

scholar-fans whose work traverses the fields of feminist media studies, television studies, and popular culture studies. These scholars make it possible for this project to thrive in a world where popular culture studies run the risk of being stigmatized, ridiculed or ignored. The value of understanding how cultural meanings are produced and reproduced through mass culture is intrinsic to a study of this kind. Without active scholarship in the areas of mass cultural production, audience reception, and cultural flow, this project could not exist. In short, I want to be sure to explain that the critical work of wading in the waters of our culture and interrogating the privileged categories of knowledge production have enabled a sharper, clearer, more focused lens for seeing what is in the water of our contemporary popular culture and how it has been constituted through the trajectory of televisual production and reception.

Finally, I would like to thank my family and friends who have endured this long road to complete a project that sounded an awful lot like just watching television and reading message boards. I write for my sons, Adrian and Adam, who have figured out that popular culture is a key element in understanding how society thinks and how culture operates. I write for my husband, who knows that without intellectual community I will surely perish. I write for my sister friends who, like me, know that more diverse and more powerful images of women on television mean the capacity for development of a bolder, more dynamic female imaginary for all of us. Thank you especially to my homegirls standin' to my left and my right, true blue and tight like glue!

Table of Contents

Introduction

As third wave feminist media critics, we recognize that pop culture is a ubiquitous part of our lives. It is therefore necessary to
address it, to develop a reading practice that attends to its contradictions in content, in its role in our lives, and in its attitudes
towards feminism.... Ladies. Love your box.
　　　　　—Merri Lisa Johnson, *Third Wave Feminism
　　　　　and Television: Jane Puts It in a Box*

　　This study represents the continuum of women and worldviews as
articulated by the female foursome shows: *Hot in Cleveland, Girlfriends,
Cashmere Mafia, Sex and the City, Living Single, Designing Women*, and
The Golden Girls. The types and tropes of female characters often repeat
on these programs; however, I argue that these female foursome shows
depict a panoply of perspectives and positionalities that invite viewers
to engage in resistant, negotiated and/or oppositional readings of mainstream, dominant culture. In this way the female foursome shows engage
viewers by offering a broad spectrum of diverse lenses and worldviews.
This is not to say, as is the case with any television program, that a preferred or straight reading is not possible. However, I argue that by providing viewers with hybrid and multi-layered standpoints vividly
represented through dynamic rather than static characterizations, these
programs produce a more politicized viewership. In her much-acclaimed
feminist essay "Performance of Feminine Discourse in *Designing
Women*," Bonnie Dow maintains that the ensemble cast of *Designing
Women* offers a wide multiplicity of viewpoints and positionalities with
which audience members may identify, thereby offering a bevy of choice
to both conservative and more liberal viewpoints (1992, 137). I concur
with Dow's discursive reading of *Designing Women*, and I argue further
that each of these foursome shows follows this model of presenting an
array of diverse characterizations while simultaneously valuing each

woman's distinct voice, vision and positionality within the narrative discourse of the program. Dow also points out the difference between ensemble cast narratives and single woman narratives. Dow notes, "The focus on a single lead character privileges a mode of character reading in which the viewpoint posited by the lead character is the most influential, offering fewer opportunities for the viewer to resist the dominant message of the program" (1992, 137).

Dow articulates the significance of offering a range of positionalities and perspectives vis-à-vis the female foursome characters as opposed to a singular woman's or feminist voice as has been historically the case, demonstrated by ground-breaking sitcoms including but not limited to *The Mary Tyler Moore Show, Maude, Rhoda, Alice, One Day at a Time, Roseanne, Murphy Brown, Grace Under Fire,* and *Reba.* This may raise questions about shows that include pairs of women. Programs like *Kate and Allie, Laverne and Shirley,* and *Cagney and Lacey* present pairs of women offering at least two worldviews or perspectives. While I agree that these programs make valuable contributions to the progressive images of women on television, they do not provide enough space for a continuum of readings or interpretations. In fact, Anne Kaler's analysis of the "four dominant stages of woman's life—as virgin, spouse, mother and wise woman—reveals the need for a balanced presentation of the four aspects of woman (1990, 49). Kaler argues that in early situation comedies, "The feminine fell too easily into stereotypes—the sacrificing mother, the housewife, the career woman, the prostitute—none of which offered a satisfactory archetypal pattern of the feminine" (1990, 50). Ultimately, Kaler maintains that *The Golden Girls* presents a pattern of completeness of the Jungian quaternity of woman that rivals Jung's masculine quaternity of the four gods coming from the four corners (1990, 49–51). In this way, the female foursome series represent a wholeness, a completeness, of a feminine quaternity equivalent to that of ancient Greco-Roman gods and goddesses. Hence the sociohistorical significance of the quaternity, as in the four horsemen of the apocalypse, the four corners of the earth, and the four winds, referenced in western philosophy, folklore, history, literature and art lends itself to an analysis of these female characters in terms of a balanced quadrant or as one quarter of a Beauvoir's category of woman.[1]

In fact, this notion of the quaternity dovetails nicely with Yvette

Lee Bowser's rationale behind the creation of the four female characters in *Living Single*. Bowser states, "I basically divided myself into four. I can certainly be kind of innocent and naïve as Synclaire. I've been as bitter as Max.... I've been as ambitious and maybe as myopic as Khadijah, when it comes to my career. And I've been as superficial as Régine" (qtd. in Brown, Malaika 1995, 42). Bowser's lived experience and creative production depicted in *Living Single* validate Kaler's claim that the complexity of the four parts of woman demand four distinct characterizations, if all are to be adequately explored onscreen. These characterizations both invite the viewer to imagine herself as a composition of four distinct parts of woman and to recognize these representations as feminine archetypes. Television critic Megan Lewit offers further explanation of the proliferation of female foursome shows in recent years. Lewit notes, "Four is a nice round number, intimate enough for each member to play a distinctive and vital role.... They allow for a variety of interactions and shifting allegiances, and avoid the odd-man-out headaches endemic to threesomes" (Lewit 2013). Lewit drills down to a fundamental element of the foursome: balance. The foursome offers the safety of an even number even when divided, and if a member of the foursome does not find support or alliance even with one other member, then clearly she would need to shift her position. However, this rarely occurs in the community of the foursome as in almost every case there is at least one member of the sisterhood who can recognize, understand and/or identify with the strife, strain, or trouble of another. Although this even-steven approach underscores the utopian construct of sisterhood within these female foursome programs, it is important to recognize how the foursome itself functions as a repeating trope of not only televisual production but one of cultural reproduction following the patterns of historical western works of myth, art, music and literature as in the case of the quintessential sisterly foursome depicted in Louisa May Alcott's *Little Women*— Meg, Jo, Beth and Amy. In this way the trajectory of the female foursome develops as a product of the literary and cultural female imaginary providing a safe space, an alternative family, and a mode for sisterhood and solidarity within the public sphere.

Communication scholar Janet Cramer similarly explains how the foursome functions on *Sex and the City* as a repeating trope, a sort of shorthand, allowing the collective relational power of the foursome to develop fully during the series. Cramer writes, "The women represent particular images of women: Miranda is the successful, serious one; Samantha is the lusty vamp; and Charlotte represents a restrained, prudish viewpoint. These, of course, are gross generalizations, but they provide a short-cut understanding of the way these characters are portrayed. Carrie is the one who holds the group together, and her narration is the thematic glue of the program as well" (Cramer 2007, 413). Here, Cramer underscores the cultural power of understanding each woman's distinct positionality and perspective, which permits the show to dig deeper into the real, lived and relational experiences of this gaggle of friends, this band of sisters who form an alternative family. Viewers can easily tune in and catch up on the plot, read the narrative and dialogue, and get up to speed with the thematic issue of the episode without having watched each sequential episode. This foursome framework allows the trajectory of the program to progress quickly while continuously drawing on the shared conceptual understanding of the repeating foursome tropes upon which viewers rely and with which fans identify.

In fact, there has been a proliferation of quizzes/surveys asking viewers to identify themselves in terms of one of the characters on the female foursome shows.[2] Similarly, television studies scholar Ashley Elaine York points out that distributors have begun to cash in on the vantage point of each of the female foursome characters on *Sex and the City* by launching one-sheet advertisements featuring each character individually. York notes that "multiple versions of one-sheets and soundtrack jackets promote ... the movie from the vantage point of all four characters. The motion picture's original soundtrack jacket and its primary one-sheet, in contrast, feature Sarah Jessica Parker's Carrie Bradshaw alone, with ad copy that reads 'Get Carried Away'" (York 2010, 17). Here, the focus on Carrie Bradshaw as the primary character suggests the inherent appeal of this character even within the framework of the foursome wherein each character provides an opportunity for the audience to engage in a more complex understanding of women's lives and women's lived experiences. These female foursome characters encourage the viewer to broaden and deepen her understanding of different worldviews and perspectives while providing a comfortable safety net through self-identification with the character who best reflects her values and tastes. These mixed, multiple and hybrid characterizations open up space for polysemic readings and create the possibility for the production of new meanings which may in turn contribute to the development of new and progressive images and articulations of the women we love to watch—TV female foursomes.

Methods

In her landmark book, *Women Watching Television: Gender, Class, and Generation in the American Television Experience*, Andrea Press examines gender identity by querying the relationship between the images of women on television and female viewers. Press supports the notion that contemporary media scholarship should combine audience reception studies with textual analysis (1991). Press argues that working-class viewers engage in oppositional or resistant readings more often than middle-class women because working-class women stand on the fringes of mainstream dominant culture (1991). Like Press, media studies scholar Robin Means Coleman engages in an ethnographic audience reception study. However, Means Coleman seeks to assess how African American viewers interpret and read Blackness in situation comedies (2000). In this way, Means Coleman broadens the application of ethnographic audience reception studies to include studies of race and, in this case, specifically Blackness. Means Coleman draws on the work of Jacqueline Bobo (1995), Andrea Press (1991) and Janet Radway (1991) to formulate her audience reception study (2000, 11). Means Coleman references Stuart Hall's work concerning the polysemic readings available to viewers (2000, 14). In his early work at the CCCS in Birmingham, Hall discovered the importance of subculture in resisting dominant cultural values. Later, in his much-cited essay "Encoding/Decoding," Hall explains that viewers may engage in preferred, oppositional or negotiated readings of television (1980). More recently, Merri Lisa Johnson expands on Hall's understanding of resistant, oppositional and/or alternative readings in her edited collection, *Third Wave Feminism and Television: Jane Puts It in a Box* (2007). Here, Johnson and her contributors move the reader beyond the well-trodden binary of cultural dupe models of television criticism versus visual pleasure readings of popular programming. Collectively, these contributors consider the performance of gendered and sexed identities found in the new millennium's post-network era of television as viewed through the hybrid and queered lens of third-wave feminist theory (2007).

Hence, I bring Hall's theories of preferred (dominant culture), oppositional (resistant), and negotiated readings of television, Means Coleman's African American reception study of situation comedies, and the queered lens of Johnson et al.'s third-wave feminist readings of contemporary television to bear on the audience reception data collected from fan-based message boards and forums. While Means Coleman, Bobo, and Radway's studies include in-depth interviewing, I engage in an online observational study of fan-based message boards and forums, focusing on fan posts as articulations of their preferred, negotiated and/or oppositional readings of these female foursome programs and characters. It seems important to note the extent to which these fan-based message boards function as a space for women's candid conversation and interaction with not only televisual critique, but cultural critique as these female foursome programs and characterizations function as lenses for fans' collective and shared perspective. Critical studies scholar Anikó Imre points to online fan communities as spaces for shared knowledge production in the United States and Britain, and notes that in Eastern Europe "postsocialist discussions of feminism are isolated from the fan venues formed around *Sex and the City* and similar programs" (2009, 403). In this way, Imre underscores the potential for consciousness-raising and politicization through fan-based postings.

Referencing online posts from fan-based message boards, forums, and blogs, I engage in the practice of an audience reception study of online communities formed in response to these female foursome shows and characters. It should be noted that the original runs of many of these shows were completed between ten and twenty-five years ago, and yet participation in online fan communities continues well into the new millennium.[3] Although I consider myself a scholar-fan,[4] the intensity of fandom for these female foursome shows as demonstrated by continuous and long-term posting in fan forums came to me as something of a surprise. As I closely read and analyzed more than one hundred pages of fan posts per series (more than a thousand messages posted per series) for programs that completed original runs as early as 1992 (in the case of *The Golden Girls*) and as late as 2008 (in the case of *Girlfriends*), I recognized the critical need for an online fan-based audience reception study.[5]

Hence, communication and media studies methodologies of online fandom influenced this study (Monaco 2010; Lotz & Ross 2004; Hills 2002). In particular, the content analysis of the repeating archetypes of the mother, child, iron maiden and sex object in *Living Single, The Golden Girls* and *Sex and the City* by communication scholar Deborah Ann Macey (2008) precipitated this online reception study. At the end of her content analysis, Macey calls for (1) a content analysis of the characters without the categories already in place; (2) a study comparing more recent recombinant[6] characters on programs such as *Girlfriends* and *Cashmere Mafia*, and (3) an audience reception study of these series (Macey 2008, 203). I intend this study to both answer Macey's call for an updated audience reception study of more recent recombinant characters on female foursome shows and to further the integration of textual analysis with audience reception data in order to advance research in the fields of cultural studies, media studies, and women studies in the subfield of feminist television studies. Indeed, this research is situated at the nexus of these three larger fields wherein popular culture studies intersect with feminist theories focused on the representations of women in media, and both cultural studies and media studies present nuanced methodological approaches to online fandom studies. That television evinces the meaning-making capacity to continue to shape viewers' shared conceptual map of the world decades after the airing of the last episode of a program suggests the profound power of the televisual experience for viewers. In fact, a *Designing Women* viewer, ML, recently posted, "My sister just gave me advice from this show [*Designing Women*], and she has an episode for every life event" (March 1, 2012).

Postings by viewers who identify with the female foursome characters of *Hot in Cleveland, Girlfriends, Cashmere Mafia, Sex and the City, Living Single, Designing Women,* and *The Golden Girls* currently continue in fan forums. Fan posts refer to favorite episodes, outlandish characters, treatment of social issues and problems, longtime program narratives, and the culture of the forum itself. In many ways, my research replicates the methodological approach of Amanda Lotz's study in which she addresses the discursive trends of fan postings in the Lifetime Lounge.[7]

Analysis of the postings revealed four discursive trends that describe many of the viewer's contributions. The first type of comment thanks Lifetime for airing the series and often expresses concern about whether the series is in danger of cancellation.... A second discursive trend is a brief, but intense discussion of an issue, often arising because of the issue-orientation of the series.... In contrast, the third discursive trend marks the discussion of a specific topic relevant to the series' long-term narrative.... The final discursive trend I consider relates less to the discussion of the series and more to the culture of the discussion space. Here I consider the way the discussants negotiate differences in perspectives among themselves [Lotz 2002, 289].

Following Lotz's model, I similarly categorize the discursive trends in this study into four areas: (1) Messages of Praise; (2) Issue-Focused Discussion; (3) Long-term Narratives; and (4) Discussion Board Culture. Like Lotz, I also chose not to post to the message boards myself, but instead collected data, coded postings and analyzed the discourse of the discussion boards. Lotz states, "I made a conscious decision not to post to the web site, at least until the conclusion of my research project. I was concerned that even when joining discussion of the series as a fan, my scholarly interest in how aspects of feminism and postfeminism appear in the series would influence discussion" (2002, 288–289). After initially making posts to the Lifetime bulletin boards, and then reading Lotz's study, I decided not to post to any of the bulletin boards or forums in this study. Over a ten-year period from January 2002 to January 2013, I reviewed and coded fan posts about these female foursome shows and characters on the following forums, message boards and blogs: imdb. com; tv.com; designingwomenonline.com; racialicious.com; ew.com; topix.com; and sitcoms and other yucky stuff on tvwop.com. For each female foursome show, I reviewed over a thousand posts. Fan comments run the gamut from delightfully funny and openly sentimental to shrewd and hypercritical. Fans quickly point out their favorite—and least favorite—episodes and characters. Discussions include detailed readings of episodes, characters' lives, relationships among the characters, background materials, plotlines, narratives, and dialogue. Through close reading, fans participate in resistant and negotiated readings even as they acknowledge preferred meanings.

My analysis of these fan-based sites of discussion reveals that fans of these programs do not blindly accept the content of these female foursome shows, but rather, they engage in a meaning-making process. Ultimately, these fan-based message boards, forums and blogs become at once a site of cultural meaning making and contestation as well as a subcultural homeland for disenfranchised television fans of shows that are often replayed on TV Land, Oxygen, the WB, TBS and other cable networks (or via DVDs that are marketed and sold), but that have long ago ceased to produce original episodes. In this way, the fandom operates as a kind of time capsule while at the same time providing a script for reading contemporary culture against a shared conceptual understanding of these shows. In other words, fans interpret contemporary culture in terms of the worldviews or perspectives offered by the female foursome shows and their respective characters. (As in, What would what would Melanie, Joy, Victoria, or Elka do? What would Maya, Joan, Lynn, or Toni of *Girlfriends* do? What would Juliet, Mia, Caitlin, or Zoe of *Cashmere Mafia* do? What would Carrie, Samantha, Charlotte or Miranda of *Sex and the City* do? What would Khadijah, Max, Synclaire, or Régine of *Living Single* do? What would Julia, Mary Jo, Charlene or Suzanne of *Designing Women* do? What would Dorothy, Blanche, Sophia or Rose of *The Golden Girls* do?) In this way, the fandom operates as a subculture which produces new knowledge and new meanings that are not only reflective of these shows, but reflective of the online fan culture. Hence, the fandom becomes a site of cultural contestation in which new cultural meanings are produced. As bell hooks notes, "Popular culture is the pedagogy of the masses" (hooks 1993).

Instead of television operating purely as a mode of one-way communication in which audiences receive cultural messages, these fan sites evidence audience contestation, negotiation and production of new cultural meanings. These forums, guided only by fan loyalty and commitment to programs and characters, offer a public archive for understanding the cultural contributions of these programs to the collective understanding of fans. Fan sites address a myriad of social, cultural, political and economic concerns, including the representations of women, gender performativity, sex roles, heteronormativity, abortion, miscarriage, menopause, breast cancer, single parenthood, interracial relationships, AIDS, the right to die, chronic fatigue syndrome, pornography, world hunger, obesity, depression, political participation, free speech, the role of women in the church, death and dying, and female friendship (to name a few).

Viewers actively compare the repeating types and tropes on these female foursome programs, but, more significantly, they point to the importance of balance among the quaternity and the trajectory of female foursomes on television.

FS compares *Living Single*, *The Golden Girls*, and *Designing Women*:

Although thinking about it Kim Fields's other show *Living Single* is very similar to *Designing Women* and *The Golden Girls* in its characters:

The book-smart, business minded one: Dorothy on *The Golden Girls*, Julia on *Designing Women*, Keedisha [sic] on *Living Single*

The Sexy one: Suzanne on *Designing Women*, Blanche on *The Golden Girls*, Regine on *Living Single*

The dim-witted one: Rose on *The Golden Girls*, Charlene on *Designing Women*, Synclaire on *Living Single* and then there was the more sarcastic/immature (at times) one: Mary Jo on *Designing Women*, Sophia on *The Golden Girls*, Maxine on *Living Single*.

FS also references *Sex and the City*:

Miranda is the Dorothy character
Samantha is the Blanche character
Charlotte is the Rose character but that's where it ends because i definitely don't see Carrie as the Sophia character!

Maybe *Sex and the City* is more easily compared to *Designing Women*:

Suzanne is Samantha
Charlotte is Charlene
Miranda is Julia
Carrie is Mary Jo?
I'm not sure it's Carrie that's tripping me up—I'm thinking she's a lot like Mary Jo but she isn't very much like Sophia at all! But Charlotte could in some ways be compared to Mary Jo as well!

LP explains the typologies on *The Golden Girls*:

I don't know—I get the feeling they just wanted to stick with characterization (Blanche loves the men, Rose is a ditz, Sophia is cranky, Dorothy is scholarly, etc.) rather than continuity.

GG agrees:

I think that all of the shows mentioned were produced using the same basic recipe for an all-female show. That recipe being: a sexy one, an intelligent one, a naïve or dumb one, and the fourth one tends to vary between the shows. Of course, the recipe is altered slightly for each show so that each show can bring something of its own to the table, but it is still the same basic recipe. Thus, there are going to be similarities between all of the shows. I personally am a fan of all the shows, but *The Golden Girls* is probably my favorite because it seems to be the "original," if you will, that paved the way for shows like *Designing Women, Sex and the City*, perhaps even *Desperate Housewives*. That's the best way i can explain the similarities.

Here, GG, LP, and FS all point to the fact that these female foursome shows reference the same typologies, the same basic recipes, suggesting that the foursome is a kind of formula or shorthand for representing the whole. These fans also suggest that the formula works and helps them to make comparisons between and among the shows. GG in particular points to the fact that each show can bring something unique while relying on the formula of the female foursome.

Fans also actively discuss the trajectory of the characterizations of the female foursome shows, noting where one show blazes a trail for the next to follow.

MV writes:

> I don't think *Designing Women* was a copy of *Golden Girls*. However I do think *Golden Girls* paved the way for *Designing Women* by proving that a sitcom with four female leads could be successful.

MG notes similarities between *Designing Women* and *The Golden Girls*:

> Julia was Dorothy (the leader, and the one you don't mess with)
> Suzanne was Blanche (the sexy one; vain and self-centered)
> Charlene was Rose (the naïve, (sometimes dim-witted) one)
> Mary Jo may be a combination of all 3 and Bernice was Sophia (the former nursing home resident, lacking some of her [faculties])

OO agrees with MG and expands the comparison:

> The similarities are uncanny and pretty obvious...
> Julia and Dorothy were (more or less) the leaders of each group of women. They were the intelligent, witty women who put things in perspective.
> Charlene and Rose were the naïve ones of the group. When Charlene left, she was replaced by her sister Carlene ... who was the naïve one of the group.
> Suzanne and Blanche were the Southern Belles, the Beauty of the group, the one whom all men were attracted to of the group. They were each wealthy, due to their ex husbands (and later, BJ—who replaced Allison—who replaced Suzanne—was the southern wealthy beauty as well).
> Berniece [sic] and Sophia were the senior citizens, the 'mother' of the group. They are both former nursing home residents, who had a medical problem which allowed them to speak their minds without thinking first.
> The "Girls" lived together, and gathered around the kitchen table to discuss life in general and solve each other's problems.

The "Women" worked together, and gathered around the living room (of Julia's home) to discuss life in general and solve each other's problems.

"Girls" took place in Miami, while "Women" took place in Atlanta.

FS refutes the easy comparison by OO and argues:

Well on the surface there are some similarities in character type and some overlapping plots, but i don't really see much beyond surface comparisons in these two.

Sure they both have characters that might be considered dumb (Rose, Charlene), or trampy (Suzanne, Blanche), etc, but other than that i feel they are very different series.

The Golden Girls created by Susan Harris tends to veer more towards straight out slapstick and broad comedy and goes for quick one-liners whereas Designing Women seems to have a more realistic, political tone to it. Each of the characters on Designing Women grew enormously over the course of their run and learned valuable lessons about themselves, whereas on The Golden Girls characters tended to learn a lesson one week and be back at square one the next week, their [sic] wasn't much character growth.

Now i love both shows, but it's clear to me that Designing Women found its niche very early on and totally came into its own. By the end of the first season it had fine-tuned its characters and plots to the point it had its very own distinct point of view.

I admire both Susan Harris and Linda Bloodworth-Thomason but i don't belive [sic] Designing Women was meant as a copycat at all. The characters and plots of Designing Women were based very closely on Linda's life growing up in Poplar Bluff, Missouri, so i don't think she intended to copy any other show.

Furthermore, Designing Women had a clear point of view—it was a show about these women finding themselves and making it in the world. It had a very clear political viewpoint—and was able to tackle very topical issues that other shows couldn't have dreamt of tackling in such a way. I can't think of a single other show that would have been able to do an episode like "Killing All the Right People" or "Julia Runs over the First Amendment" and gotten away with it. The Golden Girls was a great show but was too focused on slapstick and one-liners that even its most serious episodes never packed quiet [sic] the same punch that a serious Designing Women episode had.

I love both shows but in this case i say Designing Women wins. It's not really a competition though as they are both superb in their own right but other than some surface comparison in the fact the main characters are women i can't see much of a resemblance.

Here, FS points out the distinctions between Designing Women and The Golden Girls, and explains the more intensive politicized viewpoints evinced by the women of Designing Women, particularly Julia. FS understands the value of the more focused, feminist and politicized viewpoint on *Designing Women*, and gives credit to the creator of *Designing Women*, Linda Bloodworth-Thomason. However, FS is also quick to point out that this is not a competition between *Designing Women* and *The Golden Girls*, but rather that both programs make a valuable contribution to the progressive image of women on television.

Certainly, a primary concern of this study is the progressive image of women on television, and many fan posts discuss the changing representations of women on television through active discussions of the trajectory of female foursome shows on television. While some fans credit *The Golden Girls* and/or *Designing Women* with making space for *Sex and the City*, other fans argue the women of *Living Single* are the clear precursors to the women of *Sex and the City*.

KK writes:

> Amazing how you bring this up with the anticipated release of [the movie version of] *Sex and the City*. I've always thought of *Living Single* as the original, with Khadijah as the black SJP [Sarah Jessica Parker] and Synclaire as Charlotte.

JL agrees and notes:

> *Living Single* WAS the unspoken archetype of *Sex and the City*—and I still love that show. I wish it could be brought back.

Both KK and JL suggest that the series that most influenced the creation of *Sex and the City* is *Living Single*. Perhaps the city itself plays a major role in this theory as New York is the site of both *Living Single* and *Sex and the City*. However, *Living Single* takes place in Brooklyn while *Sex and the City* takes place in Manhattan. Although *Living Single* emphasizes many of the same messages as *Sex and the City*, including the importance of an alternative family, woman space, woman culture, and sisterhood and solidarity in the city. Clearly, fans recognize and value the individual contributions of *Sex and the City* and *Living Single* as well as their larger contributions to the continued development of the trajectory of TV female foursomes.

1

Beyond the Binary
Femininity & Feminism on Television

Growing up female with the mass media helped make me a feminist, and it helped make millions of other women feminists too, whether they take on that label or not.
—Susan Douglas, *Where the Girls Are*

Initially this study was intended to identify the repetition of types and tropes in the characterizations of women in comedic dramas and sitcoms where the primary cast featured four females. Identifying the stereotypes was eye-opening in itself, and the tropes of these TV women followed archetypal patterns recognized by many academic fields such as psychology, sociology, and cultural anthropology as well as aesthetic disciplines, including literature, theatre, music, and film. Adding to the critical discourse of the representations of women in the field of media studies continues to be the centralizing goal of this project; however, looking through the lens of critical feminist cultural studies inquiry illuminates other key elements of female foursome—focused shows. Indeed, each of these female foursome programs, *The Golden Girls*, *Designing Women*, *Living Single*, *Sex and the City*, *Girlfriends* and, most recently, *Cashmere Mafia* and *Hot in Cleveland*, evidences a form of solidarity among the characters, a sisterhood, a woman culture, and perhaps most significantly a space for women's candid conversations. The bonds of friendship and alternative family are also represented through a myriad of scenarios challenging women's social, economic, cultural and political empowerment. Both femininity and feminism are negotiated and combined in each of these programs as they depict strong women as feminine, thereby complicating the stereotypes of traditional female characters on television. In fact, all of these programs complicate female stereotypes even as they draw on them as polyvalent images of women and women's perspectives cutting across dialogue, narratives and plot-lines.

While there remains much work to be done in the casting of female roles in film and television, these comedic dramas and sitcoms move us beyond the independent working woman[1] of the 1980s and the soccer super mom[2] of the 1990s and encourage a vision of women as mixed, multiple, hybrid, strong, beautiful, dynamic and often painfully human. In every series, the characters seem to fit into some tried and true typology of the myth of woman and into existing dichotomies, such as the virgin/whore, mother/daughter, or wise woman/naïf; however, even as these characters and their foils reveal themselves, they work with and against one another to confront the social, economic, cultural and even political concerns of everyday American women.

This is not to say that the programs do not succumb to the hegemonic discourses of popular culture, but, rather, to suggest that alternative and resistant readings may be produced as viewers negotiate between these stereotypes and the multiple perspectives represented by the various female foursomes. Each of the series addresses ageism, racism, sexism, heterosexism, and social class oppressions; however, certain structural inequalities predominate in some series and are therefore treated more thoroughly. For example, *The Golden Girls* combats ageism through depictions of active female desire of women over the age of fifty, while upward mobility and racism are addressed in virtually every episode of *Living Single* and *Girlfriends*. Female sexuality and heterosexist values are challenged by *Sex and the City* and traditional Southern femininity and contemporary feminism collide in the plotlines of *Designing Women*. The ways in which these programs employ stereotypical female foursomes to confront and disrupt mainstream cultural ideologies, hierarchies and power relations enables them to contribute to the growth and development of the third-wave feminist movement.

The appeal of these programs is such that avid male and female viewers identify with these characters and the very real life problems with which they struggle. That these programs use humor to deal with larger social, economic, political and cultural issues does not diminish the significance of the problems. Immigration, the HIV/AIDS epidemic, infertility, finance, employment, business ethics, infidelity, religion, death, birth, marriage, friendship, personal success, failure, health and many more issues are all encountered through the lens of heartfelt humor. In *What Would Murphy Brown Do? How the Women of Prime Time Changed Our Lives*, Allison Klein argues that the use of humor by feminist sitcoms is a common method for questioning the status quo (2006, 11). Klein references early sitcoms, including the ground-breaking *Mary Tyler Moore Show* and later programs, including *Maude* and *Rhoda*, noting that these programs paved the way for series such as *The Golden Girls*, *Roseanne*, *Designing Women*, *Murphy Brown*, and *Living Single*, which Klein describes as "the African American precursor to *Sex and the City*" (2006, 28). Hence, Klein marks the trajectory of these provocative and challenging women's sitcoms and connects the dots between the cultural production of a progressive version of feminism on television and the changing conditions of social, economic, political and cultural life experienced by mainstream American viewers.

Indeed the historicity of women on television is most significant in this study of contemporary female foursome programs as is critical evaluation of the stereotypes and tropes evidenced in these shows. The need for more and better audience reception studies is called for both in order to map out the location of this genre of women's television in terms of where it has been and where it is headed. Feminist cultural studies practitioners of audience reception studies continue to examine the negotiation of the complex processes of meaning making, including mass mediated articulations, appropriations of dominant cultural signifiers and significations, reappropriations of subcultural signifiers and identifications, and critical evaluations of dominant cultural values, hierarchies and power relations as they relate to subcultural values, identifications and power relations.[3] Hence, this research incorporates each of these methods of analysis with data from online fan-based message boards in order to evaluate the impact of these programs, storylines and characterizations on contemporary and future characterizations.

The longevity of these programs (except for *Cashmere Mafia*, which I will address later), points not only to successful audience reception of these shows, but is also suggestive of the depth of character development taking place over many seasons. In the case of *The Golden Girls*, the program ran on NBC from 1985 to 1992 for a total of seven seasons and 180 episodes and was shown in syndication on Lifetime Television, the Hallmark Channel, and TV Land (where, as of this writing, it still airs). *Designing Women* ran on CBS from 1986 to 1993 for a total of six seasons and 163 episodes. The show subsequently aired on Lifetime for more than a decade, then on TV Land until 2008. *Living Single* was created by Yvette Lee Bowser, the first African American woman to create a successful primetime series for network television (Zook 1999, 67). *Living Single* ran on FOX from 1993 to 1998 for five seasons and 118 episodes and is still aired on Oxygen. Both *Designing Women* and *Living Single* were threatened with cancellation in the first season, but were saved by fans[4] who wrote the network (9 Lives of *LS*, 1997). *Sex and the City*, created by Darren Starr and based on the book and columns of writer Candace Bushnell, opened up a whole new arena for alternative programming. *Sex and the City* ran from 1998 to 2004 on HBO for six seasons and 94 episodes, was syndicated for a while on TBS and WGN, and is currently aired on E! and Oxygen. *Girlfriends*, created and produced by Mara Brock Akil, is often referred to as the black version of *Sex and the City* or the 21st century version of *Living Single*. *Girlfriends* ran for eight seasons and 172 episodes, commencing in 2000 on UPN and ending in 2008 on the sister network, The CW. Arguably, the 30-something women of *Girlfriends* represent the next generation of mature, independent, professional black women. A more recent comedic drama with a female foursome cast, *Cashmere Mafia*, is also produced by Darren Starr and while it only aired seven episodes, beginning in September of 2008 on ABC, it follows, not surprisingly, a very similar pattern to *Sex and the City*, but with a bit of a twist. In *Cashmere Mafia*, women's careers are not secondary to their lifestyle. Their careers are the core of their lives, which perhaps indicates the reason for its early cancellation. One of the newest female foursome shows, *Hot in Cleveland*, created by Suzanne Martin, began airing in 2010 and remains in syndication on TV Land. Filmed before a live audience, the cast hails from some of the most popular sitcoms in television history: Betty White from *The Golden Girls*, Valerie Bertinelli from *One Day at a Time*, Wendie Malick from *Just Shoot Me* and Jane Leeves from *Frasier*. Fan posts point out the mixed acclaim to which the series opened on TV Land; however, curiosity generated by the extratextual personas of the four lead women characters drew large audiences. BBC writes in TVWOP in 2010:

They got almost 5 million viewers, which is pretty impressive, and can probably thank Ms. Betty White for about 4 million of those! Her comedic timing is still great, and she definitely elevates the show. Jane Leeves is good, she's the only one of the 3 who seems to have a bit of snark, which I like. Wendie is good also, but basically playing the same character she did on *Just Shoot Me*. It works for her, sure, but it's nothing new. Valerie ... I just don't like her as much. She always comes off as sort of fake and too chipper or something, and I don't feel like she's really acting at all in this. More than any of the others, she seems trapped in the late 80s/early 90s range of sitcoms.

However, I would argue that it is indeed the longevity of the core female foursome programs enabling the full development of these women characters that complicates the stereotypes, tropes, and archetypes with which we have become so familiar. The refusal of these characterizations to remain completely static, to instead operate as both familiar but dynamic characters is precisely what makes these programs fascinating. Referencing existing stereotypes and archetypes, I have formulated a framework for categorizing the typologies found on each of these programs.

In a 2007 article entitled "Feminine Archetypal Patterns of the Complete Woman," Anne Kaler uses Carl Jung's four-sided mandala symbol and the division of the human personality—the quaternity—as a framework for reading the characters in *The Golden Girls* as virgin, spouse, mother and wise woman (49). Kaler specifically identifies the presence of the quaternity in the characters of Dorothy as Athena/Minerva figure, Rose as the virginal Artemis/Diana, Blanche as the Aphrodite/Venus and Sophia as the dual Sybil/Hecate figure. Kaler notes, "From episode to episode, the triad shifts slightly to allow the Hera/Juno aspect of the mother of the gods to be subsumed by Dorothy as the strongest person or by Sophia as the wisest. In the same manner, Rose occasionally subsumes the mother's role" (52). Although this is an oversimplification of the types of female characters on *The Golden Girls* and its successors, the fact that Kaler uses the quaternity to read the four female characters indicates that the number four is not arbitrary but supports the notion that the characters are underpinned by a complex set of power relations that simultaneously allow plotlines to play out while maintaining a sense of balance. This is not a purely formulaic occurrence, although this formula of four may come into play as the number appeals in an aesthetic way within ancient and modern western thought. It may come as no surprise that these characters act as foils for one another throughout the programs and keep the audience from going too far afield. In this way, these characteristics may contribute to the wholeness of a single woman as she moves through the traditional life cycle as virgin, spouse, mother, and wise woman. A fan post from 2010 points out the extent to which Betty White's character on *Hot in Cleveland* reinforces, reinscribes, and rearticulates the extra-textual elements of each character from *The Golden Girls*. SSG writes:

> Are the writers trying to make Betty into ALL 4 *Golden Girls*? She's a mix of Rose (when she colored her hair red and not understanding the "downtown" comments), Sophia (with the meanness), Blanche (she's got a steady guy but wants the other one to fight over her AND she's still going out looking for guys) and Dorothy, who periodically says something to center all of them. Betty's playing everyone making little room for the other actresses to have a clear part.

Clearly, each of these characters provides another perspective, a different voice, and another lens through which fans may view social problems, issues and situations.

However, stereotypical characterizations of women pervade American television and cinema. Diana Meehan's provocative book, *Ladies of the Evening: Women Characters of Prime-Time Television*, profiles ten types of female characters appearing on mainstream American television between 1952 and 1982. These types include: (1) the imp—a mischievous child-woman and rambunctious rebel who was only intermittently heroic and seldom womanish (21); (2) the goodwife—miss domestic, a paragon in the home (34); (3) the harpy—an aggressive single woman, strong and overpowering while on the hunt for a man (50); (4) the bitch—no explanation needed; (5) the victim—the most passive of all female characters (64); (6) the decoy—looking weak and appealing, and naïve as the victim, the decoy walks the television streets as bait (73); (7) the siren—insidiously sexy, harmful yet enticing, her seduction of a male character led to his demise (85); (8) the courtesan—an entrepreneur whose satin skirts and saucy tongue suggest a prostitute (89); (9) the witch—sometimes the courtesan gives the impression that she can take advantage of men but she chooses not to do so. The witch leaves no doubt about her power over men and her inclination to use it (95); and, finally, (10) the matriarch—powerful, heroic, prominent, competent, forceful and courageous (101).

Hence, I refer to the types presented by Kaler and Meehan and other tropes that have been widely explored by media studies scholars, including vamp, femme fatale, tragic mulatto, Dixie bitch, unruly woman, gold digger, sapphire, grotesque/monstrous woman, exceptional woman, every woman, and moral interlocutor.[5] Referencing these types, I create a framework combining categories where there seems to be an overlapping or redundancy in the typologies of characters populating these programs (represented in Table 1.1). While each woman exhibits some stereotypical stock character behavior, it is important to emphasize the character development and shifting roles of these women throughout the life of the series. In each case the type of character exists as a foil for another character and, as such, follows certain plotlines, but there are surprises.

The most common foil comes in the form of the virgin/whore dichotomy. The naïve Pollyanna, dumb blonde character appears in each of these female foursome programs. On *The Golden Girls* Betty White plays Rose Nylund, from Saint Olaf, who frequently tells stories about her native town that may or may not have anything to do with the issue of the episode. Lynn Searcy, the *Girlfriends* equivalent of the naïf, is book smart with four master's degrees, but often lacks common sense. Although Synclaire James is a non-blonde African American, she shares with Rose Nylund the characteristics of a naïve small-town girl. Lynn Spangler comments, "As her cousin Khadijah's secretary/receptionist at *Flavor Magazine*, her [Synclaire's] naïveté and insecurity sometimes manifest themselves as incompetence" (Spangler 210). While Charlene Frazier-Stillfield of *Designing Women* represents the classic Pollyanna character, unlike Synclaire and Rose, her competence at work is never questioned. Instead, Charlene's judgment concerning men is frequently under fire. Similarly, Charlotte York of *Sex and the City*, Charlene Frazier of *Designing Women* and Melanie Moretti of *Hot in Cleveland* are depicted as hopeless romantics caught up in the fairy-tale myth of finding Prince Charming. Caitlin Dowd and Mia Mason of *Cashmere Mafia* are also naïve about love, and in the early episodes Mia is crushed when her fiancé leaves her after competing with her professionally and losing. Caitlin is confused about healthy relationships and flits from man to man to woman. Her naïveté is grounded in her confusion over sexual relationships. Additionally, each of these characters exhibit daughter and imp qualities as they are mothered by other characters and by their

Repeating Types and Tropes on *The Golden Girls, Designing Women, Living Single, Sex and the City, Girlfriends, Cashmere Mafia* and *Hot in Cleveland*

	Unruly Woman / Iron Maiden / Wise Witch	Mother / Matriarch / Good Wife / Daughter/Victim / Tragic Mulatto	Naïve/Pollyanna / Dumb Blond / Virgin/Imp / Gold Digger	Jezebel / Whore / Courtesan	Every Woman / Moral Interlocutor / Voice of Reason	Super Woman / Exceptional Woman / (Dangerous Woman)	Femme Fatale / Vamp/Siren / Sapphire (Dixie Bitch)	Grotesque/ Monstrous Woman
The Golden Girls 1985–1992	Sophia Petrillo	Sophia Petrillo	Rose Nylund	Blanche Devereaux	Dorothy Zbornak	Dorothy Zbornak Sophia Petrillo	Blanche Devereaux	Blanche Devereaux
Designing Women 1986–1993	Julia, Suzanne, Mary Jo	Julia Sugarbaker Mary Jo	Charlene Frazier-Stillfield	Suzanne Sugarbaker	Mary Jo Shively Julia Sugarbaker	Mary Jo Shively	Suzanne Sugarbaker	Suzanne Sugarbaker
Living Single 1993–1998	Maxine Shaw	Khadijah James	Synclaire James	Régine Hunter	Khadijah James	Khadijah James	Régine Hunter	Maxine Shaw
Sex and the City 1998–2004	Miranda Hobbes	Carrie Bradshaw Samantha Jones	Charlotte York	Samantha Jones	Carrie Bradshaw	Miranda Hobbes	Samantha Jones	Samantha Jones Miranda Hobbes
Girlfriends 2000–2008	Lynn Searcy	Joan Clayton Maya Wilkes	Lynn Searcy	Toni Childs Lynn Searcy	Maya Wilkes Joan Clayton	Joan Clayton	Toni Childs	Toni Childs Joan Clayton
Cashmere Mafia 2008	Mia Mason Juliet Draper	Juliet Draper Zoe Burden	Caitlin Dowd Mia Mason	Caitlin Dowd Mia Mason	Zoe Burden	Mia Mason Zoe Burden Juliet Draper	Juliet Draper	Juliet Draper
Hot in Cleveland 2010–Present	Elka Ostrovsky	Elka Ostrovsky	Melanie Moretti	Victoria Chase	Melanie Moretti	Victoria Chase	Joy Scroggs	Joy Scroggs

Table 1.1

childlike views of the world. They are impetuous and loving and given to heartbreak.

Heartbreak, however, is rare for the whore/jezebel/courtesan characters. Blanche Devereaux, an aging Southern belle who is most proud of her initials spelling out BED (Blanche Elizabeth Devereaux), is the owner of the home in Miami where *The Golden Girls* foursome live together as an alternative family. Like Blanche, Suzanne Sugarbaker of *Designing Women* is a Southern belle. She epitomizes white, heterosexual, ruling-class femininity and is given to running through men and money in a hurry. Maxine Shaw, from *Living Single*, goes through men as fast as Suzanne, but is characterized as a "man-eater" and is an aggressive and accomplished attorney in her own right (Spangler 211). Toni Childs, from *Girlfriends*, similarly evinces an aggressive attitude toward men and her career. Like Maxine Shaw attorney at law (S2 E4), Toni Childs talks about herself in the third person and publicly sets career goals. Although men and money are more important to Toni, success for Max tends to be measured by the number of court cases won rather than specific financial gains. The softness and femininity of Blanche and Suzanne are not found in Max, Toni or Samantha Jones of *Sex and the City*. Max, Toni and Sam, with their masculine names, are much more vamp and much less siren than Suzanne and Blanche. Thus, Max, Toni and Sam appear to be more dangerous than Suzanne and Blanche; Sam, for example, comes on to a priest, a celibate yoga instructor, and gives her new boss a blow job in his office ("The Agony and the 'Ex'-tacy" S4 E1; "The Drought" S1 E11; "The Good Fight" S4 E13).

While Caitlin Dowd and Mia Mason of *Cashmere Mafia* are impish and almost girlish, they are sexually empowered and given to fits of wild sexual abandon, as demonstrated by Mia's one-night stand with Zoe's manny, Adam ("Stay with Me" S1 E5) immediately after her breakup ("The Deciders" S1 E4). Caitlin similarly conveys her sense of sexual empowerment when she gives a guy her cell number at the bar in spite of the fact that she is attending a baby shower with her lesbian lover. Media studies scholar Angela McRobbie argues:

> But this is not simply a return to the past, there are, of course, quite dramatic differences between the various female characters of current popular culture from Bridget Jones to the girls in *Sex and the City* and to Ally McBeal, and those found in girls' and women's magazines from a pre-feminist era. The

new young women are confident enough to declare their anxieties about possible failure in regard to finding a husband, they avoid any aggressive or overtly traditional men, and they brazenly enjoy their sexuality, without fear of the sexual double standard. In addition, they are more capable of earning their own living and the degree of suffering or shame they anticipate in the absence of finding a husband is countered by sexual self-confidence. Being without a husband does not mean they will go without men [2004, 262].

Hence, the trajectory of stereotypical jezebels, whores, and courtesans is skewed as the earlier sexy, Southern sirens are replaced by hip, urban players. In this way, coy femininity takes a back seat to female sexual pleasure.

However, it is the interplay between the foils and among the foursomes that evokes the most interest. The quaternity—the representation of the four parts of a complete woman—is played out effectively in each of these programs. In fact, Yvette Lee Bowser created *Living Single* as a slice-of-life comedy about four women who are extensions of different parts of herself (Zook 1999, 66). In *Redesigning Women: Television after the Network Era*, Amanda Lotz argues, "Series such as *The Golden Girls*, *Designing Women* and *Living Single* preceded *Sex and the City* with ensembles of diversified female characters and located voices of reason distinctly within one character (Dorothy Zbornak, Julia Sugarbaker, and Khadijah James)" (Lotz 100).

However, I would argue that the voice of reason is somewhat fluid in many of these shows. In the case of *Designing Women*, Julia does not always emerge as the voice of reason. Mary Jo oftentimes assumes this role when she criticizes Julia for her sanctimonious attitude. In episode 144, entitled "Mary Jo versus the Terminator," Mary Jo asks Julia to proof a letter to the editor, and Julia rewrites the entire letter. In the end it is Julia who must apologize for her behavior. In fact, Julia is given to obsessive/compulsive behavior in several episodes. In episode 85, "Payne Grows Up," Julia is not coping well with Payne's decision to graduate early and marry his pregnant girlfriend. Julia drinks too much at the reception and sings a raucous rendition of "Sweet Georgia Brown," complete with kicking her heels up and draping herself over the baby grand piano. Julia wakes the next morning in the bed of Payne's roommate, and it is Suzanne who breaks into the dorm and brings Julia back to her senses. In yet another episode, Julia takes to living a double life as Jazelle,

24

a nightclub singer. When the friends find a matchbox from the Blue Note Club and crash her performance, she tells them that she is tired of being sensible and socially responsible Julia (read feminist Julia); she just wants to do something so completely unlike herself ("How Long Has This Been Going On" S5 E15). Finally, when Julia takes up jogging in the midst of a fitness craze and loses all perspective, her friends (Mary Jo in particular) bring her back to reality ("Nowhere to Run" S5 E8).

If the voice of reason is shared in these programs, then excessive behavior is also exhibited from time to time by all of the cast members. In "Ms. Representation: The Politics of Feminist Sitcoms," Lauren Rabinovitz argues that excessive femininity operates in the feminist sitcom as a counter balance to feminism, the other end of the extremist spectrum (Rabinovitz 149). Hence, the performances of excessive femininity and feminism as portrayed by these stereotypical characters parody the lived experiences of women in American culture while at the same time evoking humor and inviting resistant readings of hegemonic portrayals of real women. Excess is exhibited in these shows: by unruly woman Max and her "prevenge" rather than revenge logic ("Just Friends?" S1 E9); Samantha and her "I'm not having a baby (ever) shower" ("The Baby Shower" S1 E10); Suzanne Sugarbaker and her infinite knowledge of beauty pageants, her obsession with tiaras and hair pieces, all of which are later challenged by her body size; Julia Sugarbaker's quintessential feminist rants; Lynn and her endless stream of dead-end jobs; Blanche and her love of sex and men; Rose and her endless Saint Olaf stories; Régine and her wigs; Carrie and Toni with their four-hundred-dollar shoes and designer handbags; Juliet Draper and her perfectionism; Joan Clayton and her holiday-themed parties; Charlotte York and her fairy tales; Victoria Chase and her blind ambition, and Elka and her bedazzled track suits.

However, in every case, these excesses invite us, the viewers, to recognize the contradictions in ourselves and in the lived experiences of so many women we know. Viewers watch, looking for some common ground, some life experience, something that will resonate.

As Laura Tropp attests in "Faking a Sonogram":

> The over-sexualized Samantha and the prissy Charlotte pose extreme attitudes about motherhood, playing on the paradox to make us laugh. In fact, these two characters represent the two extremes of the Whore/Madonna

> dichotomy. Charlotte represents the desexualized "good" woman and potential mother, while Samantha is the over-sexualized "bad" antimony. Miranda, though, struggles with definitions of what is a good mother and what she feels are her limited skills in achieving ideal motherhood [Tropp 2006, 863].

In this way, the excessive stereotypical behavior of Samantha and Charlotte play off and against each other even as Miranda represents the third space in the binary. Miranda actually mediates the binary opposition between Samantha and Charlotte, providing us with the every woman voice while offering us the conflicted agency of the "trying to be a good enough mother" (Tropp 2006, 863).

This issue of the good-enough mother is also broached by Charlene and Mary Jo in season five of *Designing Women* (97 "Working Mother"). Tensions boil over when Charlene finds out that she has missed seeing her daughter, Olivia, take her first steps. Charlene decides to become a stay-at-home mom, and Mary Jo is simultaneously jealous that Charlene has the luxury to choose this lifestyle and angry that Charlene is so willing to give up her career to stay home. Mary Jo chides Charlene for watching soap operas and lying around the house all day. Charlene defends herself, arguing that she wants what is best for her daughter. Later, Mary Jo states, "Whatever choice a mother makes, she feels guilty about it, and that women who choose to work outside the home and women who choose to work inside the home need to support one another" (97 "Working Mother"). This notion of choosing how to mother in a world that creates tensions between these groups of women complicates the cultural production of motherhood. For Mary Jo, who is a divorced, single mom, working is not a choice. Charlene must confront the guilt of her economic privilege as well as the guilt of leaving her work and her workplace friends behind.

Although this conflict is inevitably smoothed over in classic sitcom style as the friends make up, the problems faced by working moms and stay-at-home moms are clearly not completely addressed. However, as Charlene accepts the delivery of a desktop computer that will allow her to telecommute, the stereotypes of working moms and stay-at-home moms become more complicated, and there is an allusion to the complex network of social relations undergirding the relationships among women, work, and family. Both the *Sex and the City* and *Designing Women* episodes may be viewed as examples of third-wave feminist logic as they suggest ways to negotiate the role of motherhood in very real ways that would likely not be possible without a female foursome cast.

Representing the complete woman in the form of the quaternity and providing multiple lenses for viewing situations, issues and concerns, the female foursome marks a change in television production. This shift is, in part, attributable to competition for target audiences. As Jackie Byars and Diane Meehan argue, cable narrowcasting provides an environment for women's television and the Lifetime network fills one niche (1994). The syndicated runs of *The Golden Girls* and *Designing Women* are well documented on Lifetime. Also, the Fox Network, UPN, and others provoked the big three networks to target female audiences. Byars and Meehan attribute Reaganist deregulation of the airwaves with the network's invasion of the cable industry (1994, 22). The result is the proliferation of specialty channels and narrowcasting that opens up new niche markets for television programming and advertising. Thus, it is no surprise that *Sex and the City* emerges from a secondary phase of network expansion as premium cable channels, such as HBO, Showtime, and Cinemax, garner a chunk of the independent working-woman target market.

This invocation of a new market of TV consumers calls into question the brand of femininity and feminism being proffered by these female foursome programs. Critiques of these shows are frequently concerned about what brand of feminism is trafficking on what programs. Contemporary critics often designate these programs and women's television in general from the 1980s onward, including such programs as *Cybill, Ally McBeal, Suddenly Susan,* and *Caroline in the City* as postfeminist and indicative of a consumerist telefeminism which targets middle-class women with white collar jobs who control their disposable income (Meehan and Byars 2000). Angela McRobbie argues that tropes of freedom and choice that have been proffered as a form of "young women" feminism that operates as a complexification of Susan Faludi's backlash thesis and could perhaps best be described as a double entanglement of freedom and control resulting in a re-invented feminism (McRobbie 2004). Indeed, the representation of privilege, upward mobility and female consumerist "choiceoisie" pervades each of the female foursome programs (Lotz 2006, 115). Bambi Haggins addresses the notion of the incomplete fulfillment of the American Dream in African

American sitcoms as she illuminates the problematic relationship between being black and "movin' on up" in America (Haggins 1999). The depiction of four upwardly mobile black women on *Living Single* is indeed ground breaking. However, Haggins concludes that the myth of the American Dream, which she defines as unlimited consumerism, is only truly accessible to privileged African Americans, once referred to as the talented tenth (1999, 34). In this way the American Dream remains unfulfilled for many Americans because of the requirement of affluence, privilege and social mobility. However, women and people of color are disproportionately denied access to the kind of upward mobility and consumption proffered as the American Dream as depicted by the *Living Single* lifestyles. Similar criticisms of *The Cosby Show* explain the double-bind of representing upwardly mobile images of people of color while producing a homogenized, consumerist image of black American families (Bogle 2001; Means Coleman 2000; Smith-Shomade 2002). Yet, for those who achieve the socioeconomic status necessary to obtain a piece of the American Dream, the dream still remains unsatisfying because of the postmodern shift away from valuing social mobility and a better life to an entrenchment in extreme, fetishized commodification and consumerism: the American obsession with having it all.

This obsession with material wealth becomes a focal point for the women of *Girlfriends* as they judge one another based on material success. Joan struggles to decide whether to leave her profession as a lawyer to engage her dream of becoming a restaurateur. She finds little support for her dream as all of the girlfriends point out that she is giving up her financial success. In fact, when the J-Spot (Joan's restaurant) is not an instant success, Joan begins to panic.

Similar criticisms may be made of each of the female foursome programs. *The Golden Girls*, the *Designing Women* and the *Cashmere Mafia* are privileged in terms of race, education, extended family relationships, social class and personal wealth. Charlotte, Carrie, Miranda and Samantha of *Sex and the City* are arguably the most affluent and privileged representations of women on television. *Sex and the City* shamelessly proffers a liberal choiceoisie lifestyle in the form of fetishized commodities, complete with Manolo Blahnik and Jimmy Choo shoes, Birkin Handbags, and Canary diamonds, signifying the attainment of the bourgeois bohemian or bobo lifestyle (Arthurs 2003, 86). The conflation of consumerism, privilege and independent working women obscures contemporary feminist visions. Indeed, many critiques of these programs dwell on the mediated or re-mediated, repackaged, co-opted, re-appropriated form of hegemonic postfeminist discourse sold by these programs (Brown 1990; Press 1991; Feuer 1995; McDonald 1995; Rabinovitz 1999; Meehan and Byars 2000; Kim 2001; Arthurs 2003; Brasfield 2006). In fact, the discourse of feminist media scholarship is rife with debates over what type of feminist and/or postfeminist trajectories are signaled by the progression of these female foursome programs and indeed women's television in general. In *Bad Girls: Cultural Politics and Media Representations of Transgressive Women*, Susan Owen, Sarah Stein and Leah Vande Berg argue compellingly that although *Sex and the City* directly challenges patriarchal power structures through representations of contemporary sisterhood, alternative family, female sexual empowerment, women's agency and a new addition to the feminist cultural imaginary, *Sex and the City* confuses consumptive pleasure with real political power (2007, 117–129).

However, third wave feminist scholars are quick to point out that we have moved beyond the binary of feminism versus femininity, and that there is no monolithic form of feminism. Third wave feminism is decidedly mixed, multiple and hybridized, albeit infused with consumerist values that problematize both its legitimacy and its political verve. In spite of the diversified feminist positionalities, feminist media scholars focus on the alternative images of female empowerment as well as ways for women to navigate through the interstices of the interlocking systems of oppression decried by bell hooks as imperialist, white supremacist, heterosexist, capitalist, patriarchy (hooks 1992b). The ways in which women in the female foursome programs move against these oppressive power structures and/or negotiate around them is the fodder for much third wave feminist media scholarship. The palpable tension between feminism and femininity in these programs brings to the fore a shared discovery that women can be both feminine and empowered. Women in these female foursome programs demonstrate how to both grow old gracefully and fight ageism every step of the way. They portray women who feel boxed in by definitions of femininity and motherhood, but whose ways of being in the world fly in the face of traditional femininity while maintaining their womanism. They approach controversial (and seemingly not so controversial) cultural identities for women as leaders, bosses, single mothers, lesbian, bi and trans, cross-dressers, drag kings, breadwinners, and autonomous and desiring subjects. In every case, the women on these shows confront social stigmas while relying on a sisterhood, an alternative family and tapping into a social network of friends, providing not only a forum for discussion but a safe space for personal inquiry and decision making. The woman culture, woman space, and woman talk that emerges from these programs provides an image of female solidarity, alternative family, and cooperative environment for growth and development. While debates will certainly rage on about whether these shows are feminist or postfeminist, the reality is that these programs move beyond the binary and occupy the third space that is third wave feminism, enabling viewers to engage in resistant readings of contemporary culture.

The palpable tension between femininity and feminism in these series, particularly as conveyed through the dynamic relationships between characters who continually act as foils for one another, is precisely what keeps viewers watching. The fuller development of these characters moves us beyond the binary of feminism and femininity as foils collide and sometimes even switch positions in unpredictable ways. For example, in an episode of *Sex and the City* titled "Frenemies," Charlotte comes around to Samantha's way of thinking about sex (S3 E16). Charlotte—the classic, naïve, Pollyanna, virgin—prefers to idealize sexual relationships as an expression of deep and abiding love within a committed, monogamous partnership; Samantha—the embodiment of the jezebel, vamp, whore, unruly woman stereotype—engages in sex for pleasure. At brunch, Samantha is regaling her friends with her tales of her latest sexual conquest, and Charlotte stops her saying, "I can't take this anymore. Sex is something special that is supposed to happen between two people who love each other." Samantha retorts, "Or two people who love sex." Frustrated, Charlotte implies that Samantha is vulgar, sexually promiscuous, and a wanton woman, such a whore (S3 E16).

Charlotte decides that she needs to distance herself from Samantha and calls up her Kappa Kappa Gamma sorority sisters from college, believing that their conservative viewpoints on sex, marriage and love will be more in keeping with her own. Charlotte sits in an uptown restaurant, talking with her new, old, friends about being newlyweds. Her friend Sydney comments, "I remember being a newlywed. We hardly ever got out of bed" (S3 E16). Charlotte takes this opportunity to discuss her sexual relationship with Trey. Charlotte shares too much, saying, "My husband can't get it up. I'm so frustrated. I mean don't you ever just want to be really pounded hard? You know? Like when the bed is moving all around and it's all sweaty and your head is knocking up against the headboard and you feel like it just might blow off? Damn it! I just really want to be fucked, just really fucked!" However, Charlotte's sorority sisters disdain her vulgar oversharing and overtly treat Charlotte as a wanton woman and maybe even a whore. In that moment, Charlotte knows exactly what she has done to Samantha

The dialogue has come full circle. Charlotte is asking the same question of these women that Samantha asked of her. The question might be asked: Am I a whore? Am I a slut? Am I a loose woman for talking this way about my sexual pleasure? In this case, Charlotte occupies the same subject position as Samantha, and in that very uncomfortable spot, she understands the problematic binary relationship of sexual empowerment and femininity. This moment of recognition blows the virgin/whore dichotomy right out of the water and challenges the viewer to define the cultural identity of the whore. This moment is at once freeing and a damning indictment of Charlotte's façade and her moral pontifications above love, sex, and relationships because for now, at least, the ground has shifted.

Shifting ground between characters is common in each of these series, and becomes the focal point of the often fraught relationship between Max and Régine on *Living Single*, with Khadijah frequently operating as intermediary. In the inaugural episode of *Living Single*, Régine finds out that Brad, the man she has been dating who is "fine, educated, wealthy and has a good butt," is married ("Judging by the Cover" S1 E1). Régine is hurt and angry and asks why this always happens to her. Max comments, "Because you keep looking for someone to carry you." Khadijah adds, "And they keep dropping your ass. You gotta start taking care of yourself, put Régine first, do what you gotta do for you" (S1 E1). Throughout much of the series and all of the first season, Régine takes the heat as she represents the most stereotypical image of patriarchal womanhood while pining for a man to fulfill her desires.

In a later episode, titled "Love Takes a Holiday," Max, the unruly vamp, shrew feminist, again squares off against the gold digger jezebel Régine as they watch Kyle become too quickly entangled with a woman on the rebound from a recent break up (S1 E13). Régine explains how a man becomes impaired and his judgment may be clouded when he is in love, leading him to spend too much money on expensive gifts he cannot afford. Max retorts, "Régine, every time you open up your mouth, you set sisters back about a hundred years." Régine quips, "Max, next time you're marching for women's rights look up, that's me in the box seat; and I'll have fur on my back and a man on my arm" (S1 E13). Although they both see their friend, Kyle, making a fool of himself over a woman, Régine and Max disagree on how a woman should comport herself in a relationship with a man. While Max cannot imagine depending on a man for anything, Régine is waiting for a man who will provide for her. Thus, the oppositional relationship between Max and Régine is firmly established in the first season and continues in some form throughout the series.

In spite of the fact that Régine appears as the most stereotypical character in the series and is mocked for her materialism, her reliance on men, and her many hair changes, both Régine and Max operate as transgressive and unruly women. Their oppositional characterizations enable their dynamism to avoid complete co-optation by hegemonic forces. For Régine, this means that her over-the-top and stereotypical femininity evidenced through ever-changing hairstyles, shop-a-holic mentality, and gold digger behavior arguably present a politics of resistant femininity and choiceoisie feminism (Sheppard 2007, 88). Régine is repeatedly ridiculed by Max and others for wearing horse's hair wigs, but she defiantly refuses to succumb to the idea that a progressive black woman should be limited in her expression by her hair. Régine changes her hair to match her clothes, her environment, and her mood. Beretta Smith-Shomade argues, "Through her variant Black hair Régine formed a quasi-resistance to the homogeneous identity imposed by White culture ... her hair contributed to progressive Black women's representation beyond the stereotype" (2007, 64). In this way, Régine politicizes her hair. Indeed, she uses her wardrobe, her hair, her body and her femininity as tools to resist a singular identity. Régine refuses to be cowed by Eurocentric beauty standards, and she defies the image of the already racialized, exoticized other.[6] Régine is not a victim, and while she plays the part of the gold digger, jezebel, courtesan, the power of her character comes from her willfulness, her unruly desires, and her outright refusal to be limited or reduced to an image of passive femininity.

This resistance to idealized traditional femininity and stereotypical militant feminism is exemplified by each of the female foursome series. In fact, the stereotyped foils complicate the longstanding binary between feminism and femininity. These programs ultimately open up a space for mixed, multiple and hybrid female identities as they reject what Bonnie Dow names as "monolithic definitions of femininity or feminism" (1996, 119). Indeed woman space, woman talk, woman culture, alternative families, sisterhood and female solidarity are all evidenced through an embrace of the multiple identities of characters on these female foursome programs. Dow notes, "The focus on personal interaction and women's talk in *Designing Women*, the possibility for identification with multiple characters, and the resistance encouraged by some episodes' open endings contribute to construction of feminist discourse that challenges postfeminist assumptions in popular culture and in other television programming" (1996, 121). Thus, Dow argues that the blurring of lines between work as public space and home as private space contributes to the capacity for consciousness-raising and feminist discourse.

While Dow specifically addresses this phenomenon in terms of *Designing Women*, I would argue that each of these female foursome programs presents a similar forum for consciousness-raising. In the case of *The Golden Girls*, Blanche, Dorothy, Sophia and Rose hash out their problems and celebrate their successes around the kitchen table with cheesecake, ice cream and whipped cream. For the women of *Girlfriends*, Joan's home and her home cooking are most often at the center of their candid conversations. On *Sex and the City*, Carrie, Miranda, Charlotte and Samantha share their hopes, fears, desires and problems over brunch or cocktails, with each woman's beverage or food reflecting her personality or mood. *Living Single*'s Khadijah, Max, Régine and Synclaire mix things up by watching television, sprawled out over the living room couch or in the kitchen, but food remains as a centerpiece for these heart-to-heart discussions. Finally, Zoe, Caitlin, Mia and Juliet always rally round for drinks before engaging in heavy conversation. In the case of each series, the female foursome's friendship, solidarity, and sisterhood are undergirded by gathering together in a woman space, to engage in woman talk and to share their individual struggles and successes in what can only be described as woman culture. In this way, these programs are indicative of a kind of woman talk, woman space, and woman culture that resonates with viewers and promotes opportunities for women to follow through on some of the goals of consciousness-raising groups.

This is not to say that the conversations are always feminist, particularly because they rarely address structural oppression and neglect to contextualize personal struggles within a broader social context. However, these shared experiences among these female foursomes do often seem to get to the heart of the matter even when resolution is not reached. The friends reassure one another that no matter what happens, they will sustain one another. They are one another's support and comfort, even if they have to share the burden of bad news. In the pilot episode of *Cashmere Mafia*, Zoe calls an emergency meeting to tell Juliet that her husband, Davis, is having an affair with a mutual acquaintance, Cilla Gray. Mia, Caitlin, and Zoe meet with Juliet prior to a charity dinner party. Zoe explains that she had witnessed a passionate kiss between Davis and Cilla. Juliet intones, "Look at what a man gives up to be with one of us. We make more money. We rise higher. We take up more space. We are as far from the idea of a wife he grew up with as it's possible to be and still wear his ring and go by his last name" (Pilot). Juliet explains that she is not defending Davis's cheating behavior, but she is articulating how the success of the *Cashmere Mafia* flies in the face of conventional gender roles in both the public and private spheres. Juliet describes the price for this professional success as coming at a cost. She is buying into the binary logic that there is a cost to being a wife, mother and professional. She is questioning the potentiality for a blended, hybrid, mixed and happy life. Juliet hints at her problem in the context of a wider social phenomenon concerning exceptional women. There is a price to be paid for being this exceptional woman, and those who pursue professional careers while juggling marriages and families are at risk. The suggestion is that these women are not balancing their personal and professional lives, but, rather, they are careening toward certain collapse of their marriage, their careers, and/or their families.

This problematic tug-of-war between the public and private spheres, among the gender roles of wife, mother, and career professional come to the surface again when Mia calls the Cashmere Mafia together to celebrate her promotion to magazine publisher. She is promoted after winning a competition to sell more advertising dollars than her colleague and fiancé, Jack Cutting. Zoe, Caitlin and Juliet rush to toast her victory, but when they arrive, Zoe quickly brings the others up to speed and comments, "Mia got the job, and Jack called it off." Caitlin replies, "Oh my God. I'm so sorry. And screw him!" Mia quips, "Well, not anymore" (Pilot). In spite of the cause for celebration, the mood is conciliatory. Mia explains, "Well, I got the job whether I won or not I'm not so sure." Zoe responds, "That whole having-it-all thing, I think it's a crock." (Pilot) The message from Juliet's monologue still hangs in the air suggesting how hard it is for men to be in relationships with members of the *Cashmere Mafia* because, as professionals, they consistently out perform their male counterparts.

In this way the pilot episode of *Cashmere Mafia* sets up the binary relationship between having it all or having nothing, between the public and private spheres, between women and men, the battle of the sexes. While fan-based criticisms of *Cashmere Mafia* suggest that the cancellation of the show after one season is partially attributable to its thematic, cinematic and character replication of *Sex and the City*, I argue that *Cashmere Mafia* comes on too strong for avid viewers of *Sex and the City*. There is too much at stake, too much of a threat in the über-intelligent super achiever women of *Cashmere Mafia*. They are *too* exceptional, and their identities do not jive with mainstream dominant culture. Setting the pilot up as a winner-take-all, sudden-death competition between fiancés, Mia and Jack, does nothing to ameliorate the very real struggle of viewers to balance gender roles as mothers, partners and professionals. In making the statement that having it all is a crock, Zoe does not resonate for viewers, as it offers them no hope. Media studies scholar Kimberly Springer argues, "Having it all discourse implies that women are lacking something that they need to go out and get: career and family" (2007, 74). Springer situates this argument within the broader framework of postfeminism, and, like Zoe Burden, suggests that having it all is indeed a crock.

Hence, I argue that this postfeminist depiction of Mia losing her fiancé over a job in the first season kills the show. The postfeminist narrative that denies the possibility of balance and having it all denies viewers hope. However real or accurate this depiction, it is undesirable.

Viewers simply turned postfeminism off, or better still, changed the channel to a rerun of another female foursome program.

However, the pilot ends with the Cashmere Mafia making a toast to friends in high places as Mia sighs wistfully, "I don't know what I would do without you girls" (Pilot). This ending to the pilot episode solidifies the female solidarity and sisterhood of the Cashmere Mafia with that of their predecessors from *Girlfriends, Sex and the City, Living Single, The Golden Girls* and *Designing Women*. The female foursome casts from sitcoms and comedic dramas continue to depict the development of televised woman talk, woman space and woman culture for new generations of viewers. In this way these female foursome programs represent a viewing continuum.

2

Matriarchs, Naïfs, Jezebels & Virgins

> Any work of popular culture is successful as long as it replicates a familiar psychological pattern of completeness. Until recently, no television show approached this healing pattern of the complete woman—the autonomous androgynous blend of the four dominant stages of a woman's life—as virgin, spouse, mother and wise woman.
>
> —Anne K. Kaler, "*Golden Girls*: Feminine Archetypal Patterns of the Complete Woman"

Despite the best efforts of western feminism (as first articulated by Simone de Beauvoir in *The Second Sex*[1]) to deconstruct the virgin/whore dichotomy, these female archetypes persist in western culture and continue to be further reified through the lens of contemporary American cinematic and televisual milieus. The matriarch, naïf, jezebel and virgin live large on the small screens of female foursome television series. Although postmodern feminist theorists (Bartky 1988; Beauvoir 1989; Bordo 1993; Collins 2000; hooks 1992b) continue to critique the virgin/whore dichotomy, it still remains as a repeating and dominant trope in these progressive women-centered programs. Frequently, the role of the naïf, often a childlike daughter character, overlaps with that of the virgin in female foursome series. In contrast, the matriarch rarely embodies the characteristics of the whore. Instead, the modern-day whore appears either in the form of a dangerous woman—femme fatale, vamp, siren, sapphire—or she comes in the form of a jezebel, diva, or gold digger. Women's studies scholars Dionne Stephens and Layli Phillips argue that the archetypal roles of the matriarch, jezebel, mammy and welfare mother proliferate under postmodern hip-hop culture to produce contemporary images of African American women as divas, gold diggers, freaks, dykes, gangster bitches, sister saviors, Earth mothers, and baby mamas (2003, 6). Although these stereotypical mass-mediated images of African American women dominate mainstream culture, the evidence of negotiated and/or resistant readings by viewers of *Girlfriends* and *Living Single* prevail in online fan-based forums and blogs.

In her *Racialacious* blog titled "TV Flashback," LaToya Peterson explains her reading of *Living Single* more than ten years after its original run (April 2008). Peterson writes:

A few things that stand out to me now:

1. The show was excellent with its portrayals of black love. Just excellent. Sinclair and Overtons' relationship was a given, but all the other characters had dalliances back and forth that were for the most part, respectful and loving. I'm wondering what happened to these kinds of portrayals of black romance.

2. Their lifestyles look decidedly normal. Though I remember reading criticism somewhere that the kind of brownstone they had in New York would probably be out of reach, watching the show as an adult reinforces to me that the '90s were a time of more realistic TV. There are four successful professional women on the show, but only one lives alone (Max). More often than not, the people on the show were dressed down in jeans, jerseys, and in Sinclair's case, overalls. And what's even better to me is that they *act* like friends. Even within the ridiculous comedy setups, the dialogue is gifted in showing how people actually talk and relate to each other.

3. Everyone was doing something of note—check out the descriptions of the characters:

The series focuses on two different households in one brownstone (although, as the later seasons revealed, there are more apartments in the building): one shared by a trio of upward[ly]-mobile women and another shared by a pair of male friends who have known each other since they spent their youth in Cleveland, Ohio. Khadijah James, a hardworking editor and publisher of the fictional urban independent monthly *Flavor*, shares an apartment with her sweet but naïve cousin Synclaire (originally the role of Synclaire was to be played by British rapper Monie Love, a long-time friend and music collaborator of Queen Latifah), an aspiring actress who works as Khadijah's receptionist and has an affinity for Troll dolls; and her childhood friend Régine Hunter, an image-conscious boutique buyer who was in constant search of a well-to-do man to spend her life with, often referring to said potential man as her "Chocolate Ken" and later became a costume assistant for a soap opera called *Palo Alto* with a fondness for gossip and wigs. Maxine "Max" Shaw, a sharp-tongued attorney and Khadijah's best friend, stops by frequently to share her unique insights and make sure the girls' refrigerator isn't overstocked.

Living in the apartment above are Overton Wakefield Jones, a friendly handyman who holds deep affection for Synclaire; and Kyle Barker, a handsome stockbroker whose constant verbal sparring with Max does little to mask their obvious sexual attraction.

And the best part is by the end of the show, all of the characters have shown some kind of growth within their careers.

4. It occurs to me that Kyle and Overton may have been the first metrosexuals on TV. Watching some of the back episodes I was shocked to see how nice their apartment was—especially when compared to Khadijah's. They devote themselves to their grooming habits with almost religious devotion and are much more image conscious than their female counterparts. After watching one episode in which Kyle complains that Overton got hair in his oatmeal soap, I started to wonder if *The Metrosexual Guide to Style* owes them a check.

5. The *Living Single* intro is still on the internet, though it is cut out of most of the videos on YouTube. Still as good as I remember.

Here, Peterson praises *Living Single* for its positive representations of Black love, friendships and community. Peterson also points to the significance of upward-class mobility as a key signifier of progress and character development in the series. Finally, Peterson underscores the value of alternative representations and masculinity and femininity as the characters are depicted as successful career women and men who are attuned to fashion, homemaking, and personal grooming. In this way, Peterson provides a resistant reading of *Living Single* that is supported by other fan posts praising the show for its positive representations of bright, creative, dynamic and socially mobile African Americans.

FF writes:

I've been watching the Oxygen reruns all summer and had to say that this show [*Living Single*] is hilarious! It's not often I literally laugh out loud while watching a sitcom, but I find myself doing just that—most especially at Max and Régine (both actresses were terrific in their roles: Erika is great at physical comedy as well as drama and Kim's line readings and reactions were just perfect). Even though I've seen each episode multiple times, I still get a kick out of something in each show (for instance, I wait to see Max fall off the stage in the *Dreamgirls* spoof—kills me every time).

I wish there were more shows like this on TV right now. It was a smart, funny, warm and witty show and everyone associated with it should be very proud. But how is it that, out of that terrific cast, no one except Queen Latifah made it really big? Erika should have had her own sitcom and become a huge star, and it's a shame that Kim Fields hasn't had another great vehicle (she's gorgeous and talented).

SV notes:

> I love, love, love this show. I am so glad I get to watch it on Oxygen daily. I tend to schedule after work errands around the show. I didn't see the last season in its original run, so I am hoping to catch [it] on reruns. Although, the first and second seasons were my favorites.

PP comments:

> God, this show. This is one of my favorite shows in EVAR [sic]. Question—They're still airing it daily on Oxygen, right? Please?
>
> And I ... loved all the characters; couldn't pick a favorite character or actor. Seriously. Well ... I hated Tripp. But out of Khadijah, Synclaire, Régine, Max, Overton, and Kyle—don't make me choose. I loved when Synclaire got kissed by that guy while she and Overton were ... engaged, I believe? And she feels so guilty about it and during dinner with Overton at a fancy restaurant, she just bursts out with "Oh, Overton! I'm a slut!" Synclaire was hilarious. Oh, and when Daryll (I think? Whoever Heavy D played—he was good too) was getting married and the bride was cheating on him, Regine yells out "THE BRIDE'S A TRAMP!" and Synclaire's all "Regine! You're in the House of God! The proper word is Jezebel!"

These fan posts, along with Peterson's analysis of *Living Single*, point to the complex negotiation between onscreen depictions and audience reception of these archetypes that remains a central issue for media scholars. Katrina Bell claims that viewers not only negotiate the meanings that they derive from televised representation in terms of reflective social values, but also negotiate these meanings within the frame of their own roles in everyday life (1999, 214). Bell states:

> On the one hand it appears that the mere fact that updated representations of African American womanhood appear on *Living Single* serves as a kind of resolution of the past. But inherent in this resolution is the recognition among these women that archetypal representations of African American women are still widely circulated. In other words, my co-researchers[2] appear to negotiate rather than criticize the meaning that they attach to questionable portrayals of African American womanhood—likely because the show and the experiences tap into their own experiences [1999, 214–216].

Although the women of *Living Single* may arguably fit into traditionally racist archetypes: Max as sapphire, Khadijah as mammy, Régine as jezebel, and Synclaire as tragic mulatto, Bell's co-researchers resist these traditional identifications and recognize and negotiate their own identities through the progression of characterizations on the show. Katrina E. Bell's in-depth interviews with African American female fans of *Living Single* reveal that the show evokes problematic archetypes of African American women from early cinema and television roles (1999, 213). Bell argues, "My co-researchers identified Synclaire, Khadijah's younger cousin and member of the foursome, as the Tragic Mulatto figure, Maxine as the Sapphire, Régine as the Jezebel, and Khadijah as the Matriarch (1999, 213)." Fans' comments complicate the archetypes while providing negotiated and resistant readings. MP writes about the typologies of her favorite characters:

> Max—loved her realness, sarcasm and sense of humor...
>
> Synclaire—loved her silliness, craziness and always staying true to being so unique and different from anyone else, despite all of the criticism.

KK comments on the similarities of the repeating types on *Sex and the City* and *Living Single*:

> Amazing how you bring this up with the anticipated release of *Sex and the City*. I've always thought of *Living Single* as the original, with Khadijah as the black SJP [Sarah Jessica Parker] and Synclaire as Charlotte.

JL agrees and notes:

> *Living Single* WAS the unspoken archetype of *Sex and the City*—and I still love that show. I wish it could be brought back.

Like Bell's co-researchers, I would argue that these easy archetypes do not fully represent the complexity of the *Living Single* female foursome, nor do I accept that these white supremacist paradigms leave space for the progression of sisterhood, solidarity, woman talk, woman space, or collective growth that is central to the development of the *Living Single* characters over the course of the series.

However, the repeating tropes of jezebel, virgin, matriarch and naïf operate as foils for one another throughout all of the female foursome shows. The role of the jezebel in each of these female foursome series is to offer comic relief for episodes that frequently contain weighty subject matter. Frequently, the jezebel character infuses the dialogue with risqué double entendre and celebrates women's sexual empowerment and pleasure. Hence, the role of the jezebel in contemporary comedic dramas and sitcoms becomes one of politicization and social reform despite its reprise of the role of the wanton woman.

Matriarchal Power and Mothering

Matriarchs of these female foursome programs include: Sophia Petrillo of *The Golden Girls*, Julia Sugarbaker of *Designing Women*, Khadijah James of *Living Single*, Samantha Jones of *Sex and the City*, Joan Clayton of *Girlfriends*, Juliet Draper of *Cashmere Mafia*, and Elka Ostrovsky of *Hot in Cleveland*. However, in the case of *Sex and the City*, *Girlfriends*, *Hot in Cleveland*, and *Cashmere Mafia*, the role of matriarch stands in contrast to the mother of the foursome. Although Samantha is the matriarch of *Sex and the City* based on her life experience and age, Carrie plays the role of mother. This pattern repeats on *Designing Women* and *The Golden Girls*, wherein Julia Sugarbaker and Sophia operate as primary matriarchs and Mary Jo and Dorothy frequently mother the foursomes, but, as previously noted, roles of matriarch and mothers sometimes shift by episode. Among the *Girlfriends*, Joan occupies the position of matriarch, but Maya mothers all of the girls including Joan. Similarly, Juliet leads the Cashmere Mafia as their true matriarch, but Zoe mothers Caitlin, Mia and, to some extent, Juliet. On *Hot in Cleveland*, Elka's age and seniority make her the undisputed matriarch while Melanie Moretti is both the voice of reason and the mother for the series.

In contrast, the role of the mother and/or matriarch serves as an anchoring fixture for other women in these television series. The matriarch protects, leads, and legitimates the sisterhood. In many cases, this character simultaneously functions as matriarch and mother, although this is not always the case. Anne Kaler notes,

> From episode to episode, the triad shifts slightly to allow the Hera/Juno aspect of the mother of the gods to be subsumed by Dorothy as the strongest person and by Sophia as the wisest. In the same manner, Rose occasionally subsumes the mother's role with her caring attitude and her maintenance of the household; it is she who bakes or brings food home [1990, 52].

As Kaler explains in the case of *The Golden Girls*, the role of mother and matriarch often shifts. This is also the case in the other female foursome series. Referencing the archetypes of woman from ancient mythology, philosophy and literature and drawing on Jungian analysis of the four-sided mandala symbol, a four-sided division of the human personality, the quaternity, Kaler produces an archetypal analysis of the four primary *The Golden Girls* characters. Kaler states, "While all of these aspects fluctuate among the characters of *The Golden Girls*, the easiest way to categorize them is through the Greco-Roman triad of Dorothy as the Athena/Minerva figure, Rose as the virginal Kore/Artemis/Diana, Blanche as the Aphrodite/Venus, and Sophia as the dual Sybil/Hecate figure" (1990, 52).

However, communication scholar Deborah Ann Macey troubles Kaler's reading of the series even as she draws on Kaler's analysis. While Kaler presents the quaternity as virgin, spouse, mother and wise woman, Macey references Wood's stereotypes of women in the workplace as the iron maiden, the sex object, the child and the mother (Macey 2008, 4). Although Macey, Kaler and Wood each provide foursome paradigms for understanding representations of women, these paradigms may be overly reductive and may not leave enough space for the kinds of resistant, oppositional or negotiated readings evidenced by fan postings on message boards, forums and/or blogs. I would argue that integrating the archetypal readings of Kaler, Wood, and Macey provide a more polyvalent framework for understanding the character dynamics. It should be noted, however, that discrepancies of analysis exist within the typologies. While Kaler refers to the goddess Artemis as a virgin, daughter character (1990, 52), Macey articulates Artemis as a huntress and a warrior reflective of the iron maiden archetype (2008, 6). Still, Kaler describes Dorothy as the Athena/Minerva portion of the triad, the intelligent warrior goddess (53) while describing Rose as the virginal Kore/Artemis/Diana (1990, 52). I point this out, in part, to suggest that even these archetypal roles evidence a breadth of characterization, but I also want to underscore how these characters shift positions throughout the series.

In fact, this case of shifting positionalities is perhaps best evidenced in an episode of *Designing Women* titled, "The Strange Case of Clarence and Anita" (S6 E8). Here we see Mary Jo Shively, who most frequently serves as the show's everywoman character and moral interlocutor. Although Julia's position in this instance is closely aligned with Mary Jo's, it is Mary Jo who flips the script and becomes the mouthpiece for feminism (Butler 1993, 21). Media studies scholars agree that, in this episode, Mary Jo represents the position of advocacy producer Linda Bloodworth-Thomason and her preferred reading of the Clarence Thomas confirmation hearings (Spangler 1996; Sullivan & Goldzwig 1996; Butler 1993). In fact, Sullivan and Goldzwig maintain that there were, in fact, "four stories within stories—plays within plays" (1996, 233). The first story is that confirmation hearings are being conducted for Clarence Thomas, and that Anita Hill is testifying that Thomas sexually harassed her. The second story is that Mary Jo and Julia are playing the principal characters in a local theatre production of *Whatever Happened to Baby Jane?* The third story is that Allison, who has never had a slumber party for her birthday as a child, is planning one for this very night. The fourth is that Allison supports Thomas's confirmation and is wearing a T-shirt that reads "She lied," while Mary Jo's T-shirt reads "He did it." Not surprisingly, Mary Jo actively advocates Thomas's censure throughout the episode. Although the sexual politics of Thomas's confirmation hearings operate as the background story of the episode, Mary Jo's reading of the hearings and her matriarchal feminist discourse stand in stark opposition to the patriarchal good old boys' network, thereby underscoring what is at stake in the episode not just for Anita Hill, but for all women. Mary Jo declares:

> Most women ... don't want to call themselves feminists because George Bush and Phyllis Schlafly want to make people believe that feminists are all these big mouthed, bleeding-heart, man-hating women who don't shave their legs. Well, I shave my legs, and I'm a single parent, a working mother, and if believing in equal pay and mandated child care makes me a feminist then I am damn proud to be one [S6 E8].

It would seem here that Mary Jo nearly returns to the voice of reason, the moral interlocutor of the season, but her use of the f-word marks her as another angry feminist. Later in the episode, after Thomas is confirmed as a Supreme Court justice and Mary Jo and Julia are driving home from a dress rehearsal in full costume as Baby Jane and Blanche Hudson (iconic camp characters played in the 1962 film by Bette Davis and Joan Crawford, respectively). Mary Jo cannot contain her anger at the outcome of the confirmation hearings any longer, proclaiming, "I am mad as hell and I'm not going to take it anymore" (S6 E8). Sullivan and Goldzwig comment, "When Mary Jo/Jane/Bette and Julia/Blanche/

Joan drove to Allison's house for the slumber party, Thelma and Louise intertextualize the narrative. As Mary Jo and Julia drove along, they echo the sentiments of *Thelma and Louise* suggesting that they simply would not live by patriarchal norms" (1996, 237). At the end of the slumber party, a news reporter seeks a response to the confirmation of Thomas. Mary Jo grabs the microphone and looks directly into the camera saying:

> All we want is to be treated with equality and respect. I'm sorry, I don't mean to be strident and overbearing, but nice just doesn't cut it anymore. Like a lot of women out there tonight, I'm mad! ... What I'm going to do is get into my car and drive to the center most point of the United States of America and climb the tallest tower and yell, "Hey, don't get me wrong, we love you, but who the hell do you men think you are?! [S6 E8].

Mary Jo's female gaze is trained directly into the camera, and at this moment she becomes an empowered female subject focused on her own desire to be treated with equality and respect. Her underlying anger becomes exposed and raw, but her speech defines her role as subject, not object. In this way, Mary Jo's appropriation of the male gaze, returning the look, evokes the female gaze popularized in the 1991 feminist film *Thelma and Louise*. Film studies scholar Brenda Cooper maintains that resistance to male objectification, returning the look and celebrating women's friendships construct the female gaze in *Thelma and Louise* (2000, 285). Following Cooper's analysis, I argue that Mary Jo, like her feminist film counterparts, Thelma and Louise, also resists male objectification as she stands squarely looking into the camera as empowered female subject returning the look. Mary Jo's defiant gaze in complete Baby Jane Hudson costume and her words of solidarity and sisterhood distinguished by her use of the first person plural pronoun *we*—resonate with the viewers and cultivate a matriarchal feminist connection. Thus, Mary Jo moves beyond the seemingly harmless, mousy, divorced mom stereotype and into the active role of feminist matriarch, rivaling Julia Sugarbaker as a force with which to be reckoned.

Certainly, matriarchs are imbued with significant cultural power in their television families. However, Joan, of *Girlfriends*, realizes early on that sometimes the burden of matriarch is too much for her to bear. In an episode titled "Childs in Charge" Toni decides to overextend herself financially to start her own upscale boutique real estate business. Joan, however, warns Toni against taking such a risk. After Toni storms out and leases an office and begins to plan for the opening of her new business, Joan realizes that her overbearing matriarchal behavior stems from being trapped in the role of "Mama." Joan arrives at Toni's new offices, which Maya and Lynn are cleaning, when Toni returns from an investor's meeting (S2 E17). Joan tells Toni that she should have been a better girlfriend, more supportive, more affirming and less judgmental. Joan truly feels trapped in the role of mother, and she explains to all of the other women that she wants desperately to escape this role and to be just another girlfriend. Toni comforts Joan and says, "It's ok. I know you're happy for me. You just have to be 'Mama.' That's you. If I'm gonna eat up all your food and borrow all your money, guess I gotta take the good with the bad." Lynn points out that Joan has the soul of an old woman, and Maya makes jokes about Joan also having the ankles of an old woman. Joan responds "Seriously, guys, I'm tired of being the practical one, the voice of reason. I just want to be a girlfriend, who cracks jokes at the expense of her other girlfriends." Finally, Toni hugs Joan saying, "Joan, you *are* a girlfriend. You're my best girlfriend" (S2 E17). Here, Joan embodies what Dionne Stephens and Layli Phillips describe as the evolution of the matriarch into the earth mother (2003, 32). Joan operates as the voice of reason, moral interlocutor, and independent working woman in the foursome. As such, she is bound to what Stephens and Phillips describe as a cultural script. Joan's desire to step away from her matriarchal role mark a breakthrough for the sitcom. Joan manages to break out of her matriarchal role to be a part of a collective identity of girlfriends. The shared culture of woman space, woman talk, and alternative family constitutes a continuing trajectory for female foursome shows. Although the long-standing trope of the matriarch remains visible on *Girlfriends*, this episode illustrates the potential for power shifts within the foursome and for a collective identity as a sister-friend and girlfriend to transcend the restrictive category of matriarch. On the other hand, the responses of the other characters (Maya as sister savior, Lynn as a freak, and Toni as a gold digger) still reinforce the sociohistorical construction of African American women's stereotypical identities.

In fact, these constructions are similarly reflected on *Living Single* when Khadijah James refers to herself as "mother" in two episodes

("Great Expectations" S1 E6 & "Ride the Maverick" S4E2). In "Great Expectations," Khadijah sits back at Club Zina and turns down many men who ask her to dance. When Synclaire questions her rejection of so many potential suitors, Khadijah replies, "Believe me when the right guy comes along, mother will be macking" (S1 E6). Here, Khadijah assumes the role of mentor, teacher, and mother as she shows Synclaire how to mack, how to flirt, and how to pick up the right kind of man. Later in "Ride the Maverick," the day after Max accuses Khadijah of assuming the role of mother of the foursome, Khadijah sarcastically notes, "Mother hasn't thought about you all day" (S4 E2). Here, Khadijah's sarcastic appropriation of the term "mother" reifies her as the legitimate leader and matriarch in the foursome. In each of these cases Khadijah operates from a position of power and authority. This does not come without a cost to Khadijah, who is plagued by the strong black woman trope[3]; however, during the series Khadijah successfully appropriates matriarchal power and arguably revises it to produce a strengthened postmodern and postcolonial womanism.

Khadijah serves as the glue person, the counselor, the foundation and the mother of *Living Single*: she protects, encourages, listens, and directs. She is a leader, a girlfriend and confidant to her three cohorts. In *Color by Fox: The Fox Network and the Revolution in Black Television*, Kristal Brent Zook argues that Khadijah's role, played by Queen Latifah, is, in fact, enhanced by Latifah's extratextual affiliations (1999, 71). Hence, Latifah's success as actor and hip-hop artist not only inflect her role as leader of the foursome, but her role as Queen, the ultimate matriarch, reifies her matriarchal power. Zook maintains:

> In looking at Latifah's various on-screen roles, then, we see that her feminist and lesbian characterizations represent an integral part of her persona as a popular icon among African American audiences. Moreover, because she is situated within a community of hip-hop artists, a whole body of narrative possibilities is to her Characterizations—possibilities that both challenge patriarchal contexts and affirm traditional notions of mythical matriarchal Africanity [sic] with a contemporary womanist twist [1999, 73].

Zook expresses what many viewers recognize as an extratextual dimension to *Living Single* and to the role of Khadijah James. In many ways, Khadijah fulfills onscreen the promise of the cultural roles that Latifah calls for offscreen. Latifah's politicized music and lyrics, most notably, her debut album, *Ladies First*, suggests that African American women specifically should be venerated as the matriarchs of the black American family. Lyrics from the Queen's album command respect for women, and in her smash hit "U.N.I.T.Y." she directly attacks domestic violence as a gendered social problem.

This extratextuality is evoked in an episode of *Living Single* titled "U.N.I.T.Y." (1994 S1, E 23). When Kyle hosts a poker game for partners from the brokerage firm, Lawrence, a junior vice-president who is considering Kyle for a promotion, asks Régine out for a date. After the date, he begins to brag about his sexual conquest. Khadijah wins the next poker game, and Lawrence calls the ladies "bitches." Kyle confronts him, but Latifah's "U.N.I.T.Y." cuts into the script, thereby reinscribing the Queen's voice and persona into the script of the episode. "U.N.I.T.Y." also closes out the episode, reinforcing the womanist message of the show. However, the fact that Kyle defends the women instead of the women defending themselves may, to some extent, co-opt this powerful portrayal of matriarchal power. Fans' posts reflect their passion for Queen Latifah, Khadijah and "U.N.I.T.Y." JN notes: "And recently, I was thinking about how it used to be, whenever you mentioned Queen Latifah, people would be like U-N-I-T-Y. But now, folks wouldn't even know what you mean." What JN points to is a generational loss of the shared cultural understanding of the relevance of Queen Latifah's contributions to the history of rap and hip-hop as sites for political struggle and collective resistance to white supremacist, capitalist patriarchy.[4] In fact, Queen Latifah belongs to a 1980s ground-breaking, hip-hop sisterhood that includes artists MC Lyte, Monie Love and Yo-Yo. These black female artists banded together to form the Intelligent Black Women's Coalition with the goal of supporting sisters of all races. Hence, as Zook argues, Khadijah James's brand of African American, matriarchal womanism emerges from "the profound subtextual tension embodied in Latifah's persona: that is the tension between race and gender, and the struggle to reconcile feminist and nationalist desires" (Zook 1999, 71). In this way, *Living Single* becomes a vehicle for these subtextual and extratextual tensions.

Many fan posts point to the success of the show as producing a sense of community, sisterhood, and collective unity. The "U.N.I.T.Y." episode underscores the value of collective black identity on the show (not so dissimilar from the shared social mobility and collective black identity among artists, writers, musicians and black intellectuals who reconstructed the image of the New Negro through the Harlem Renaissance[5]). For many fans, *Living Single* represents a shared identity of black unity embodied in some very progressive characterizations: political activism, social consciousness, upward mobility, intellectualism, professionalism, womanism, and collectivism. These positive representations resonate with fans in many ways.

LS writes:

> There was [an] "audience choice" poll for which of the three ladies (Khadijah/QL, Régine/KF or Maxine/EA) would end up with Hamilton/MC which Khadijah/QL won. One of my fondest memories of this show is my sister and I begging our parents to let us call and vote for Khadijah, and them [sic] letting us. We felt so important and triumphant the next week when she won. I think *Living Single* is one of those rare shows where the first season is really fantastic and stands up to the later episodes. I don't know titles, but that first season was chock full of greatness—Max vs. Régine re: Charles, Club Zina, Hamilton, Greg returning, Synclaire quits Flavor, Synclaire runs Flavor ... and so on.

MM also posts a praise message for *Living Single*:

> This show is freakin hilarious. I LOVE their interaction. Max and Kyle's putdowns, Synclaire and Overton's romance, Régine's diva with a heart ways and Khadijah's expressions. Erika Alexander has to be my favorite actress on the show—I can't BELIEVE I haven't seen her on TV since. Does anyone have better comic timing and energy? The only off note to me is the actress' portrayal of Synclaire. It's usually too over the top for me—just not in sync with everyone else's ease. I like the actress and the character, but the role is often played too broad.

Although this message operates as a praise message, MM is quick to point out the character in the show that did not work for her. Her role in posting becomes one of a critic to point out the show's strengths and weaknesses. Her comments provoke the response of DD, who writes back to MM:

> Word. *Living Single* was the best sitcom of the '90s IMO. Khadijah/Regina/Maxine/Synclaire as Flo & The Flavorettes? Hilarious (one of the better latter day eps). And the first season is brilliant. Régine vs. Max over Charles, Khadijah as Max/Shaquan's sister Sabuddah, the first glimmers of Kyle/Maxine during Greg's visit, Kyle-Overton & Sanford, Régine not remembering Eastland, Max vs. Khadijah over the loan, Kyle/Stacy, the return of Goldie,

Overton-Khadijah bonding, Khadijah-Rita vs. Regine-Laverne, etc. All classic stuff.

The classic stuff that DD and MM write about are indications of the broader appeal of *Living Single*. Fans situate *Living Single* within a broader framework of ensemble casts and female foursome shows.

KS writes about the limitations of the ensemble cast:

> I can only guess that maybe the *Living Single* producers saw the success of *Friends*, and wanted to catch some of their success, making it the black *Friends*. But I think that was a tragic mistake. I never realized this until you mentioned it, though. I think that's the main thing that keeps me from *loving* the show: not enough of the female characters, too much of the men.

GD posts a comment about *Living Single*'s premature cancellation:

> That's such a weird coincidence that you posted this article on *Living Single* today, because I just watched a really good episode earlier today (the one where Khadijah and a rival reporter try to beat each other out for a major scoop). I watched this all the time back in the day when I was a young single gal myself newly moved to the D (Detroit). I always liked it because it was so much more true to life and funnier than your average lame, predictable white folks sitcom, *Friends*. BTW, I never got the hype around *Friends*, and I've never understood why it was so popular in the first place—I only watched it 2 or 3 times, and wasn't even impressed—the characters didn't do nothing for me, because they didn't come off as real, and they weren't at all funny to me. Even other white shows like *Seinfeld* and *Mad about You* were a hell of a lot funnier. I also felt like *Living Single*'s cancellation was premature—I felt they had another good year or two left.

KS questions the decision to include the men (Kyle Barker, Overton Wakefield Jones and, later, Tripp Williams) as part of the ensemble cast, and both KS and GD discuss the reproduction of a mixed male and female ensemble cast akin to the hit show *Friends*. Interestingly, several of the fan posts point to the gendered and raced identities of the characters as being more significant and richer in quality than those of other ensemble casts. Clearly fans understand and engage in critique of the limited characterizations on *Living Single*; however, GD suggests that the premature cancellation of *Living Single* did not permit the show to achieve its full potential. Even as the female foursome characters—Khadijah, Régine, Synclaire, and Max—resonate with viewers' life experiences and identities, there is a palpable sense of longing evidenced in fan posts for a fuller and more robust development of these characters and their collective identities. Many fan posts ultimately indicate that they believe that *Living Single* produced powerful and dynamic images of black American woman culture, space, identity, sisterhood and solidarity; however, the trajectory of *Living Single* was cut short and the fullest potential of these characterizations never materialized.

Daughters, Virgins and Naïfs

Like Charlene, Lynn Searcy of *Girlfriends* is mothered by the other characters of the show. With four master's degrees, Lynn is book smart, but operates as a childlike figure, lost in the world of work, bills, and commitments. Synclaire functions as the classic naïf on *Living Single*; however, her role as tragic mulatto complicates the simplicity of the daughter, virgin, naïf. Katrina Bell explains that Synclaire functions as a mirror and as a conscience for the other characters (1999, 215). Her perspectives are insightful and surprise fellow characters because their occurrence is relatively rare. In short, Synclaire's naïveté situates her as a clear reporter of truthfulness—even if she lacks sophistication. This analysis may similarly be applied to the naïve, virgin, daughter character of Charlotte York from *Sex and the City*. In an episode entitled "Three's a Crowd," Charlotte confides to Carrie that she is considering a threesome to make her architect boyfriend, Jack, happy (S1 E8). Carrie voices her concern that it seems odd to imagine that Charlotte might become closer to Jack by adding a third person to their lovemaking. The suggestion is that the third person is more likely to come between Jack and Charlotte than to bring them closer together. However, Charlotte continues to ask deeper questions about how well anyone of us knows the person with whom we sleep, make love, or partner. Carrie responds in a voiceover that just when one would write her off as simplistic, she would say something profound (S1 E8). Hence, Charlotte, like Synclaire, provides insight, perhaps not unlike direct and accurate childlike observations (i.e., from the mouths of babes). Bell explains that this vagueness about the naïf's perspective and insight suggests that there is a complexity to the character that the viewer cannot fully understand or reach (1999, 215). These insightful comments may indeed be the mark of some elemental characteristic of the naïf character as Rose Nylund, Lynn Searcy,

Charlene Frasier and Caitlin Dowd also deliver profound and direct evaluations and assessments of situations and behaviors during the series.

Perhaps naïfs Charlene Frasier and Bernice Clifton (a semi-regular on *Designing Women*) make the strongest case for this type of insight. In "How Great Thou Art" (S2 E20) Charlene realizes that her minister, Reverend Nun, does not support the ordination of women, she invites him and her girlfriends over to discuss the issue of women as ministers. Although Bernice has slept through dinner, and is known to have an arterial flow problem, she engages with the good reverend in a battle of scripture and verse. Reverend Nun begins quoting scripture, "The deacon has to be the husband of one wife" and Bernice replies referencing 1 Timothy chapter 3, verse 12: "A deacon must be faithful to his wife and must manage his children and his household well" (NIV). Bernice points out that many priests do not have children, so if Reverend Nun insists on the literal interpretation of scripture then, ministers without children should be ineligible. Julia also points out that she does not understand why this means women cannot be ministers (S2 E20). Reverend Nun implies that Bernice's interpretation of the scripture is skewed and that he can give her other verses to support his argument. Here, Bernice invites Reverend Nun to voice his rationale for not supporting the ordination of women, and although Nun is depicted as a judicious clergyman, he is neither a zealot nor a fundamentalist. In an article entitled, "What Designing Women Do Ordain," Religious studies scholar Ray Penn argues, "Not only is the depth of the arguments presented amazing and refreshing, but the characterization establishes a breakthrough in how ministers and Christians are presented" (Penn 1990, 99). I agree with Penn and would add that this episode ameliorates rather than polarizes Christian, feminist, traditional, and progressive perspectives on this issue. That Bernice and Charlene, the classic naïfs, not only bring this issue to the fore, but speak so convincingly, so compellingly, and so genuinely, hits home the notion that the naïf is an essential element in the female foursome.

The ensuing debate vividly depicts Bernice's intimate knowledge of scripture learned from her preacher father. Although tension exists between Bernice's Pollyanna qualities and her women's liberation politics, one does not undercut the other. Instead, these complex characterizations suggest that Christianity and feminism are not mutually exclusive, but that naïveté and activism might also co-exist within in a single female character. However, the debate between Reverend Nun and Bernice extends beyond mere rhetoric into a justification for women's equality. Reverend Nun then quotes from 1 Corinthians 14:34, "Women should remain silent in the churches. They are not allowed to speak, but must be in submission, as the law says" (NIV). Bernice responds with Galatians 3: 28, "There is neither Jew nor Gentile, neither slave nor free, nor is there male and female, for you are all one in Christ Jesus" (NIV). Reverend Nun continues to quote from 1Corinthians extending into verse 35, "If they want to inquire about something, they should ask their own husbands at home; for it is disgraceful for a woman to speak in the church" (NIV). Bernice fires back from Acts 2:17, "In the last days, God says, I will pour out my Spirit on all people. Your sons and daughters will prophesy..." (NIV). Mary Jo asks if Bernice feels all right and Bernice says that she does, in fact, feels like all her circuits are cooking.

In this way the dialogue between Reverend Nun and Bernice is broken up a bit and Bernice looks to Charlene and asks how she sounds. Charlene indicates that Bernice sounds wonderful and underscores the simplicity of Bernice's argument. Charlene and Bernice, the two naïfs, recognize each other as having a clear and common goal. In contrast, Julia as the matriarch steps in and argues that people are always using the Bible in ways that will support their own personal prejudices. This enables a humorous moment when Reverend Nun suggests that feminists believe that God is a woman. Julia responds that she does not know many feminists who would say that, but that she believes that God is a spirit. Suzanne, the jezebel, suggests that if God were a woman then men would be the ones walking around wearing high heels, taking Midol, and having their upper lips waxed. This break in the Bible battle invites humor and keeps the conversation in the room open, so that when the dialogue continues, Bernice and Charlene make some powerful points and end the debate with an impassioned and historically accurate image of women's contributions. Bernice points out that Reverend Nun is always quoting the King James version of the Bible, which is known to convey a very narrow and very privileged male perspective of the Bible wrought with chauvinistic tendencies and even misogyny. Bernice also critiques Reverend Nun's condescending glances, implying that only he, an ordained minister, has the power to understand the Bible. Bernice also questions a translation of Romans' wherein Phoebe is named as a slave and other translations have indicated that she would be named as a deacon.

While the accuracy of this remains questionable, the point that Bernice makes is well taken—that translators of the Bible have taken license with meanings of words, including the politics of the era in which the translations occurred. Here, Charlene intervenes and questions how Baptist ministers can be against women in the ministry when many very famous missionaries were women including Annie Armstrong and Lottie Moon. Reverend Nun tries to placate Charlene and Bernice by saying that he is not trying to discredit the women missionaries' contributions and that he would like to invite Bernice to church. However, Bernice is not quite finished, after quoting Genesis, chapter 1, how both male and female were created, she states, "I will leave you with these parting words. Just remember after Christ was crucified on the cross and all his men had gone home. It was women who stayed until the bitter end, and it was women who first heralded the news of his resurrection, so just put that in your pulpit and smoke it" (S2 E20). The naïfs, Charlene and Bernice, have the last word, which is extremely rare for this genre. Charlene's faith, it seems, is shaken and she decides to leave her church after all. She looks to Julia as matriarch and hero at the end of the episode. Charlene looks to Julia as the matriarch to solidify the bonds of sisterhood and solidarity. Julia rises to the challenge by singing one of "the highest notes in all of hymndom" (S2 E20).

Jezebels, Virgins and the Virgin/Whore Dichotomy

The virgin/whore dichotomy resurfaces in each of these female foursome series, both through the character foils of naïfs and jezebels and through the exploration of female sexual desire. In fact, *The Golden Girls* offers a provocative view of senior sexual desire through the active sex lives of not only Blanche's jezebel character, but through all of the main characters, including bookish Dorothy, octogenarian Sophia, and the classic naïf Rose. Fans frequently comment about the sexual escapades and bawdy performances depicted by *The Golden Girls*.

As NC notes:

There was a scene on *The Golden Girls* when Blanche explained that an older woman should be on top during sex so that her boobs will look good, because if she is on the bottom, they will fall to the side. Then one of the others (probably the Bea Arthur character) said, "but have you ever seen what gravity does to your face when you look down?" Of course, Blanche gets a mirror and leans over it, and discovers that her face is far more wrinkled if she is on top. I think they eventually decided that the woman should be on the bottom and keep her arms folded.

Viewer comments reinforce the notion that the characters of *The Golden Girls* were vital sexual beings of a certain age, blowing the doors off conventional wisdom regarding mature women's sexual agency. GN, LP and BG write about *The Golden Girls'* active sex life in a flashback episode where the women prepare to go on a singles cruise (S4 E15).

> GN: I loved the episode where the girls go to the store and they end up getting condoms. "Ah, Joe, I need a price check on some condoms. These three ladies here have the King George profalatics [sic]. Two of them have the regular, and the blonde has the ultra-sensitive, in black." LOL
> LP: Oh, yeah…. I love that whole scene. Blanche's voice when she takes the microphone and spits, "Now just what in the hell are you people staring at?" is hilarious.
> BG: I posted that in the "Hell, Yeah!" thread—I loved Blanche. Grade-A slut and bitchy to boot, but she never made any apologies or excuses for it, and in fact REVELED in it. You go girl.

Here GN, LP and BG identify with *The Golden Girls* and celebrate their unbridled female sexual desire. Buying condoms to prepare for the real possibility of sex on a singles cruise and to protect against sexually transmitted diseases indicates the progressive attitudes of seniors regarding their own sexual desire. Fan support of this healthy and mature sexuality underscores the reciprocal relationship found both in the community of online fandom and in the shared experience of watching the episode. Not surprisingly fans of *Hot in Cleveland* (in many cases also fans of *The Golden Girls*) recognize the similarities between the show's characters, particularly in terms of sexual agency and age.

L3 writes:

> It IS interesting to note that the *Golden Girls* ranges in age, at the outset of the show, were not far off from the women on this show (Malick is ten years older than Rue M was when the show began) … and yet they looked SO much older. I don't know if all the actors are botox'd and surgery enhanced, and I don't actually know anyone in real life who's resorted to those measures, but it is nice that styles in clothing and hair and makeup and attitudes about aging have at least changed enough that past 40 doesn't equate to frumpiness,

sexlessness, cluelessness and nursing homes. Although the *Golden Girls*, despite embracing frumpiness and bad 'dos, sure did get around.

Certainly, fans comments indicate that without Blanche Devereaux from *The Golden Girls*, Victoria Chase from *Hot in Cleveland* would not exist. JS similarly argues:

> I think this show's high concept seeks to make a statement on this, but it seems a bit outdated now, as today's women in their 40s, 50s, or even 60s are not the automatic grandmas of past generations. On *The Golden Girls*, circa 1985, the idea of women "of a certain age" living active lives was novel, and the actions of Blanche Devereaux, or Mona from *Who's the Boss?* were seen as outliers—that's why they were so funny. The *The Golden Girls* women had a mother/grandmother look to them. But because of characters like these, plus changes from the baby boomers reaching retirement age, our expectations of older women are very different.

JS notes that viewer expectations of older women have changed both because of the trajectory of the representations of women on television and because of cultural changes, including the generational aging of baby boomers. However, I would argue that the sexual agency of women over the age of 50, or perhaps even 40, remains a taboo subject. There can be no doubt that the fearless double-entendre and outright bawdiness of Blanche Devereaux, Rose Nylund, Dorothy Zbornak and Sophia Petrillo forever changed American perceptions of aging women as both sexually desirable and desiring subjects.

However, when the hospital notifies Rose that she could have contracted AIDS during a gallbladder surgery, Rose's judgmental attitude about Blanche's sexual behavior stands in stark contrast to the sexual openness that prevails during most of the series (S5 E19). Rose, as classic naïf and goody two-shoes, literally pits herself against Blanche as modern-day jezebel and suggests that Rose isn't the one who should be worrying about contracting AIDS. Rose explains that she is mad at herself for trusting the medical community, for trusting the hospital, for trusting doctors and nurses to perform the surgery and take care of her. Rose is embittered because the doctors and nurses never asked her about blood transfusions or the risks of receiving blood transfusions. Her frustration builds when she thinks that she could die because she contracted a disease through a transfusion that she did not know about or accept, and Blanche tells her it will be ok and that she should just relax. Rose retorts aggressively:

I might have AIDS, and it scares the hell out of me. And every time I open my mouth to talk about it, someone says, "There, there, Rose, take it easy." Why me, Blanche? I'm tired of pretending I feel ok, so I won't say take it easy. And I'm tired of you saying take it easy because you think I'm going to fall apart. Dammit, why is this happening to me? This isn't supposed to happen to people like me. You must have gone to bed with hundreds of men. All I had was one innocent operation [S5 E19].

Blanche tries to understand Rose's perspective, but Blanche is very hurt by Rose's insinuation that Blanche somehow should be the one on the hook, waiting to know if she has contracted HIV or not. Rose realizes her mistake in saying this out loud and suggesting that Blanche's risky sexual behavior should put her at risk in a way from which Rose should be exempt because she is not promiscuous like Blanche. Rose's victim-blaming line of reasoning is exposed, and Blanche counters saying, "AIDS is not a bad person's disease, Rose! It is not God punishing people for their sins!" (S5 E19).

Here, the naïf and the jezebel, Rose and Blanche, confront each other and, in the process, deconstruct mainstream 1980s ideology about AIDS as a stigmatized illness correlating with promiscuity, drug use and gay sex (S5 E19). Rose argues that she is a good person and doesn't sleep around like Blanche, implying that she does not deserve to contract AIDS. Throughout the series, Blanche's promiscuity operates in staunch opposition to Rose's naïf and seemingly virginal qualities. However, this episode challenges both the stereotypes and the stigmas attached to women's sexual behavior. Although fans of *The Golden Girls* generally seem conservative, they responded strongly against Rose's judgmental behavior. XD writes: "Rose was also a bitch on the "very special" HIV/AIDS episode. I understand she was flustered but to basically tell Blanche she deserved to be sick over her was pretty low."

BE comments:

I also consider that line to have been included less because the writers genuinely believed it was an organic Rose sentiment, and more because they thought *someone* would say it and Rose was the best candidate. The episode was written during a time in which plenty of people had no qualms drawing distinctions between "innocent" HIV/AIDS victims (e.g., children, those who got the virus via blood transfusion) and those who actively "brought it on themselves" e.g., gay men, "promiscuous" women). It was repugnant to the most basic sense of human decency and an unnecessary and divisive distraction when all anyone should have been focused on was finding a cure, but you heard it all the time. So I don't so much mind that they had Rose utter those ignorant and hateful words, but I do mind that she wasn't taken to task for them more than she was.

LP responds:

I agree that Rose's attitude that Blanche should get AIDS because she is a woman of loose morals is distasteful—and she never really seems to apologize for it. I understood that Rose was supposed to be really scared that she might have contracted AIDS, but I think that could have been shown without making her completely unsympathetic and insufferable. Just to try to be positive about the episode for a second, I was glad the show chose to make Rose the one who might have AIDS instead of Blanche in order to show that AIDS can happen to anyone. My stepmother's family carries hemophilia, and [a] number of her male relatives died from AIDS acquired through the blood transfusions that hemophiliacs routinely require. I applaud *The Golden Girls'* refusal to paint AIDS as some kind of disease only slutty people or drug addicts get.

HM writes:

I agree with you—no one deserves to get AIDS. I do think though that when someone has   just been told they may have contracted a deadly disease that it's understandable that they are going to get angry and lash out. To say something is understandable is not to say that it is acceptable! Since we're on the subject (somewhat) of VSE's I thought this episode was a much better "very special episode" than the one where Dorothy ends up being diagnosed with Chronic Fatigue Syndrome.

AC writes about the very special episodes:

So far Dorothy has had Chronic Fatigue and a gambling problem, Rose almost has HIV (and the fact that they keep calling it AIDS is kind of jarring, but I know it was way back when), plus they've mentioned elderly health insurance issues, pensions being cut off, saving the dolphins, saving the wetlands, age discrimination and those are just off the top of my head. Like I said, most of them aren't whole episode issues, they just contribute to the main plot in some way (Rose gets the new job because Charlie's pension gets cut off and then faces age discrimination while looking for a new job) but I kind of feel like I'm watching one of those Saturday morning things from when I was a kid, "The More You Know."

Certainly, these fans engage in an involved critique of the episode, the character dynamics, and the script; perhaps more importantly fans make arguments about social problems and the ways in which this episode contributes to their understanding of the problem and its possible solutions. Also, fan posts reveal that they integrate meaning from one episode into their analysis of other episodes and the series in general. Finally, as AC writes, the program serves as a kind of public-service message, educating viewers about AIDS and how harmful the stigma of AIDS can be to society. These fan posts compellingly demonstrate how viewers are able to decode the meaning from an episode and apply it to real-world situations and relate in new ways to people whom they know, who have AIDS. These fan posts refute cultural dupe models of televisual experience, and indicate that viewers are critical and thoughtful about the episodes, dialogue, characters, and how plotlines further underscore that viewers indeed integrate information gleaned from the series into their worldviews. In fact, *Designing Women*, *The Golden Girls*, *Sex and the City* and *Girlfriends* all confront the issues of sexual promiscuity and social stigma of AIDS and HIV through critical episodes ranging from 1987 to 2003:

Designing Women: "Killing all the Right People" (October 1987)
The Golden Girls: "72 hours" (February 17, 1990)
Sex and the City: "Running with Scissors" (August 2000)
Girlfriends: "The Pact" (March 2003)

Hence, the issue of gay sex, promiscuity, and sexual education as linked to AIDS becomes the centerpiece for a *Designing Women* episode titled, "Killing all the Right People" (S2 E4). When Ima Jean, a childhood friend of Julia's, realizes that Sugarbaker's will be planning the funeral for a young interior designer, Kendall Dobbs, who is dying of AIDS, Ima Jean's homophobia reflects the rampant social hysteria and prevailing ideology regarding the stigma of AIDS. Julia springs to action as the terminator, embodying the role of both the iron maiden and matriarch, while Mary Jo assumes the role of mother as she fights for sexual education in the schools in order to protect teens from contracting AIDS (S2 E4). Ima Jean contends that gay men deserve to contract HIV and even full blown AIDS because of their engagement in risky sexual behaviors that subvert heteronormative values. While Mary Jo intervenes and points out that gay men are not the only demographic group who have contracted the disease, Ima Jean clings to her cultural ideology that AIDS is a gay plague and has been sent to wipe out the gay male population, hence the title of the episode, "Killing All the Right People" (S2

E4). Suzanne attempts to quibble with Ima Jean's logic, asking why lesbians are not an at-risk group if heteronormative values are the primary issue. Ima Jean explains that it is not for her to say, but she has certainly not engaged in the kind of behaviors in which these people (gay men) have engaged. To which, Julia responds that AIDS is not a moral problem, but she finds it difficult to understand how the moral police (read Ima Jean and her ilk) now seem to occupy a moral high ground and blame victims of a disease for the disease itself thus conjuring up the notion of Biblical plagues sent as punishment for human iniquities. Julia responds, "Ima Jean, get serious, who do you think you're talking to? I've known you for 27 years, and all I can say is—If God was handing out sexually transmitted diseases to people as a punishment for sinning, then you would be at the free clinic all the time!" (S2 E4).

In this way *Designing Women* confronts the social prejudice of homophobia and AIDS and levels the playing field indicating that no one is exempt from this horrible disease and further demystifies the widespread belief that AIDS is a punishment from God. Both the *Designing Women* and *The Golden Girls* episodes address the religious and moral conviction that good people do not get AIDS. This thread resurfaces in a 2003 episode of *Girlfriends* (S3 E19) and is followed up with a second episode, a final tribute to the epidemic of African American women who have died from AIDS (S3 E23). That proportionally more African American women contract and die from AIDS becomes a centerpiece for *Girlfriends*. However, the linkage between each of these female foursome programs and their treatment of the issues surrounding AIDS seems to be the focus on public education and awareness. In the case of *Designing Women*, Mary Jo's final speech at the PTA forum for sex education in school boils the arguments for and against sex education down to a life-or-death argument: regardless of one's view on the morality of teenagers having sex, this is not a choice for which they should die (S2 E4). Hence, Mary Jo in a Mary Wollstonecraft–type[6] of move uses the ideological role of the mother as the moral guardian of the private sphere (guardian of hearth and home) to transcend the social problem of sexual education of children. Like Wollstonecraft, Mary Jo expands the theoretical positioning of the mother as moral and civic compass for her children to include protecting their health and well-being against sexually transmitted diseases that can kill. Mary Jo's appropriation of this line of argumentation indicates an undergirding presence of feminist consciousness and explores the very real role of mothers in the sexual education of their children, in the protection of society's children and in the decision-making role of protecting countless sons and daughters from AIDS, something far worse than the stigma of sexual promiscuity or homosexuality.

This issue of AIDS as a punishment continues as a trope on *Girlfriends*, when a college friend, Reesie, acknowledges that her husband, Joan's former college sweetheart, has transmitted AIDS to her (S3 E19 "The Pact"). Reesie talks to Joan and the other girlfriends about having HIV, saying that her medications are working and that they work to keep the strength of the virus at bay. Reesie explains that she tires easily, but she is stable. The women ask questions about the disease, including whether Reesie has HIV or full-blown AIDS. When Reesie responds that she has AIDS she is quick to point out that this disease cannot be contracted through the air, but only through the exchange of bodily fluids like blood and semen. The tenor of the discussion suggests that this episode is intended to provide education about HIV and AIDS to viewers. The particular way in which Reesie has contracted AIDS, via Brian, who also has sex with other men, is suggestive of sexual education regarding "down low" behaviors. Reesie explains, "If he put a condom in his pocket, then he would be admitting to himself that he was going out to have sex with men. And, that would make him gay—which according to him, he's not" (S3 E19). Joan says that she is sorry that she held it against Reesie all these years for stealing her boyfriend from college, and now she feels bad for bringing all of this back up again. Reesie responds, "Since we're apologizing—I *did* steal Brian. You've been right all along. I stole him. He was fine. Karma's a bitch, huh?" (S3 E19). This line, by Reesie, reinforces the idea that AIDS is a karmic response to her ill-gotten gains, stealing Brian from Joan, but Joan tells her that she should not think or say such a thing. However, AIDS as a punishment for sexual promiscuity and deviance repeats as a theme as the dichotomy of the virgin (Joan) and the jezebel (Reesie) becomes intertwined with the concept of AIDS as a literal plague or pox upon the jezebel.

In order to procure funding from a philanthropic foundation, Lynn presents a segment of her documentary film, focusing on African American women and AIDS. Lynn introduces the film and notes, "Someone once told me I'm dying. Black women like me are dying, and AIDS is our killer. I took that as a challenge, and this presentation is my answer to that challenge. I have put together a portion of my first documentary titled, *Lives in the Balance: African American Women and the AIDS Epidemic*. With funding from your foundation, hopefully we will save a life" (S3 E23). However, at the end of the episode, Lynn replays Reesie Jackson's documentary footage, and Reesie states:

> I'm proud of who I am. I am proud of my life. I have a wonderful family that supports me. I have friends who encourage me every day. I have two magnificent kids that say ... they say, "Mommy, you're my bestest friend." They say that even when I am mean to them. They find it in their hearts to say that to me. That gives me strength. You know, and I'm gonna be damned if I'm gonna let something like AIDS break their hearts or my spirit. AIDS is a condition. It's not a verdict on who I am, and I'm not gonna be demonized for having it. I won't do it, so I ain't goin' nowhere. I am too cute for that. I have a wedding to attend. I have children to love. Man, I have moments to catch [S3 E23].

Here, Reesie casts off the image of the victim and rebukes the discourse of victim blaming. In fact, even as she denies victimization, she occupies the subjective roles of active mother and survivor. Her positive attitude and refusal to accept defeat in the face of the AIDS epidemic provide a strong frame for re-visioning what AIDS means to the public. However, her message is arguably co-opted at the end of the episode as Reesie's black-and-white still photo with these dates (1978–2008) hangs on the screen. We are left knowing that HIV disproportionately afflicts African American Women as 1 in 3 will contract the disease. Although the combined episodes (S3 E19 & S3 E23) represent an attempt at public education through the character of Lynn—as classic naïf yet hyper sexualized tragic mulatto akin to Synclaire James of *Living Single*, these episodes fail to fully silence the public discourse of AIDS as a punishment for risky sexual behavior.

This problematic discourse also replays on *Sex and the City* in an episode entitled "Running with Scissors" (S3 E11). The friends realize that Samantha, the most sexually adventurous member of the foursome, has never taken an AIDS test. Samantha asks Carrie, Miranda and Charlotte about having AIDS tests, to which they all respond that they have. Charlotte admonishes Samantha to stop talking about AIDS because they are supposed to be looking at wedding gowns, and Samantha's AIDS talk is sullying the discussion. Again the harbinger of the virgin/whore dichotomy resurfaces with Samantha in the role of the whore talking about AIDS and sexual promiscuity, and Charlotte as the upholder of the patriarchy through her correct engagement in the ritual of marriage. Samantha persists and points out that the reason for her line of questioning is that she has met her man *du jour* who requests her to have an AIDS test before he will go to bed with her. Carrie indicates that she has had two tests and Miranda indicates that she has had three. Charlotte remains in denial of the conversation and asks about their feelings regarding full-length gloves. Miranda is incredulous that Samantha has never had an AIDS test and Carrie just asks her why not. Samantha confesses that she is afraid: "Sometimes it takes me a really long time to get over a cold." Carrie quips, "That's not AIDS. That's central air conditioning. Just go and get it over with" (S3 E11).

At the medical center, Samantha must revisit her sexual history. After answering yes to just about every question about her sexual behavior, including types of sex, types of protection and numbers of partners, Samantha worries that she is, in fact, at high risk for contracting AIDS. Later, as she waits for the results, she thinks to herself—please don't let them take me in that little room. When the nurse motions for her to come with her, she faints and falls to the floor. Carrie's voiceover announces, "She was perfectly healthy. The nurse just wanted a quiet place to lecture her on safe sex practices" (S3 E11). In the end Samantha's fear is allayed, but Carrie's sexual behavior is questioned when the scene cuts from Samantha at the clinic to Carrie standing in the lobby of a hotel. A Japanese businessman approaches Carrie and says, "How much? I've seen you here before—for sex, how much?" Carrie walks over to Big and says, "That's it, I'm out of here. That Japanese businessman thinks I'm a hooker!" (S3 E11). The question of promiscuity, of sexual wantonness, of the loose woman still hangs in the air even after Samantha gets a clean bill of health. The question becomes—who is the jezebel now?

Hence, the role of the jezebel remains alive and well in spite of the fact that Carrie now wears this identity rather than Samantha. The results of Samantha's AIDS test absolve her of her past sexually risky behavior. These shifts in identity on the series both suggest the need for shifting foils on the series, but also underscore the pervasiveness of these female archetypes: jezebel and virgin, matriarch and naïf as they recur in all of the female foursome shows. That these archetypes persist across all of these series further emphasizes the power of archetypal roles and the power that they hold in American television culture. Clearly, these archetypes reinscribe and reify existing sex and gender roles for women within the framework of the larger cultural systems of power and domination, including what bell hooks has named as imperialist, white supremacist, capitalist, patriarchy.[7] However, it seems important to also critically examine where and how these female foursome series resist easy stereotypical readings and where they push the boundaries of sex and gender roles.

3

Queer Telefeminism, Gender Trouble & Female Foursome Friendships

> When Carrie, Miranda, Charlotte, and Samantha discussed their escapades—oral sex, S&M, one-night stands—over cocktails and brunch, June Cleaver and Harriet Nelson must have rolled over in their TV graves.
> —Allison Klein, *What Would Murphy Brown Do?*

While these female foursome characters often succumb to stereotypical portrayals of women on television, they also step outside the boxes of conventional gender and sex roles to engage in the kind of gender trouble that Judith Butler heralds.[1] Decoupling sex from gender becomes a cornerstone for many of these foursome shows. Episodes involving lesbian characters, cross-dressing, female masculinity and transgender characters call into question gendered and sexed identities of main characters. In fact, every series involves at least one lesbian episode.

However, none are perhaps more memorable than the *Designing Women* episode wherein the fiercely feminine Suzanne Sugarbaker discovers that her long-lost friend and fellow competitor from the Miss Georgia Pageant, Eugenia Weeks, has finally come out (S4 E22). Even after Eugenia tells Suzanne and friends that she has come out, Suzanne does not grasp the full meaning of Eugenia's words. Eugenia mentions that no one else from her pageant days will acknowledge her now that she has come out, and Suzanne responds quizzically saying that is just ridiculous—just because Eugenia decided not to come out in her teens is no reason for folks to treat her badly. Suzanne's incredulity at this mistreatment turns to surprise as Mary Jo, Julia, and Anthony try to explain the facts to Suzanne. Suzanne asks, "What do I care if she's the world's oldest living debutante?" (S4 E22) Julia replies, "When she said coming out, she didn't mean at a cotillion, she meant from the closet!" (S4 E22) The humor in both the semantics of the dialogue and Suzanne's naïveté allow the episode to play with and trouble lesbian stereotypes.

The episode literally pokes fun at the ridiculousness of lesbian stereotypes as Mary Jo describes what she thought a lesbian bar would look like, as she comments, "This isn't at all what I pictured a lesbian bar to look like. This is terrible, but I saw a little dark cave tucked away under a staircase with women in gangster suits dancing the Tango and pictures of tennis stars all over the wall" (S4 E22). In this way Mary Jo, who speaks as the everywoman character, manages to articulate precisely those negative images of lesbian women that dominate the mainstream American imaginary. Through this articulation, Mary Jo calls into question heterosexist modes of thought and calls out the very darkest, deepest, elements of heterosexual fear, what Eve Sedgwick refers to as a fear of the instability of the homo/heterosexual binary (Sedgwick 1990). This fear is predicated on the understanding that heterosexuality exists in the collective consciousness only in contrast with homosexuality; however, without this binary sexual boundaries become too fluid, so these boundaries must be policed at all costs. Sedgwick maintains that heterosexuals are terrified of legitimizing homosexuality by recognition because it is a radical threat to their own identity, yet the binary opposition between heterosexuality and homosexuality is essential to stabilizing both identities on the continuum of sexual desire (Sedgwick 1990).

Mary Jo's confessions regarding her perceptions about lesbian bars and lesbian behaviors compellingly demonstrate this kind of heterosexual fear; however, the clarifying moment of the episode comes in the final scene when Eugenia confronts Suzanne in a sauna. Eugenia addresses the fear underlying Sedgwick's theory of homosexual panic when she tells Suzanne and the viewer, "I don't know what you've heard, but gay people are not out to convert the rest of the world" (S4 E22). In this final scene of the episode, Eugenia herself is able to speak against homosexual panic and lesbian stereotypes; however, it is Suzanne's statement to a woman fleeing the sauna that communication scholar Lauren Rabinovitz finds most powerful:

"Lady, who cares what you think? You got more problems than lesbians in your sauna." The naming of lesbian and women desiring women—the repressed aspect of female friendship throughout these programs—as well as Suzanne's verbal incorporation of herself as a lesbian (the plural "lesbians") shift Suzanne to a position of political resistance. It is a highly significant textual movement that yields feminist pleasure [Rabinovitz 1999, 150–151].

For Rabinovitz, Suzanne's political resistance resides in the repressed desire palpable just below the surface of the kind of female friendships depicted in this episode of *Designing Women*. I would argue that this kind of female friendship and this type of repressed desire repeat on all of the female foursome programs, and furthermore that the political resistance articulated by Suzanne Sugarbaker resides in the characterizations of many of the other female foursome programs. Communication scholar Alexander Doty points out the extent to which audiences take an active role in the queer and resistant readings of women-centered television programs. Doty argues:

> What is so interesting about series such as *I Love Lucy* (and later, *The Lucy Show*), *Laverne and Shirley*, *Designing Women*, *The Golden Girls*, *Babes*, *227*, *The Mary Tyler Moore Show*, *Kate and Allie*, and *Alice* is their crucial investment in constructing narratives that connect an audience's pleasure to the activities and relationships of women.... It is this kind of narrative construction I am calling "lesbian." The spectator positions and pleasures audiences take in relation to these lesbian sitcoms I call either "lesbian" (for self-identified lesbians) or "queer" (for anybody else) [Doty 1993, 41].

However, Rabinovitz concludes, "Suzanne's moment of woman-identified politics is ruptured through a denial of her friend's articulated desire for women, thereby ensuring that in future episodes that Suzanne may be returned safely to the realm of heterosexual feminine excess" (1993, 151). Rabinovitz argues that Suzanne's last line in the scene, "If we can put a man on the moon, we can put one on top of you" undercuts her earlier self-identification as lesbian and projects heteronormativity onto Eugenia (S4 E22). While I concur with Rabinovitz's assessment of the statement as reifying heteronormative values, I would argue that this line is not delivered with the same passion as the earlier line, "You got more problems than lesbians in your sauna" (S4 E22). The earlier line rings true and the later line is a throwaway, a laughter-evoking afterthought, that is classic Suzanne. Rabinovitz acknowledges that her reading of this scene conflicts with Alexander Doty's interpretation of

Designing Women in general and this scene, in particular, wherein Doty recognizes an ongoing lesbian dynamic between the characters (Rabinovitz 1999, 165; Doty 1993, 41). Doty similarly finds that this lesbian dynamic continues on *Hot in Cleveland*. His critical analysis of the *Hot in Cleveland* episode titled "The Sex that Got Away" reinforces his overarching theory of women-centered sitcoms as reflective of the deep bonds that form through women-centered relationships (S1 E4). Doty explains:

> True to classic women-centered sitcom form, however, this plot thread combines having one of the recurring characters mistaken for a lesbian with this character's incredible naïveté about all things Sapphic. In this case, Nash mistakes Melanie's bumbling and fumbling encounters as inept, if endearing, come-ons, while Melanie seems to be clueless about Nash's sexuality, even given that one of her albums is titled "I Like Girls" and features the song "Love My Honeypot" [Doty, 2012].

As Doty indicates, there is a familiarity evidenced by this lesbian episode that is rife with Sapphic stereotypes, but there is also something freeing in the plotline that allows Melanie to occupy an alternative space of genuine woman-centered desire. Nash occupies the space of hero and idol—a space typically reserved for male protagonists. Certainly, viewers know that Melanie is not lesbian, but her genuine admiration, appreciation and adoration of Nash opens up a space for woman-centered desire that is rarely enacted by female characters in mainstream media. In this way both Doty's and Rabinovitz's critical analyses provide structural frameworks for potentially lesbian, queer, and resistant readings of female friendships and woman-centered relationships as depicted in *Designing Women* and *Hot in Cleveland* in particular, and female foursome programs in general.

Allusions to lesbian dynamics similarly pervade the narrative structure and character depictions on *Living Single*. In particular, Maxine Shaw's masculine persona and the strong, independent, business woman, Khadijah James, played by rumored lesbian Queen Latifah, produce fireworks on the show. Communication scholar Kristal Brent Zook explains, "Latifah was known as the antidote to hip-hop sexism. A widely respected rapper, she carried with her a long history of resistance to macho bravado and, despite her protest to the contrary, was labeled both a feminist and a lesbian" (1999, 54). Hence, lesbian and feminist meanings swirl around narrative structures, dialogue and character depictions. These two very powerful women, Maxine Shaw and Khadijah James, both run things and share a history of friendship and sisterhood. While Max's overt sexuality and voracious appetite set her up as the man eater and unruly woman, Khadijah, by contrast, operates as the voice of reason.

In an episode entitled "Woman to Woman," Khadijah tries to help Max accept that her roommate from college, Shayla, is gay and plans to marry a woman, Chris (S3 E22). Khadijah jokingly suggests that Max's attitude toward men convinces Shayla that men are not worthy partners. Max questions how long Khadijah has known that Shayla was lesbian, and Khadijah replies that Shayla told her during her junior year of college (S3 E22). Max is concerned about why her roommate did not share the truth with her, opting instead to share the truth with Khadijah. Max also tries to explain to Khadijah how difficult it is for Max to imagine that Shayla is gay, given Max's pronounced heterosexuality. Khadijah comments, "Ok, so, she played it cool.... That's how much your friendship mattered to her." Max quips, "Don't make me go back and rethink this.... I've already come up with a bitterness that I'm comfortable with" (S3 E22). Here, Max gives voice to her own insecurities and discomfort, as she explains to Khadijah that she takes comfort in her hard feelings toward Shayla. Khadijah encourages Max to forgive Shayla for keeping her sexuality a secret and to accept Shayla's lesbian identity; however, Max tells Shayla that while she can accept Shayla's sexual orientation, she finds it difficult to accept that Shayla kept this secret from her. Shayla explains her reasons for keeping the secret and Max continues to believe that Shayla just did not trust her. In the end Shayla confesses that she was in love with Max, and that was why she could not possibly tell Max during college that she was gay (S3 E22). Max feels bad about this situation, but she makes sure that Shayla knows that Max was not gay then and is not gay now. Shayla responds to the question of Max's sexuality in college by saying, "Well, I did wonder that you always rambled on about how men were snorting warthogs" (S3 E22). Max explains that if Shayla told her this during their time in college, she might have been upset, but Max would like to have had a chance to do the right thing by her dear friend and roommate (S3 E22).

These scenes highlight the tension in Max's character between her masculine performativity and her heterosexuality. In this way, Max and Shayla confront lesbian and feminist stereotypes. Perhaps this episode decouples sexual orientation from gender performativity, as Shayla, a petite and overtly feminine woman, identifies as a femme lesbian, while Max, a boisterous and aggressive woman, identifies as a voracious heterosexual. Smith Shomade declares, Max occupies the position of "unruly woman—taking over the conventionally male-occupied space of aggressor—in order to usurp male potency and claim a space of her own" (2002, 53). Although Max's masculine gender performativity may be recognized as the embodiment of stereotypical second wave, equity feminism, her pronounced heterosexual desire marks her as unruly. While the preferred reading of the scene between Shayla and Max might be one of acceptance and forgiveness, wherein Max forgives Shayla for keeping her feelings a secret, Max's feelings of homophobia and betrayal become so conflated that the audience cannot know where one begins and the other ends. Hence, the resolution of the conflict between Max and Shayla (who never appears again on *Living Single*) leaves the audience wondering about the connection between lesbian desire and sisterhood.

This open-ending repeats in an episode of *The Golden Girls* titled "Isn't it Romantic" in which Dorothy's friend Jean, who has recently lost her lesbian partner, visits *The Golden Girls* and develops a crush on Rose. When Dorothy tells Sophia the news, Sophia unflinchingly responds. "If one of my kids was gay, I wouldn't love him any less. In fact, I would wish him all the happiness in the world" (S2 E5). As an octogenarian, Sophia operates on *The Golden Girls* as the elder, the wise woman, and the matriarch. Sophia's endorsement of gay relationships, particularly within the parameters of familial bonds as in the case of a child, reinforces the same kind of political resistance present in Suzanne's speech in the sauna. Fan posts also connote this theme of political resistance, noting that the queer lens of *The Golden Girls* is culturally symbolic and recognizable.

HP writes: "Man, I LOVE this show! When I was growing up, I would tape the originals and then obsessively play them back over and over again. How did my family not know I was gay?! LOL."

An article appearing in the online forum *TV Squad* (now a division of the Huffington Post) immediately after the death of Rue McClanaghan titled, "Memories of Rue McClanaghan and The Golden Girls as Gay Icons" suggests that the queer lens of *The Golden Girls* attracted gay audiences.

> Blanche, Rose, Dorothy and Sophia were identifiable peers. But NBC was delighted when the ratings showed that for other, younger viewers, they were fantasy grandmas—and their show a de facto Saturday night babysitter. If you were like me, maybe you fantasized about staying a while at Blanche's house in Miami.... *The Golden Girls* were the ultimate surrogate family, relatable to gay viewers who had constructed such relationships ourselves [Memories of Rue 2010].

In this way, the potential for resistant readings of queer telefeminism proliferate to include gay male viewers for whom the women of *The Golden Girls* represent the types of surrogate and alternative family that is both familiar and desirable. That the women of *The Golden Girls* face the realities of living alone without biological family members, that they continue to date, attend nightclubs, events, and parties, that they enjoy getting dressed up and going out on the town, that they are swinging singles who lean on each other—all of these elements resonate with gay viewers.

Certainly, the affirming queer politics of *The Golden Girls* mark it as a ground-breaking sitcom for its time and Sophia's sage octogenarian wisdom regarding gender bending and gay marriage are particularly noteworthy. This is evidenced throughout the series as she openly accepts her own son Phil's identification as a cross-dresser (S6 E12) and assists Blanche in working through her homophobic attitude when Blanche's brother, Clayton, announces that he will marry a man (S6 E14). In the episode titled "Sister of the Bride," Clayton plans a commitment ceremony with his partner, Doug (S6 E14). Blanche is very disturbed by this and she and Sophia sit down to discuss the matter. Blanche comments, "It's easier for you to say, Sophia. It's not *your* brother who's getting married to another man. Oh, look, I can accept the fact that he is gay, but why does he have to slip a ring on this guy's finger so the whole world will know?" (S6 E14). Sophia asks why Blanche and George wanted to get married, and Blanche explains, "We loved each other, wanted to make a lifetime commitment, and we wanted everybody to know" (S6 E14). Sophia points out that everyone wants to live out their days with someone, to love and to be truly loved and that Clayton and Doug are no different in this regard. Blanche seems to understand and tells Sophia that she needs to go and talk to Doug and Clayton. Sophia says that's fine, but she proposes marriage to Blanche and Blanche laughs it off. Finally Sophia retorts, "Fine, but I'm going to need an answer. I am not going to wait for you forever" (S6 E14).

Although Sophia's last line adds much-needed levity to the situation, the weightiness of the conversation and the overt politics in support of gay marriage and affirming gay partnerships prevails. The political resistance evidenced by Sophia's position as the wise woman and matriarch represents a rupture in the humorous narrative of double entendre and misunderstandings on the show. Viewers watch *The Golden Girls* for laughs, but find themselves opening up to new ideas, queer perspectives, and excessive female characters. TQ writes about Jean falling in love with Rose:

> OMG, one of my many favorite Blanche moments is that whole scene in Dorothy's room when they tell her Jean is a lesbian and she thinks they mean Lebanese, and after they correct her, they tell her Jean is in love with Rose, and instead of finding it as funny as they do she's offended that Jean has fallen for Rose rather than her. Evidently Blanche's belief in her own desirability crossed all gender lines, lol.

What TQ points to is the place where Blanche's idea of herself as universally desirable offers a radical reading of sex. Both Suzanne Sugarbaker and Blanche Devereaux reveal the depth of their self-absorption and narcissism when lesbian characters (in these cases, Eugenia and Jean) do not fancy Suzanne and Blanche, respectively. Suzanne and Blanche experience this absence of lesbian desire as an insult in spite of their decidedly homophobic worldviews. Although the ridiculousness of Suzanne and Blanche's excessive narcissism tempers the political implications of the radical possibility of universal desirability in a polyamorous and/or bisexual world, TQ's post glimpses the potential for alternative and resistant reading of this episode of *The Golden Girls*.

Later, in the same episode, when Rose and Jean finally talk about Jean's feelings, Jean tells Rose that she felt so very alone after her partner Pat died, and that she became confused about her feelings for Rose. Rose tells Jean that she is flattered, and asks if her friendship is enough. Jean responds saying it's enough. Although Rabinovitz might argue that Rose's response undercuts Sophia's endorsement of queer desire, and Blanche's assertion of her universal sex appeal, Rose's ability to remain friends with Jean in spite of the fact that Rose does not reciprocate Jean's lesbian desire, evidences a different kind of political resistance. Jean and Rose can still be friends, and can still engage in the bonds of female friendship, even if lesbian desire is not something they share. In this way, the episode moves beyond the rhetoric of tolerance to a celebration of sexual difference. While this does not discount Rabinovitz's critique that lesbian desire[2] in that female friendship is not fully explored in these shows, I argue that the trajectory for articulating this repressed lesbian desire through female friendships continues to be evidenced in later female foursome shows.

Clearly *Sex and the City* marks a dramatic shift in the televisual exploration of sex and gender roles as the confluence of heterosexual behaviors as linked to conventional gender performatives and biological sex become fair game for female sexual pleasure and empowerment. While some critics argue that *Sex and the City* reifies heteronormativity and traditional femininity, there is no doubt that Charlotte, Miranda, Carrie and Samantha explore repressed lesbian desire through their female friendships. In a sense, their female friendship makes a safe space for exploring multiple sex and gender identities. In an episode entitled, "What's Sex Got to Do with It?" Samantha comes out with a shocking statement (S4 E4). Samantha tells the girls that she is dating someone new, someone she likes: a woman named Maria. Charlotte is confused and asks if it's her friend Maria from the gallery. Samantha replies sharply, "Well, she's *my* Maria now. We're having a relationship. Yes, ladies, I'm a lesbian" (S4 E4). Just then, Maria walks into the bar and Carrie, Miranda, and Charlotte stand shell-shocked by the announcement. When they leave the restaurant, they begin to address the implications of what Samantha told them. Carrie asks, "How does that work? You go to bed one night; you wake up the next morning, and—*poof*—you're a lesbian?" Charlotte retorts, "I don't think she's a lesbian. I think she just ran out of men" (S4 E4). Miranda adds, "Then you go on strike, you don't eat pussy" (S4 E4). Once again, lesbian stereotypes resurface, but Samantha, who oozes sensuality and who arguably demonstrates the broadest range of sexuality and sexual desire, surprises her friends both because she uses the terms *lesbian* and *relationship*, both of which seem completely foreign to Samantha's way. She moves beyond the scope of the classic femme fatale into the positionality of unruly, wanton woman, one who is willing to do whatever it takes to prove that she cannot be pinned down to a single typology of woman. Samantha moves beyond the identity of the vamp, siren, femme fatale and into the category of dangerous woman. In some ways, this identification or disidentification with the traditional role of heterosexual femme fatale underscores the excessiveness of Samantha's sexual desires which transcend the sex and gender binaries of love objects and relationship labels.

Some might argue that Samantha's sexual freedom transcends and/or defies the traditional categories of sexual desire and moves toward more contemporary notions of polyamorous relations. This is also the case for the *Girlfriends* character of Lynn Searcy, who becomes engaged to a woman after rescuing her from a suicide attempt. However some viewers of *Girlfriends* were not convinced of this shift in Lynn's sexual desire, as DN argues:

> But Lynn's lesbian stage isn't much of a stage, she just got engaged to keep the woman from killing herself, it's not like she loves her. That might become the plot twist but as of right now Lynn isn't some sudden lesbian.

KB 2005 also argues that the *Girlfriends* lesbian storyline fell flat:

> After last night's episode I have an idea where this show is going, nowhere. This whole lesbian storyline was stupid from the beginning but last night it entered a new realm of stupidity. We know Lynn wasn't a lesbian but now we find out Jennifer isn't one either, she just pretended she was one to keep Lynn. So they bore us with a lesbian storyline and it turns out there really wasn't a lesbian storyline.

However, DD 2005 maintains that Lynn as a heterosexual freak is an important element of the show.

> Well I'm glad they finally dropped that storyline. It was kind of weird though, because Jennifer sold the lesbian thing all too well. But I liked when Lynn was like "I'm still a freak though" and held out her arm twice, then kicked up her leg. When they laughed after that it seemed like it was real laughter and I thought that was cute.

This part of Lynn's character, her wild (sex)ploitations are grist for the dialogue and the plotlines on the show, but the extent to which Lynn maintains her heterosexual frame is underscored when viewers are told that, in fact, there was no such sexual move as the "Lynn Spin."

However, when Charlotte joins a circle of New York power lesbians, her idea of female friendship and sisterhood come into question (S2 E6). When Carrie, Miranda and Samantha ask Charlotte to come out for a drink, she tells them she has other plans and is meeting Lydia and some of her friends for the evening. Miranda comments, "Haven't you heard Charlotte's a lesbian?" and Charlotte replies that she has some new lesbian friends that she likes very much because they are stylish and chic and into art and they don't need men (S2 E6). Charlotte explains that she enjoys the friendship of these women and that it's refreshing to avoid the topic of men. She falls into a wonderland of womanliness. But later, Patti Austin, the power lesbian queen bee confronts Charlotte and asks her if she is lesbian. Charlotte must respond that she is straight, but she wants Patti to know that she feels connected to all women through the bonds of sisterhood and that joining the power lesbians makes her feel spiritually empowered and connected. Patti's reply is short: "Sweetheart, that's all very nice, but if you are not going to eat pussy then you're not a dyke" (S2 E6). Hence, Patti defines the bottom line for lesbian identity as it is reduced by mainstream dominant culture into a singular sexual performance. Charlotte's desire for female friendship becomes conflated with lesbian desire, but the sex/gender boundary police (in this case the power lesbian queen bee, Patti) rules that unconsummated lesbian desire does not equal lesbian identity for Charlotte. Patti quite literally revokes Charlotte's lesbian backstage pass and guest I.D. card. In this way, female friendship becomes detached from lesbian desire both reinforcing strict sex/gender boundaries and reinscribes the homo/heterosexual binary. Charlotte almost makes it as a femme lesbian, but now she returns to the trope of heterosexual white ruling-class femininity.

Although this episode of *Sex and the City* depicts lesbian desire as constituted by sexual performativity, a later episode entitled "Boy, Girl, Boy, Girl" troubles this easy identification and perhaps represents a move toward gender bending (S3 E4). When Carrie becomes infatuated with a hot, young, guy named Sean, he immediately opens the ex-file, and tells her about his history of monogamous relationships with Kaylynn, Leslie and Mark. Carrie is shocked, but attempts to play it cool, and tells Sean it's not a problem. Later with her friends Carrie vents her fear and frustration. Carrie comments, "I'm not even sure bisexuality exists. I think it's a layover on the way to gay town" (S3 E4). Of course Samantha thinks bisexuality is super sexy, but Miranda thinks it's a sign of promiscuity and indecision. The classic naïf Charlotte believes that everyone should choose a sexual identity and remain in that box. Charlotte very much believes in labeling sexual identity and the roles that relate to that identity (S3 E4).

In this scene each woman voices her perspective on the matter of bisexuality, but more than this they express how they feel about gendered and sexed identities. This scene validates the claim of Rebecca Brasfield: "Carrie, Miranda, Samantha and Charlotte represent a continuum of women's views and dilemmas when it comes to sex, love and dating. The range of perspectives may be one of the reasons why *Sex and the City* sparks so much interest, enthusiasm and criticism" (2006, 132). Except for Samantha, each woman indicates discomfort with gender bending and polyamorous behavior. However, later in the episode, Charlotte's infatuation with an artist, Baird Johnson, who paints portraits of drag kings, challenges her rigid views of gender performativity. Baird tells Charlotte, "Every woman has a male inside of her" (S3 E4). When Baird asks Charlotte to pose for one of his portraits, she initially resists, but bolstered by her desire for Baird, she acquiesces and as they both admire her masculine reflection in the mirror, she becomes aroused and asks him to add another sock to her trousers. In this moment, Charlotte is a woman dressed as man who desires a man, and Baird is a man who desires a woman dressed as a man. Charlotte's outward signification of masculinity through attire and performativity operate to expand the categories of sexual desire and gender performativity. That Charlotte, the most conservative, naïve and repressed character reaches this point of sexual freedom underscores the capacity for sexual empowerment and liberation in this episode specifically, and in the series in general.

Although *Sex and the City*'s approach to the theme of liberation through heterosexual cross-dressing, vis-à-vis the naïve character of Charlotte York, may be considered ground-breaking, Carlene Dobber of *Designing Women* similarly engages in gender bending seven years earlier when she discovers that her new boyfriend, Eric, enjoys dressing as a woman (S7 E20). In an episode titled "The Lying Game," Carlene (the naïf and replacement for Charlene, appearing in the last two seasons of *Designing Women*) dresses as a man in order to gain insight into her boyfriend's psyche. Eric has told Carlene that he finds dressing as a woman to be freeing as he is able to experience his feminine side. Although this aspect of cross-dressing is not seriously explored, Carlene's performance as a man demonstrates the invisible privilege of ruling-class, white males.[3] Carlene solicits opinions from the other women about how to enact masculine performativity in order to tap into her masculine side. Each of the women offers suggestions: (1) Men put their hands in their pockets and hitch up their pants; (2) Men give themselves permission to be aggressive—kinda like the guy who has to poke at you to make his point; (3) Men make noises to indicate that they have made some kind of effort.

Suddenly, Mr. Reynolds, a potential client with a hotel business, comes in and tries to low ball Sugarbaker's design quote for his job. BJ states, "Everything is negotiable." Mr. Reynolds declares, "Only to a woman." Mr. Reynolds asks who Carlene is, and BJ introduces her as Mr. Carl Lean of Lean Industries. Carl Lean retorts, "That's right and I'm here to bid for their time. (Grabbing thigh) I'll give you $50K, but I need you to start a week early" (S7 E20). Mr. Reynolds suggests that they settle this in a civilized manner between gentlemen asking what is the highest bid that Mr. Lean will entertain. Mr. Lean and Mr. Reynolds discuss a very high bid of fifty-five thousand dollars, and then Mr. Reynolds tops it at sixty thousand dollars (hitching up his pants). Mr. Lean replies jams his finger into Reynolds chest, "Well, I guess the best man won. But, that's the last time you ever play hard ball with me" (S7 E20). After Mr. Reynolds leaves, Mary Jo comments, "It's amazing the credibility that men have just by right of gender" (S7 E20). Carlene's decision to take up space like a man, talk like a man, and engage in masculine comportment, underscores the weightiness of Mary Jo's statement. It is important to note the extent to which the *Designing Women* interrogates this complex system of white, ruling-class, male privilege as it resides in the bodies of men through the performance of masculinity, thereby marking a significant milestone of oppositional gender performativity in the trajectory for female characters in mainstream American television. Hence, in this episode, *Designing Women* does the hard work of not only exploring gender identity through cross-dressing, but also challenges the power relations of masculinity by posing the following question: Can a woman perform like a man? While the question of passing as a man has certainly been a part of the American imagination onstage, in the cinema and on television, the idea of gender performativity as the site of that power springs to life as Carlene occupies the power position of Mr. Carl Lean of Lean Industries.

When a version of this question is asked on *Sex and the City*—can a woman have sex like a man?—Samantha decides to engage in revenge sex with her former lover in order to get even with him (S2 E11). Samantha calls Carrie and tells her that she is going to woo Dominick into falling in love with her, and that then when they are about to have sex, Samantha will dump him just like he dumped her. However, in the end when Samantha gets caught in her own game of cat and mouse, she realizes that she still has feelings in spite of her hybridity (a man's ego inside a woman's body) and she is surprised but happy to know it (S2 E11). For Samantha, the ability to operate as a scoundrel and to use Dominick for sex and then walk away when she is satisfied is ultimately not fulfilled. Carrie's voice-over allows viewers to know that Samantha is a "powerful hybrid," suggesting that Samantha is, at once, both masculine and feminine. In this way, Samantha represents a whole and complete human containing both masculine and feminine qualities—what feminists have been saying for years. However, the fact that the scene ends with Samantha recognizing that her feelings, her humanity, prevent her from moving further down the gender performance continuum reinforces the gender binary, leaving the viewer with the sense that the gender norms have been restored.

Performing like a man or like a woman is a problem that is also addressed on an earlier episode of *Designing Women* titled "Blame It on New Orleans," when Suzanne and Charlene dispute whether a lounge singer, Lolita DuPage, is a man in drag or not (S5 E19). Suzanne does not believe that Lolita DuPage is a man in drag: "I'm telling you, Charlene, Lolita is a woman pretending to be a man, pretending to be a woman. I mean haven't you ever seen *Victor Victoria*?" (S5 E19). However, Julia is exhausted and unamused when she shouts, "I don't care if he is George Bush in Drag!" (S5 E19). In this case the arguing over the category of sex and gender and sexuality leads to the most radical idea of the 1980s: George H. W. Bush in drag. The point here is both why should we care about the sex, gender, and sexual identities of this lounge singer in New Orleans? That, in fact, it is both extremely radical to argue the merits of this case, and extremely impertinent to feel empowered to argue about someone else's very private sex, gender and sexuality identities and performatives.

However on *Sex and the City*, Carrie's experience with Sean at a party may be read as the ultimate genderbending experience. When Carrie plays spin the bottle in mixed company and the bottle spun by a girl lands on her, she responds saying, "Whoops, it's a girl. Spin Again" (S3 E4). Instead of spinning again, the girl leans in for the kiss, so Carrie kisses her. Of the kiss, Carrie says, "It was nice, kinda like chicken." Carrie stands and excuses herself saying that she needs more cigarettes. In a voice-over Carrie explains, "I was in confused Alice in Wonder/Sexual Orientation Land." Carrie justifies her departure to herself, saying, "I took my hot, old fart ass home." Carrie implies that this wonder/sexual-orientation-land stuff is for young people, and she is too old to understand. Her ultimate reaction reifies rigid sex and gender categories, and unlike Charlotte, Carrie does not reach the point of sexual liberation by resisting dominant culture norms. Rather, in this episode, Carrie represents the hegemonic culture, and Charlotte represents the resistance. This flipping of character typologies invites resistant readings, consciousness raising about sexual binaries and gender performativity as well as offering an open ending that allows audiences to consider their own perspectives, experiences and visions for gender and sexed identity.

Although *Sex and the City* may offer some kind of sexual and consumptive power, critics argue that the series reflects the values of traditional white ruling-class hegemonic femininity and its concomitant heteronormativity. Deborah Ann Macey maintains, "As it turns out Carrie is simply not comfortable with fluid gender roles or the sexualities of Sean [her new bisexual boyfriend] or other party guests. This resolution privileges heteronormativity and denies bisexuality" (Macey 2008 168). Macey's reading aligns with critics who view *Sex and the City* as embodying what Amanda Lotz names as female consumerist choiceoisie (2006, 115). However, Karin Vasby Anderson and Jessie Stewart explain this reading of *Sex and the City* as "what happens when third-wave logic gets appropriated and infused into political culture: a homogenized, sexualized version of woman as consumer stands in for the woman as citizen" (2005, 610). Although Carrie's discomfort with Sean's bisexuality may be read as a classic case of heteronormative snobbery, she may also be participating in a choiceoisie that allows for a continuum of sexual desires and sexual behaviors, albeit, in this case, conservative hetero-sexuality. In fact, one might argue that Charlotte foils Carries "old fart" behavior in this episode by enacting an adventurous attitude toward sex, sexual desire and gender bending as depicted both by her willingness to pose in drag for Baird Johnson and her desire to join the social circle of power lesbians in the aforementioned episode (S2 E6). There is a real sense in which Charlotte tests the boundaries of her own sexual desire and gender performativity. Through both her drag performance and in the bonds of lesbian friendship, Charlotte literally tries on these gen-dered and sexed identities, thereby demonstrating the complexity of her seemingly simple characterization as a virginal Pollyanna.

Gender roles are similarly tampered with on *The Golden Girls*, as Dorothy frequently flirts with masculine personas. In particular, this occurs when she plays a sheriff with a serious beer belly in play, and a later episode when the girls are wrongly imprisoned as prostitutes. How-ever, she is often depicted as the masculine foil on the show as even her wardrobe is constructed as a form of failed femininity. Dorothy's mas-culine energy also operates as a foil for Blanche's über-sexuality and Rose's über-naïveté, both elements of über-femininity. In fact, Dorothy and her extra-textual personas Maud and Bea Arthur are well-known for their deep voices, towering height, and aggressive behavior.

RM discusses Dorothy's masculinity:

> Ahhhhhh I love that one too—where Dorothy "growls"!! There's great humor to be found in Bea Arthur's masculine side. Like when the girls do that play where Blanche (as well as the rest of the cast) is going out w/the director—and Dorothy plays the sheriff b/c she's the only one big enough to wear the costume!

In an episode entitled "Ladies of the Evening" *The Golden Girls* stay at a hotel with a discount rate because their house is being fumigated (S2 E2). The women dress for a concert with Mr. Burt Reynolds, and they meet in the hotel lobby for a drink. The hotel is raided for prosti-tution, and while in jail, Dorothy warns the other inmates against both-ering her or her friends. Dorothy sates, "Listen, you punk. You wanna fight with someone, you're gonna have to fight with me. But I warn you, I did time in Attica" (S2 E2). The other woman points out that Attica is a men's prison, but Dorothy comments that she was in for a year before anyone knew she was a woman. The other women are amazed at Dorothy's masculine bravado and they ask how she ever managed it. To which Dorothy replies that being a public school teacher requires a lot of tough love and it's not that different from being in jail (S2 E2).

PK writes about Dorothy in this episode:

> I came across an old episode on tape the other day and it was one of my favorites—when the girls are mistakenly imprisoned for prostitution and one of the hookers tries to start a fight with Blanche and Dorothy steps in saying "Listen, you punk! If you want to fight with someone, you'd better fight with me!" and the hooker backs down. Hee! Even criminals are frightened of Dorothy.

RML notes:

> Long time lurker, 1st time poster!
>
> I agree, KMG—I always thought of Bea Arthur as a "handsome woman." Particularly when coupled w/her booming voice! One of my favorite lines is when Dorothy sings a line from "Old Man River."

LC writes:

> Bea Arthur seems like a striking, handsome woman. Why does society have this agenda of making her seem like an example of ugly? I think Bea Arthur is a striking woman in the same way that, say Gina Davis or Angelica Huston is striking. That's why I'm glad that Dorothy was the Golden Girl to get married at the end of the series.

LC's concerns about Dorothy's depiction as ugly and masculine are perhaps best demonstrated in Season 5, Episode 23, when Dorothy prepares for a date. Dorothy asks, "Which goes better? The silver chain or the pearls?" and Rose suggests the chain. Blanche exclaims, "An amateur's mistake! Can't you see that the chain accentuates the many folds of that turkey-like neck?" Rose quips, "Well that may be, but the pearls draw attention to the non-existent bosom!" Blanche replies curtly, "Yes, but the chain leads the eye even lower to that huge spare tire jutting out over those square, manly hips!" Noticeably angry, Dorothy comments, "Fine! Why don't I just put a sign on me that says, "Too ugly to live?" To which Blanche replies, "Fine, but what are you going to hang it from? The chain or the pearls?" Dorothy growls, "None! I'm going to spray paint it on my hump!" (S5 E23). Here Dorothy's body becomes the site of gender policing that is so profound even viewers wonder how Bea Arthur feels about being cast in such a negative light.

Viewers also wonder at Dorothy's odd wardrobe in spite of Miami's heat. LB writes:

> Word. Miami is totally hot—at least that's what I hear. And those boots were fugly as hell. But I love Dorothy, no matter what she wears, for the awesome way in which she delivers all her snarky lines.

RM comments:

> Good point, I think b/c she is tall & has that deep voice she acts as a good foil for more feminine actresses out there. The artist John Currin painted a Bea Arthur Portrait that satirizes our culture's desexualization of the elderly.

Overturning this idea of the desexualization of the elderly operates as a repeating theme on *The Golden Girls*, and Betty White as Elka Ostrovsky's on *Hot in Cleveland* frequently draws on the taboo power of aging sexuality to produce some rather revolutionary conversations regarding sexual mores among aging populations. An example of this involves Elka's use of the term "downtown" in a season one episode of *Hot in Cleveland* (S1 E3).

> Melanie Moretti: So, Elka, when are you going to make it official?
> Elka Ostrovsky: Oh, that's over. We started having problems.
> Melanie Moretti: What happened?
> Elka Ostrovsky: Well, we got along fine but... he wouldn't go downtown. If you know what I mean. (the three girls are stunned)
> Elka Ostrovsky: What! I mean there are so many good restaurants and, and shops downtown. (the three laugh, relieved)
> Elka Ostrovsky: I can't give that up!
> Victoria Chase: Why should you?
> Elka Ostrovsky: [going to answer the door] What did you think I was talking about?
> Joy Scroggs: So you meant shops.
> Melanie Moretti: Nothing, nothing at all.
> Max: Hi.
> Elka Ostrovsky: M-Max.
> Max: Listen, Elka, I don't want to lose you, so if you're still up for it, I'm willing to try going downtown.
> Elka Ostrovsky: You are?
> Max: Yes. Just hope I don't get lost down there.
> Elka Ostrovsky: Oh, you won't. I have no trouble telling you where to go.
> Max: It's just that it's so dark and scary there.

The double entendre hangs in the air as the live audience roars with laughter, and the reference to Elka's vagina as a dark and scary place akin to that of Eve Ensler's description of "The Flood" monologue from *The Vagina Monologues* (Ensler 2001).

> THE FLOOD
> [Jewish, Queens accent]
> Down there? I haven't been down there since 1953. No, it had nothing to do with Eisenhower. No, no, it's a cellar down there. It's very damp, clammy. You don't want to go down there. Trust me. You'd get sick. Suffocating. Very nauseating. The smell of the clamminess and the mildew and everything. Whew! Smells unbearable. Gets in your clothes. No, there was no accident down there. It didn't blow up or catch on fire or anything. It wasn't so dramatic. I mean ... well, never mind. No. Never mind. I can't talk to you about this. What's a smart girl like you going around talking to old ladies about their down-theres for?

Elka dares to talk about her "down there," albeit only through double entendre, but what is revolutionary about this is that it is not some late-night theater play off, off Broadway, with some unknown feminist actress. Instead, this is Betty White in primetime acting as an octogenarian character, and she is empowered as the Wise Woman character to raise the question of going downtown. The end of "The Flood" monologue raises similar questions.

> What would it wear? What kind of question is that? What would it wear? It would wear a big sign: "Closed Due to Flooding." What would it say? I told you. It's not like that. It's not like a person who speaks. It stopped being a thing that talked a long time ago. It's a place. A place you don't go. It's closed up, under the house. It's down there. You happy? You made me talk—you got it out of me. You got an old lady to talk about her down-there. You feel better now? [Turns away; turns back.] You know, actually, you're the first person I ever talked to about this, and I feel a little better.

As the viewer considers Max's last line "it's just so dark and scary there" the power of talking about "down there" registers. That Elka, at her age, could consider ending a relationship because her lover wouldn't "go downtown" upsets the delicate apple cart of mature sexuality. Instead of Elka being depicted as a benign old woman or a desperate spinster, she appears on the crest of active female sexual empowerment. Her sexual desire remains intact, and she is able to engage in the robust sexual banter of women nearly half her age. Elka holds the attention of the audience and guides them to a narrative of mature female sexual empowerment that draws from the trajectory of female foursome shows while engaging in the cultural critique of taboo sexual subjectivity of female sexual power and the generational decline in sexual desire.

Although the reifying of heteronormative sexuality may be arguably present in each of the female foursome shows, the bonds of female friendship, alternative family and shared female pleasure in woman's space and woman's talk inspire queer readings of the series. Cultural historian Jane Gerhard argues, "What made *Sex and the City* different was that it regularly suggested that this family of four could be enough to make up a life, a life still worth living without the husband and baby, a life led outside the historic feminine and feminist script" (2005 46). What Gerhard suggests is that there is a liberatory power in the formation of the alternative family of Carrie, Miranda, Samantha and Charlotte. Gerhard links the historical production of alternative family by survivalist gay men and lesbians to the construction of alternative family by postfeminist women (2005, 44). While I concur with Gerhard's analysis of the appropriation of the queer alternative family model by the women of *Sex and the City* and the other female foursome programs, I dispute her use of the term *postfeminist* here. Indeed, Gerhard points to the interrelationship of the four women in *Sex and the City* and finds that the bonds of female friendship expand beyond the boundaries of 21st century female friendship and reach back to the intimacy of 19th century female friendships. Gerhard states, "Women's historians have argued that these private bonds were passionate, that they involved psychological and physical intimacy, and provided support and love that women living in racial/gender hierarchies could not get from men, who like women, lived largely in homosocial worlds" (2005, 44). Gerhard argues provocatively that these female friendships extended beyond the bounds of conventional heterosexual friendship.

This intimacy is similarly present in the candid sex talk by Carrie, Samantha, Miranda and Charlotte. Gerhard argues that the sex talk both serves as a form of feminist consciousness-raising and as space for shared female pleasure (2005, 45). Hence, Gerhard maintains that the queering of *Sex and the City*'s narrative structure and woman's talk produces an alternative space for the feminist project and women's liberation (2005). In *Third Wave Feminism and Television: Jane Puts it in a Box*, Merri Lisa

Johnson and her contributors similarly argue that the queering of television opens up a liberatory space for feminist audiences and may actually have the potential to move viewers beyond the binary oppositions that have plagued our collective psyche for far too long (2007). However, unlike Gerhard, Johnson and her contributors argue that the queering of sexuality, whether it is bisexual, heterosexual, homosexual and/or some of each of these, underscore the crucial point that the third wave of feminism is queer (2007). Hence, I support Gerhard's assertion that the queering of narrative structure, woman's talk and the depiction of these larger-than-life women characters open up the space for the feminist project and women's liberation. And, also, like Johnson and her contributors, I recognize the potential for resistant readings of popular culture and media as the products of a queer third-wave feminism— what may be referred to as *queer telefeminism.*

4

Unruly Women, Femme Fatales, Gold Diggers & Dixie Bitches

> In traditional bourgeois cultures unbridled sexual appetites or loose speech are a mark not only of the lower classes but of the unruly woman, who inverts the power relations of gender and has sex like a man.
>
> —Jane Arthurs, "*Sex and the City* and Consumer Culture: Remediating Postfeminist Drama"

Stereotypes of unruly women, femme fatales, gold diggers, and Dixie bitches dominate the casts of *Girlfriends*, *Hot in Cleveland*, *Cashmere Mafia*, *Sex and the City*, *Designing Women*, *Living Single* and *The Golden Girls*. These too much women of television are truly the ones we most love to watch. They remind us of extraordinary women in our daily lives: our mothers, aunts, cousins, sisters and friends. However, in every case, these over-the-top TV women invite us, the viewers, to recognize the contradictions in ourselves and in the lived experiences of so many women whom we know culturally, socially and intimately. Allison Klein suggests that it is precisely these unruly types that inspire viewers. Klein states, "While my mother's generation grew up with role models like June Cleaver, we now have single mothers, career women, smart alecks and ballbusters" (2006, 251). As ballbusters, these women punctuate the continuum of unruly women on television. Communication scholar Jeremy Butler argues, "The unruly woman is not satisfied with woman's conventional role as object of masculine desire and spectation. Rather the spectacle she creates is one that serves her own desires and needs" (1993, 14). Butler articulates precisely what is so groundbreaking about the characters appearing in these female foursome shows as unruly women, femme fatales, gold diggers, and Dixie bitches: their female subjective desire. This refusal to exist only as object coupled together with an unflinching female desire constitutes the unruly women of these female foursome shows.

The Dixie Bitch

Film scholar James Kirby coins the term Dixie bitch in his landmark book, aptly titled *Media-made Dixie: The South in the American Imagination* (1978, 72). Scarlett O'Hara serves as the iconic, big screen Dixie bitch, whose fiery temper, fierce independence, flamboyant flirtations, and beguiling femininity make her a match for any man. Arguably, *Designing Women*'s Suzanne Sugarbaker, played by actress Delta Burke, dominates the small screen as the postmodern embodiment of the Dixie bitch. Ethel Goodstein evokes Kirby's image of the Dixie bitch to describe the sharp contrast between antebellum architecture and the characterization of a particular kind of Southern woman. Goodstein states, "Like the controlled, classical elegance of the plantation house, she [the Dixie bitch] was a foil for the demagoguery and oppression that were equally mythic in Southern history" (1992, 178). Certainly, the Dixie bitch belongs to the larger category of unruly woman; however, I argue that the Dixie bitch operates as a monstrous woman, a grotesque and frightening woman. Communication scholar Kathleen Rowe describes the unruly woman typology in western art, literature and history as threatening to the conceptual categories and upsetting Foucaultian power relations in terms of subjective power (1990, 77). Rowe notes, "She [the unruly woman] evokes not only delight but disgust and fear. Her ambivalence, which is the source of her oppositional power, is usually contained within the licence [sic] accorded to the comic and the carnivalesque. But not always" (1990, 76). Certainly, *Designing Women* actively invokes Delta Burke's extratextual persona as a former Miss Florida 1974 through the characterization of Suzanne Sugarbaker as the super beauty queen, Miss Georgia World. The carnivalesque of the pageant circuit as signified by the trappings of excessive femininity (big hair,[1] stage make-up, manicured nails, high heels, waxed legs, denture gripped bathing suits, and Vaselined teeth). Each of these tricks of the trade demonstrate feminine performativity, and remind us of Jonathan's Swift's metaphysical poem, "A Beautiful Young Nymph Going to Bed," in which femininity is debunked as a most unnatural processes wherein its elements must be put on like a suit of armor to cover up the natural and the real woman underneath, who, in the case of the poem, is a prostitute named Corinna.[2] An excerpt from the poem appears below:

> Then, seated on a three-legged chair,
> Takes off her artificial hair:
> Now, picking out a crystal eye,
> She wipes it clean, and lays it by.
> Her eye-brows from a mouse's hide,
> Stuck on with art on either side,
> Pulls off with care, and first displays 'em,
> Then in a play-book smoothly lays 'em.
> Now dexterously her plumpers draws,
> That serve to fill her hollow jaws.
> Untwists a wire; and from her gums
> A set of teeth completely comes.
> Pulls out the rags contrived to prop
> Her flabby dugs and down they drop.
> Proceeding on, the lovely goddess
> Unlaces next her steel-ribbed bodice;
> Which by the operator's skill,
> Press down the lumps, the hollows fill,
> Up goes her hand, and off she slips
> The bolsters that supply her hips.

Here, Corinna dismantles her femininity as she takes off her wig, wipes her glass eye and places it on the table, removes her teeth, untethers her corset and lets her breasts hang down, and takes out her hip enhancers. Swift's satire of the trappings of femininity can be extrapolated to critique Suzanne Sugarbaker's performativity as a retired beauty queen from the pageant circuit. Suzanne's increasing size does not diminish this critique, but rather furthers the parody of excessive and now grotesque femininity. Proffered by Suzanne Sugarbaker, Miss Georgia World, it constitutes the quintessential iconography of perfomative femininity not unlike that found in a drag queen. Jeremy Butler argues that as Delta Burke's character gained weight and continued flouting the conventions of ideal beauty, she began to occupy the space of the unruly woman (1993, 15). Butler notes, "She had shed the masquerade of femininity that women must preserve if they wish to remain visible and powerful in patriarchal culture" (1993, 15).

These trappings of femininity signify the construction of gendered performativity akin to drag performances of idealized white, ruling-class femininity. This case of putting on the armor of femininity repeats in many episodes of the series. Including an episode entitled "Stranded" also known as meet me in "St. Louis, Louis," wherein Suzanne and Anthony get caught in a blizzard on their way to a pageant event and design expo (S2 E10). Anthony is permitted behind the curtain of Suzanne's closet of femininity as he preps her wig, discusses her dress, shoes and hosiery choices. This also occurs in an episode titled "Blame it on New Orleans," wherein Suzanne refuses to believe that a drag queen, Lolita DuPage, is a man. When the man removes his wig, Suzanne likewise removes hers and states, "Oh, that doesn't prove diddly" (S5 E19). Tara McPherson comments, "With their stocking-capped heads and over-the-top makeup, the two look remarkably alike, spinning Southern femininity and its constructions in new directions" (179). In this way, Suzanne Sugarbaker's power on the show stems not only from her body, her beauty and her overt Southern femininity, but also her ability to engage in a parody of idealized, white ruling-class femininity.

Viewers cannot be sure whether Suzanne is playing the straight character or the parodied carnivalesque version of the femme fatale, and it is this uncertainty that keeps viewers watching. The polyvalent meanings of Suzanne as at once straight, traditional, and seemingly conservative blue-blood are offset by her excessive eccentricities during the series. For example, viewers see her wearing a pink negligée while toting a semi-automatic rifle in order to protect Noel, the pig in her parlor (S3 E15). Suzanne calls attention to and recognizes the disjuncture of this dissident disidentification at times. For example Suzanne says it wouldn't look right for she and Anthony to spend the night in the hotel in St. Louis in spite of the fact that they kvetch about her wigs, hosiery and make-up during the trip (S2 E 10). When they arrive at the hotel in St. Louis, Anthony and Suzanne work like a fashion and make-up design team behind the closed bathroom door. The other women listen with great interest as Anthony tells Suzanne that she can wear the hosiery that he wore last night, and that he will roll out her wig for her since she doesn't have time to wash and dry her own hair (S2 E10). The feminizing of Anthony definitely plays into the series as Anthony may be read as "the help" for many episodes.

However, Suzanne's continual suggestion that there is a disjuncture in the gendered and raced relationship between she and Anthony underscores her failed performance of white ruling-class femininity even as she tells him that she enjoys his company and she can be herself around him. Stranded on the way to St. Louis, this disjuncture is exposed. Suzanne wonders aloud to Anthony about what it might have been like for them if they had both been born into white privilege. She suggests that their friendship would have been natural, and that Anthony's blackness stands in the way of their current relationship. Anthony responds that perhaps Suzanne should consider what it would be like if they were both black, and Suzanne capitulates and says, "Oh, okay we can both be black. That way I can be the first Black Miss America because Vanessa Williams doesn't count" (S2 E10). Anthony's sarcastic reply indicates that Suzanne does not fully grasp the differential in their raced, classed, and gendered power relations. The fact that Suzanne assumes that even if she were black she would occupy a privileged class position, as the first Black Miss America demonstrates her inability to interrogate her own privilege in terms of white ruling-class femininity as it is reified by the dominant power structures of white supremacist, capitalist, patriarchy. Even as white supremacy dominates the power relations between Anthony and Suzanne there is an interrogation of the categories of whiteness and blackness, and they are temporarily deconstructed as Suzanne imagines herself as the first Black Miss America. Her trivialization of Blackness serves to underscore the power of white supremacy, its impact on dominant mainstream culture as evidenced by the beauty industry and pageant circuits; however, this exchange queries the naturalness of whiteness and Blackness as categories of value.

In this way, Suzanne transcends her role as the embodiment of white ruling-class femininity as she imagines a world in which she and Anthony might be equals. Although race maintains its dominant cultural meaning in this exchange, there is a critical discussion of how race separates these characters who might otherwise be friends. This allows for the possibility of friendship under exceptional circumstances, and Suzanne allows Anthony and her viewers to see her authentic self. Suzanne and Anthony concur that they are glad to have spent this time together and that within the confines of these special circumstances (in a crisis, in a blizzard, and in a small hotel in the middle of nowhere), they can be friends.

However, this does not so offset the power relations that she becomes unaware of the cultural norms. Suzanne clearly recognizes social conventions and generally adheres to them except in cases where those exceptions would benefit her. This occurs in many episodes, including "La Place Sans Souci," in which Suzanne and Charlene become members of the "heavy duty" group and suffer through a boot camp for big people. Charlene notes that she does not like being referred to a big person as she has just had a baby, and Suzanne retorts, "I guess the implication is that the rest of us are just childless and fat." Later all four women are thrown out of the spa and resort, La Place sans Souci, for fighting in the mud bath. As Anthony drives them home, Julia notes, "Well, Suzanne, we look odd, but then again I suppose I always knew in my heart we would end up like this.... It's kind of fitting, isn't it? Here we are going down the highway into the dark Georgia night: four aging Southern belles, war-torn hair, dirty faces, a nanny, a baby, and a crippled black man" (S4 E28). In a later episode entitled "EP Phone Home," Suzanne notes this disjuncture again: "This was one of the weirdest weekends I've ever had in my life. Driving seven hundred miles to spend two days in a cheap motel with a bunch of Elvis Presley cooks, and now Julia is dating a truck driver" (S3 E3). Here, Suzanne interrogates class difference and recognizes how she does not fit in with this scenario. However, Suzanne's recognition of her excessiveness, her "too muchness" constitutes her as both unruly woman and Dixie bitch. For example, when Suzanne goes to the beach with the whole gang (Charlene, Bill and Olivia, Mary Jo, J.D. and their children, Reese, Julia and his grand-children) they decide to hire a nanny to watch the children and grand-children. Suzanne immediately recognizes that the large-breasted, spandex-wearing, blonde bombshell—nanny Ursula—threatens the social order of the group (S3 E1). Suzanne confronts Ursula and explains, "Ursula, let's get serious. This is not an unobtrusive outfit. I mean, these are not clothes that scream—yes, my job is taking care of small children.... I think you are just one of those people who are too much.... Julia and Charlene and Mary Jo would never tell you this because they're too nice, but I can tell you because I am too much, too" (S3 E1). This too-muchness is precisely what constitutes Suzanne as an unruly woman and Dixie bitch.

Certainly, Suzanne and Julia Sugarbaker (and, to some extent, Blanche Devereux) demonstrate the characteristics of Dixie bitch; however, Julia Sugarbaker's frequent outbursts, ranging from high-flown blue-blood exclamations to vitriolic diatribes of Southern outrage, mark her as the stereotypical Dixie bitch. This is perhaps best depicted when Julia reads a newspaper article written by a New Yorker about Southerners eating dirt. She quickly jettisons her gentility in favor of scathing commentary (S3 E4). Julia calls the newspaper and leaves a message for managing editor, Jackson Weeks informing him that she could attest to the fact that although Southerners eat a lot of things (grits, homemade biscuits and gravy, fried chicken and even crow), they never eat dirt.

Julia's frequent diatribes evince a form of Southern feminist, righteous indignation rarely captured on television. I maintain that Julia Sugarbaker is the quintessential Dixie bitch and that her viewpoint perhaps most powerfully conveys the sentiments of her writer, Linda Bloodworth-Thomason. Nonetheless, Bloodworth-Thomason's creation of this explosive character Julia Sugarbaker builds on prior images of the Dixie bitch, and produces a powerful and provocative image of the contemporary Southern woman for the American imaginary—a form of Southern femininity that is at once feminine and profoundly feminist.

Unruly Women and Their Bodies

Ultimately, I argue that unruly women characters provoke resistant and oppositional readings, particularly in female foursome shows, because each character represents a point on a worldview continuum, ranging from conservative and traditional to liberal, and sometimes radical. Communication scholar Lynn Spangler explains, "In a discursive reading of *Designing Women*, each of the women can be interpreted to represent a particular world view or ideology" (1996, 220). Similarly, film and television studies scholar Samantha Sheppard maintains that *Living Single* presents four successful Black females of varying sizes, skin tones and worldviews who engage in a female community that is not based in struggle (as seen in previous series, such as *227*) but rooted in a more ideal reality" (2007, 97). Each female foursome character represents a different ideological standpoint, and, as such, they invite viewers with a variety of worldviews and positionalities to engage in perspective taking and, in many cases, to walk a mile in someone else's shoes.

In this way, my fan-based research supports previous findings by television scholars that fans watch programs more avidly when they identify with the program's characters (Press 1991). Furthermore, this project builds on earlier television scholarship and confirms that fans post most often on message boards and forums in the following cases: (1) when they identify with a character or episode, (2) when their own experience resonates with that of a character or episode; and (3) when characters inspire, encourage, or challenge viewer's positionalities.[3] The unruly characters, femme fatales, gold diggers, and Dixie bitches of these female foursome shows do inspire, encourage and challenge viewer's positionalities; therefore, this chapter is reflective of the power of these excessive women who frequently move outside of their designated stereotypical boxes. Each female foursome show depicts more than one excessive character, and even characters who are generally mild mannered are given at one time or another to flights of fancy and terrific excess. Identifying with the characterizations on these programs provides access for viewers to a visual imaginary they might otherwise never see. LP writes about her experience watching *Living Single*:

> Watching those shows as a little girl (I was also in late elementary/middle school when they were in syndication!) was a really positive experience. To know that I could grow up and be beautiful, smart, single, and still fly was awesome. I love that the show's main focus wasn't them trying to get a man; they were so much more than just that.

LP underscores the importance of experiencing a visual imaginary reflective of possibility for the kind of woman she could grow up to be. Similar responses emerged from Robin Means Coleman's ethnography of African American sitcoms, wherein participants engaged in resistant readings. "Participants exhibited a pattern of seeing themselves in only those female characters who are powerful, strong, and independent in the face of dominating structures (e.g., patriarchy, racism, social-class inequalities). The constructions, then, tended to reveal that the female participants negotiate dominant messages by resisting characters and portrayals that lack empowerment" (2000, 246). Thus, Means Coleman's findings are validated by BB who writes about both *Living Single* and *Girlfriends*:

> I loved the show because I knew all of those people! My sister's best friend was Khadijah, my little sister was Synclaire, I always had a Régine in my life, [and] I had another sister who was Max. The extra skinny/hair-weaved cast of *Girlfriends*—not to knock the show, but I don't know any of them.

Although BB and LP both identify with the characters of *Living Single*, BB does not recognize the kind of women from *Girlfriends* as any of her friends or family members. While LP identifies with the characteristics of the women of *Living Single* as "beautiful, smart, single and still fly," BB indicates that she cannot move beyond the physical representations of the *Girlfriends* as "skinny and hair-weaved." In fact, many fan posts indicate that the voluptuous bodies of the women of *Living Single* enabled them to resist the Eurocentric standard of the slender ideal body and embrace their own ample bodies.[4]

That these bodies housed successful, driven, independent, and strong women resonates with *Living Single* fans. CS writes about the variety of body sizes, skin tones and hair styles on *Living Single*.

> Wow! I was in my 20s and living in Ohio when the show was on, and I *knew*I wanted to be Maxine. I was in love with the show's variety of body sizes and skin tones and 'dos (yeah, even Régine's ever-changing wigs).

While CJ writes about the visible image as well, she also comments on the realness of the women of *Living Single*:

> Looking back on *Living Single* makes it all the more obvious that we (black women) are missing from the TV landscape. Enough with the ABW [Angry Black Woman] or Crazy BW on reality shows, we need updated versions of funny shows that go beyond the surface. Of course, the thing that stuck out for me the most was not only the nods to the wigs, but the shows inclusion of the variety of ways we wear or hair. Priceless!

Black hair and voluptuous body types pervade cultural studies and media studies readings of *Living Single*. Beretta Smith-Shomade explains that Régine's wig wearing is a form of politics.[5] Régine's frequently changing hairstyles reject simple stereotypes of black hair, and instead involve a politics of difference. Régine's bourgeois hairpieces and wigs reflect the character of the black bohemian lifestyle. Robin Means Coleman maintains, "Most recently, the Boho has followed in the footsteps of the

B-boy/girl character in that they can be seen as achieving educational, economic and material success without shedding the Black, urban identity, without favoring assimilation, or without striving to move in and out of Black and White worlds" (2000, 134). Régine's hairdos resist Eurocentric beauty standards and operate as signifiers of the Black bohemian lifestyle proffered by *Living Single*.

However, the women of *Living Single* not only resist Eurocentric beauty standards when it comes to hair, their ample bodies also resist the female cult of thinness that dominates American television. Communication scholar Lynn Spangler argues that "there is pleasure to be had in the lives of these four women who are not stereotypes physically. Three of the four are "full figured," and part of the pleasure is watching women whose body size is accepted and not an issue when it comes to attracting men" (2003, 208). This resistance to mainstream dominant culture's ideal body marks the women of *Living Single* as physically unruly.

However, unlike the black mammy stereotype of earlier sitcoms, the women of *Living Single* move into a postmodern construction of unruly femininity evidenced by the voluptuousness of their bodies. I argue that the character of Suzanne Sugarbaker from *Designing Women* paves the way for this representation on *Living Single*, and in many ways parodies and questions the mainstream dominant culture's construction of both the ideal feminine and the ideal female body. Film scholar Jeremy Butler argues that Suzanne troubled conventional femininity by showing that as she grew in size, she became the quintessential unruly woman (1993, 15). While certainly Delta Burke's history as a beauty queen (Miss Florida 1974) becomes conflated with that of her character (Suzanne Sugarbaker as Miss Georgia), the overt Southern femininity, classic hour-glass figure and movie star face, present Suzanne Sugarbaker as the embodiment of the feminine ideal. As such, Suzanne gets away with outlandish behaviors, including traveling with big "ole" Louis Vuitton luggage, demanding expensive gifts from suitors, collecting thousands of dollars in alimony from ex-husbands, owning a pig and a semi-automatic machine gun, constantly looking in the mirror, and acting as if the world owed her a living. As Suzanne literally takes up more space on the show, her wardrobe is adapted to camouflage her growing figure; however, even as she loses her ideal female body by becoming larger and larger, Suzanne becomes more powerful and more demanding. Suzanne refuses to relinquish status as former Miss Georgia as it is tied to white ruling-class femininity. Rabinovitz explains how Suzanne Sugarbaker's position as a former beauty queen marks her as "the epitome of culturally, objectified, commodified femininity" (1999, 149). However, Suzanne's fatness threatens to undermine this codified femininity, so the wardrobe assistants work overtime to ameliorate the size of Suzanne's body. Kathleen Rowe argues, "For women excessive fatness carries associations with excessive willfulness and excessive speech" (1997, 76). Suzanne's weightiness, indeed her fatness, threatens her position as beauty queen, and indeed there is an episode in which Suzanne is asked to give back her crown, but at the last minute she is vindicated when it is revealed that Donna Jo Carnes slept with one of the pageant judges (S4 E3 There She Is). Jeremy Butler points out that as Suzanne/Delta became larger and larger, she becomes more and more unmanageable (1993, 15). Although Butler insists that Burke's departure from the show is evidence that she and her character, Suzanne, are thwarted by the patriarchy, I argue that the lasting impact of Burke's contribution to female depictions in the role of Suzanne Sugarbaker transcend the momentary victory of patriarchy. Viewers love to watch Suzanne and her outrageous acts of sisterhood and womanhood. TP comments:

> My favorite moments in this show were when Suzanne showed her sisterly side. Here was a character who was shallow, self-absorbed and had a tendency to say all the wrong things but she had Julia clocked and she always came through in a crisis. Whenever Julia was throwing a temper tantrum (like the episode where Reese fails to propose) or when she was in deep distress, Suzanne would take over, do what needed to be done and take Julia in hand kindly and firmly. And Delta Burke did it brilliantly. It was at moments like that where Suzanne was really humanized for me. I also enjoyed it when Suzanne had the opportunity to be truly charming—again, Delta could pull it off with a smile and a laugh. That made me believe that she really was a hard to resist Southern Belle.

ON states:

> I always like Suzanne when she went into her competent and in-charge mode. In the episode after Reese dies, she goes into it big time and just takes over everything for Julia. My favorite line. Charlene says something like "Look at her, most of the time she doesn't have the sense God gave a goose, then in a crisis she turns into Scarlett O'Hara. I think if she needed a new dress, she would take down the blinds and hammer them into tiny credit cards.[6]

ON and TP share their thoughts about some of the pivotal moments when Suzanne takes on the full Dixie bitch persona and occupies the position of a survivor and crisis leader. This role as leader in a crisis juxtaposed with her stereotypical behavior as self-centered, aging beauty queen produces a dynamic character capable of inspiring and challenging viewers' perspectives.

BW writes about the extra-textual persona of Delta Burke:

> I used to watch *Designing Women* religiously when it was originally broadcast, but have missed the run on Lifetime. Suzanne was always my favorite, followed by Mary Jo, Julia and then Charlene. I just didn't realize until Delta Burke left how much the show's humor depended on her. Julia's rants didn't bother me until the last few seasons, and frankly I welcomed having a show with liberal opinions to balance out some of the other conservative shows. But after DB left, Julia's rants started to grate.
>
> I am glad that Delta has her panic attacks under more control and that everyone has gotten past the disagreements. And while I know the official story now is that DB left because of creative differences and the fact that she was having a meltdown, I remember reading a few truly nasty remarks by the show's producers about her weight gain, and being very angry about it. Suzanne to me was even funnier and had much more depth after she got heavy. I could totally empathize with her, because she was used to thinking of herself as beautiful enough to win a beauty contest, and then after she gained weight, people regarded her very differently. And I think most of us can identify with that, whether we gain weight or just get older and are no longer the way we were at 20. In our mind's eye we still think of ourselves as young and beautiful, and then sometimes something happens that makes you realize you're not young and beautiful any more. That's why I loved *They Shoot Fat Women, Don't They*, because Suzanne suddenly had to confront the fact that because her body had changed, people who used to admire her were now laughing at her. She handled it much better than many women would have.

BW's comments confront the real-life drama of Delta Burke leaving the program and underscore how Suzanne Sugarbaker's character confronted the real-life problems of Delta Burke as former beauty queen struggling with her body.

Hence, I argue that Suzanne Sugarbaker's unruly and unconventional voluptuous female body paves the way for the full-figured women of *Living Single*. Synclaire James's curvaceous body takes center stage as Synclaire appears nude in play in an episode entitled "Raw Talent" (S2 E24). Synclaire considers backing out because she worries about showing her breasts in public. Max encourages Synclaire to apply herself to the role. Max explains that Synclaire should think about this like going to a nude beach. Synclaire comments, "Yeah, but you don't have fifty people staring at you with their mouths wide open" (S2 E24). Max quips, "Speak for yourself" (S2 E24). This dialogue between the modest Synclaire and the aggressive and provocative Max sets up the conflict in the episode as Synclaire must come to terms with her own insecurities about her body. Synclaire also discusses her situation with Overton, who states, "You don't have to use our relationship as an excuse not to pursue your dream. I find plenty of time to practice the oboe. And it doesn't interfere" (S2 E24). Synclaire gets confused and off-track and tells him that she did not know about his musical penchant for the oboe, and Overton tells her that he did not know that she had acting head shots taken. In spite of these exchanges with Max who tells Synclaire that she needs to feel comfortable in her own skin and with Overton, her boyfriend, who supports her career but is not happy about Synclaire appearing in the nude, Synclaire must make her own decision. She chooses to take the part when she sees a poster that refers to her as the star of the show. As Synclaire runs naked across the stage, the theme from *Chariots of Fire* plays indicating that she and her body have championed over the stage, and she has achieved her dream to be an actor.

Hence, Synclaire's body resists the politics of the slender body, and with the music from a Eurocentric film playing, *Living Single* appropriates the power of white masculinity or at least parodies it in classic Judith Butler style. Judith Butler describes in *Gender Trouble* how the repetition of gender performatives leaves space for gender transformation, as "the arbitrary relation between such acts, in the possibility of a failure to reappear, a de-formity, or a parodic repetition exposes the phantasmatic effect of abiding identity as a politically tenuous construction" (1999, 179). In the moment that the nude Synclaire dashes across the stage, she engages in a performance that both deconstructs the filmic moment of the foot race in *Chariots of Fire* and parodies the power of white masculinity that is considered to be part of the shared cultural experience of the audience. This appropriation and rearticulation indicates the danger of the unruly women who both physically and verbally step outside the boundaries of the accepted feminine roles. Kathleen Rowe argues, "These figures, I believe, can be found in the tradition of the unruly woman, a topos of female outrageousness and transgression from literary and social history" (1997, 75). Although Synclaire's body politics in the aforementioned episode of *Living Single* deem her as capable of unruly behavior, Synclaire is perhaps the least transgressive of the *Living Single* women as she and Overton maintain a monogamous, heterosexual bond throughout the series, and her gender performativity readily conforms to the conventions of traditional femininity.

In contrast, Régine's intense femininity designed to ensnare handsome, successful and marriageable men, culminates in the classic topos of femme fatale and moves her into the realm of the gold digger. Communication scholar Jeremy Butler declares, "Like the femme fatale or 'spider woman' of the film *noir*, this expression of desire makes the unruly woman dangerous and invites retribution from patriarchy" (1993, 14). Régine makes no apologies for her desire, and all the other *Living Single* women watch her work her womanly wiles. When Khadijah interviews Grant Hill in an episode entitled "On the Rebound," Régine quite literally sets a man trap for him complete with gumbo in a crockpot (S3 E3). After Khadijah decides she must not get involved with the basketball superstar, Régine quickly scampers out the door exclaiming, "No reason to let him go hungry." In this way, Régine maintains her über-femininity as a femme fatale, but she also remains a dangerous siren threatening to subvert patriarchy with her own desire.

However, Maxine Shaw's brand of patriarchal subversion runs counter to the Régine's femme fatale, as KG notes:

> I would either watch the show on FOX or watch reruns and I would laugh hysterically.... Max was funny too, although for different reasons. The way her [sic] and Régine would go at it, it was too perfect. They are the true definition of frenemies. I think they did a lot on the show to portray strong, beautiful, successful black women.

KG points out the importance of the rivalry between Max and Régine in terms of their depictions of "strong, beautiful, successful black women." Communication scholar Deborah Ann Macey describes Régine as embodying the archetype of the sex object in contrast to the iron maiden archetype of Maxine Shaw (2008, 78). Régine and Max arguably act as foils for one another as Régine's excessive femininity chafes against Max's female masculinity. Smith-Shomade situates Max in the position of the "unruly woman—taking over the conventionally male-occupied space of aggressor—in order to usurp male potency and claim as space of her own" (2002, 53). In this way, Max's character represents a second-wave feminist standpoint while Régine deploys traditional femme fatale behaviors. Max actually describes herself as a man eater, but she also presents herself as an independent woman who does not need a man. SW explains:

> I love Max in the premiere episode, where the girls go to a club and she complains that she only gets hit on by gold-toothed losers. Then, when she seems to find a nice guy behind the bar and begins to relax a little bit, he smiles to reveal a mouthful of gold teeth. Max's eye twitching, almost seizure like reaction was priceless.

In this same episode, "Great Expectations," discussed above by SW, Régine throws a drink at a woman who shows up to the club wearing the same designer dress (S1 E6). Régine comments, "This club ain't big enough for the both of us."

In both cases, Régine and Max occupy the position of the unruly woman because they refuse to allow their desires to be dictated by outside forces. Régine will get her man, and Max will be a success and stand on her own two feet come what may. Sheppard explains how Régine voices the ideological perspective of desperation in sharp contrast to Max's womanist discourse of female superiority (2007, 123). In an episode titled "A Kiss Before Lying" Max must decide whether to give up her career for her man or to stay with him. Khadijah and Régine each weigh in on Max's choice (S1 E4). Khadijah explains that Max does not need to give in to ultimatums or engage in relational power struggles. Max points out that she does not need a man to feel complete, and Khadijah agrees, noting, "She'll appear stronger alone" (S1 E4). Régine disagrees and retorts, "She'll appear alone, alone" (S1 E4). Here, Régine voices what Sheppard calls the desperation ideology, while Khadijah holds up the womanist positionality of standing on her own two feet. Sheppard argues, "Max walks away coolly saying goodbye and leaving him wanting her. In fact, Max is now in the driver's seat of her happiness. The original theme of desperation is used here to show how a woman can find herself again outside of her longing for a man and then be empowered and secure in that reality" (2007, 122). In this way, Max defines her own empowerment and sets the terms of her own desire.

In a later episode titled "The Hand That Robs the Cradle" Régine plans a cocktail party for Khadijah's associates at Flavor, but wants to include ice swans and live doves which will exceed Khadijah's two hundred dollar budget (S1 E17). Régine argues that Khadijah should expand the party budget because the party is a reflection of Khadijah's social status and class. Khadijah comments, "I don't recall any ice swans where I'm from. And if you take a closer look underneath all those wigs, you'll find your roots" (S1 E17). Régine retorts, "I am all that I pretend to be" (S1 E17). Khadijah metaphorically critiques Régine's emphasis on appearances, as she reminds the audience that she and Régine come from the same working-class neighborhood in New Jersey. Meanwhile the subject of appearances comes up later in the episode as Max begins to date a younger man. In the ensuing discussion Max and Régine square off (S1 E17). Max argues that she will not be held hostage by the court of public opinion. Régine coyly comments that she never really puts much stock in what other people think. Khadijah replies, "*What?* You base your whole life upon what other people think" (S1 E17). However, Régine holds her ground, saying, "Not true. I base it on what other people *say*. There's a big difference" (S1 E17). Max responds, "Régine, you are not talking to me about relationships. You who cannot even commit to a hairstyle" (S1 E17). Khadijah points out the extent to which Régine focuses on appearances, and Max articulates how shallow and superficial Régine can be. Hence, Régine concerns herself with social climbing and appearances, while Max fights to carve out her own space in the society. Max threatens patriarchal power as she claims control over her own destiny and chooses a younger man. Sheppard concludes, "Max's feminist characterization serves to put a televisual representation on the screen for Black feminists who felt ostracized by both the feminist movement and African American culture" (2007, 93). In this way Max presents both as an unruly woman and as a Black womanist. Smith-Shomade argues that Max's "sexuality coupled with her quick wit defied containment. She not only harbored feminist articulations but extended them to their logical conclusion—the woman handled things" (2002, 53). Thus it is not surprising that Erika Alexander earned an NAACP Image award for Outstanding Actress in a Comedy Series in 1995 and 1996 for her portrayal of Max on *Living Single*. In contrast, some fans point out that Kim Fields's character, Régine, reinforces traditional patriarchal ideals of femininity that limit and confine both the character and the actor. AD writes:

I remember from one of those Intimate Portrait episodes that Kim Fields HATED playing Régine Hunter. She had spent most of her life playing the role of the all-American black girl on and off camera, so when she got the role of the urban Blanche Devereaux, it was a major culture shock that she never quite recovered from.

However, a majority of the *Living Single* character postings indicate fan identification with Max. Max is the character that most want to be, as GD notes: " Loved all the characters on the show—including Maxine, who was the closest to my crazy self—it was nice to see a crazy, smart, offbeat sister holding her own in a show like that."

RE concurs: "I am Maxine Shaw!"

RM explains:

Max was my favorite character. She was so damn funny. I really loved her relationship with Kyle. She was so afraid of letting go, so she did/said all these really mean and stupid things to keep him at arm's length. He was so patient with her, and it broke my heart when they broke up. The best thing about them was that the sniping never stopped, even during the relationship.

In an episode titled "The Best Laid Plans," Max explains, "I need a man in my head not just in my bed, someone who can challenge my mind as well as feed my soul" (S5 E5). Thus, Max articulates her desire for a life partner, an equal who challenges her and cares for her. Max's desire exists in sharp contrast to the superficial, rich man of Régine's design.

Femme Fatales, Socialites and Gold Diggers

Blanche and Régine share the position of femme fatale, but they are not looking for just any man. They want handsome, successful, powerful, wealthy men. Blanche, like Régine, uses her womanly wiles to lure men into her bedroom. Both of these women plot, plan and scheme to land a man who can fulfill their dreams. Blanche may be viewed as unruly in terms her excessive Southern, white, ruling-class femininity. In fact, the most noteworthy distinction between Blanche and Régine may be their regionalisms as Blanche paints herself as a gentile Southern belle, and Régine assumes the identity of a New York socialite. In spite of the fact that Khadijah continually reminds Régine of her working-class roots, Régine strives to transcend these roots by appropriating a pretentious bourgeois persona. This sense of pretense also emanates from the character of Toni Childs on *Girlfriends,* who refers to herself in the third person in an episode entitled "Childs in Charge" (S2 E17). Here, Toni's self-centered, egoism, and materialistic ideology parallel her personal journey from a poor, black girl in Fresno to a professional, upscale realtor in L.A. Toni declares to Joan and the other girlfriends, "Although I'd like your blessing, Joan, I really don't need it. There has never been a challenge that Toni Childs hasn't met. When I was eight years old, I spotted you across the playground; I told myself we would be best friends. We are. I wanted to get out of Fresno. I did. I wanted to get into UCLA. I busted my butt, doctored some transcripts, and got in. I think that sounds like I get everything I want" (S2 E17). Toni's raw ambition and determination reinforce the meritocratic values of the American Dream while spinning them into a web of spider woman, femme fatale, deception that make a Régine Hunter, Blanche Devereaux, or Suzanne Sugarbaker pale in comparison. On the other hand, this places her squarely in the ring with man eaters Maxine Shaw attorney at law, and Samantha Jones public relations director. Max, Sam and Toni not only share masculine names, but they possess the drive and ambition that rival their male counterparts. In this way, they may be identified as the ultimate rivals to their male counterparts. Although Maxine Shaw maintains a clear sense of second-wave feminist ethics, Sam and Toni convey a sense of post-feminist values or at least third-wave feminist values, wherein they feel comfortable using their femininity and their masculinity to achieve their own objectives.

However, when Toni solicits an investor named Anthony to back her business plan, Anthony confronts her about her reputation as a gold digger. He does not take her seriously and talks to her in a condescending tone, questioning her ability to open up her own real estate office. Toni replies, "It's not just a real estate office. It's a boutique agency that caters to a discriminating clientele who demand a certain level of attention" (S2 E17). Anthony still makes light of the situation indicating that she did not have to go to all this trouble just to get him to ask her out on a date. Toni tells him that she is serious and that he should review her business plan and prospectus. Anthony is not convinced and he chides Toni, saying that the only thing she has ever applied herself to is dating wealthy men. Toni questions him, "So, you think I am just a gold digger?" Anthony confirms this, noting that he never called her a gold digger, but that sums up his estimation of her approach to men (S2 E17). Toni allows him to get away with this supposition, but responds, "Isn't possible that she does her very best to make men feel complete and add exponentially to their happiness quotient?" Anthony looks confused and asks where she is going with her argument. Toni replies, "The point is whether it's separating people from their money or making them feel complete, both are essential components in selling high-end real estate" (S2 E17). In this way Toni re-appropriates the term gold digger and attempts to co-opt the powerful materialism of the term in order to make a case for her boutique, upscale, real estate firm. In this way, there is a shift in the dynamics of imperialism and capitalism, as Toni moves against colonizing white discourses to get financial backing from an African American man for a company that she will run. While the exploitation inherent in capitalism is not overturned by Toni, her ability to co-opt the system for her own goals represents a possible break in the interlocking system of imperialist, white supremacist, capitalism. However, patriarchy remains as a linchpin in this scenario as Toni still must gain the approval and support of a businessman in order to move forward with her own project.

Comparing Types

Viewers point out the similarities and differences of characters on each of the female foursome shows. It is important to note that like other fans, I recognized the repeating character typologies in the shows during my initial viewings, and only later recognized that episodes focused on similar themes. Viewers' sophisticated comparisons indicate their in-depth knowledge and understanding of these female foursome shows and the repeating character types. Fan posts evidence their ability to critique and compare character types and program types. SM writes about *The Golden Girls*:

> WOW! Ok, I thought I was the only *The Golden Girls* fan. I used to watch this every Saturday night w/ my grandma. My cousin and I even named the "girls" after older women we knew (we were always with my grandma and her friends during the summer). This show is like comfort food to me. No matter how bad a day I have had I feel better watching this show.

Here, SM notes the intergenerational appeal of *The Golden Girls* and the way in which the community of viewers—her grandmother, her grandmother's friends and her cousin—identified with the characters and how watching the show collectively produced a shared space for community and a kind of comfort akin to eating comfort food. This is significant as SM is able to reflect on his/her collective viewing experience and explain how the program cultivated a shared community among family and friends through watching the show. Certainly, the intergenerational elements of the show resonated with SM's viewing experience and although SM does not expressly say this, it seems clear that the program offered generational appeal to multiple audiences.

A discourse study by Jake Harwood and Howard Giles in 1992 supports SM's perspectives and reveals that *The Golden Girls* reached a high level of popularity with the mainstream media and younger viewers (406). The shift in the representation of women of a certain age is indicated through the following media reviews:

- *The Golden Girls* is surprisingly mature for prime-time television in both its characters and characterizations. But it is innovative mainly in its demographics… [the producer and director] have dared to create a comedy that revolves around three older single women [*The Christian Science Monitor*, Thursday, 12 September 1985: 26].
- Week after week, TV's dynamite "Golden Girls" prove that mature women can still be sexy and beautiful [*National Enquirer*, 22 January 1991: 16].
- [paraphrasing a producer of the show] Take some women around 60. Society has written them off, has said they're over the hill. We want them to be feisty as hell and having a great time [*New York Times*, 22 September 1985, Section II: 1].
- [discussing the appearance of *The Golden Girls* on prime-time schedule] [Senior Citizens] are trendy right now, having supplanted yuppies as the demographic darlings of the media [*TV Guide,* 19–25 October 1985: 6; quoted in Vande Berg and Trujillo, 1989: 179–80].

These reviews underscore the extent to which the aging representations of *The Golden Girls'* female foursome impacted contemporary discourses surrounding aging women's agency. Although Harwood and Giles point out the extent to which Blanche's character in particular operates as a counter-stereotype for aging women, particularly in terms of sexual agency, ultimately Harwood and Giles argue that the counter-stereotypical behaviors involving Blanche's sexual agency are limited and co-opted by the humor that pervades her sexual escapades (1992). However, fan-based message boards and blogs of both *The Golden Girls* and *Hot in Cleveland* seem to counter Harwood and Giles's conclusions by insisting that although ageism is an element of our collective visual culture, fans actively support the empowered agency of aging characters and their depictions. ON explains how these images repeat in *The Golden Girls* and *Hot in Cleveland*:

> I was watching last night and they showed the scene where the three are sitting around the table and Betty White's character offers to make them breakfast and all of the sudden it hit me, this is the Golden Girls—with Betty White as the Sophia character and 10 years subtracted from the ages of the others. Fabulous house—check, cantankerous old lady—check, slutty roommate—check...

JS concurs and writes:

> Sure, "Hot" appears as a variant on "Golden Girls," a show that I can still watch today, if I come across an episode. This week's episode further gives the appearance of this show as a parody of, or homage to, *The Golden Girls*—versus being a fully-realized show in its own right, worthy of its own following and appreciation.

In contrast, NS points out the repeating foils and types on *The Golden Girls, Sex and the City*, and *Living Single*:

> I miss living single!!!!! i was probably too young to watch it when it was coming on but i saw it anyway (i was in elementary). But, I have now come to appreciate it even more as a 20 yr old, lol. There are three shows that I always felt were linked together, *Golden Girls, Living Single*, and *Sex and the City* mainly because of their characters and their traits. *Golden Girls* was representing older women, living single represented black women *Sex and the City* represented white women not old but not young. BUT i felt *Sex and the City* definitely copied *Living Single*.
>
> Carrie = Khadijah (Queen Latifah), Carrie wrote for a column, Queen Latifah was the executive of a magazine,
>
> Samantha = Régine (sex appeal),
>
> Charlotte = Synclaire (dumb characters),
>
> Miranda = Max (independent and hardworking lawyers) those parallels are no coincidence.

NS's fan posts suggest how the shows have intergenerational appeal and stand the test of time. She also draws parallels between Khadijah and Carrie as writers. I would add that both of these characters serve as moral interlocutors and culture readers on the shows. Carrie's column, "Sex and the City," and Khadijah's magazine, *Flavor*, serve a populist market. Their audience is made up of young upwardly mobile women like themselves. They both like to think that they have their fingers on the pulse of what is happening in mainstream, dominate culture. While Carrie's column's focuses on dating and relationships, she still is very concerned with the status of women in terms of power, position, and agency. Khadijah similarly seeks to challenge high culture with street culture. Khadijah produces *Flavor* for a growing demographic of upwardly mobile urban African American professionals in the metro area of New York City. Both Carrie's column and Khadijah's magazine politicize the perspectives of the audiences that they serve with Khadijah coming down hard on issues of equal access to education, health care, transportation, and Carrie pointing out how women are frequently trapped by the glass ceiling, super woman syndrome, and patriarchy. Both women address feminist issues, but in very different and often subtle ways. They both use other characters and scenarios to provide examples of oppression and to move beyond barriers to social justice. However, the politicization is often co-opted by other things happening on the shows or by their own reluctance to take action. Frequently, the social justice issue is only highlighted but not fully engaged. NS also notes the similarity between Miranda Hobbes and Maxine Shaw, both strong willed, motivated, successful and feminist attorneys. NS comments that it is no coincidence that these super woman characters exist on these female foursome shows. In fact, it may be argued that they operate in the most radical and extreme space of feminism on the show. Their representations are necessary as foils for Charlotte York and Synclaire James who are the Pollyanna characters of their respective programs. These foils are a critical part of the continuum of perspectives on the female foursome shows, and they permit viewers to experience difference vis-à-vis the lens of the character with whom they most identify. Rather than viewers being jilted out of their identity and identification with their preferred character, they can experience the difference of some very challenging and unruly women, and still occupy the position of their preferred or safe character.

However viewers are also critical of the female foursomes typologies, as AG compares and critiques *Sex and the City* and *Hot in Cleveland*:

> I guess expecting the worst was good for me because I was surprised to discover it wasn't half bad. The three main girls actually, kinda, sorta do work, though they are broadly drawn stereotypes (Malik is the Samantha, Leeves is the Miranda, Bertinelli is the Charlotte/Carrie). Betty White seemed cobbled in, as if producers are taking advantage of her sudden popularity. "Hey, let's put Betty White in for viewer draw and have her say "whore" a few times!

AG's comments suggest that she is disenchanted with the repeating typologies, but, more importantly, that Betty White's character, Elka, does not fulfill a single role. Instead, Elka serves as comic relief and her character seems muddled and reliant on one-liners, sexual innuendo, and crass language to keep the show moving. This critical view underscores the sophistication of viewers who are frequent watchers of many of the female foursome shows. Fan posts, like AG's, consciously push for a more progressive trajectory of women characters on television by expecting more from programs predicated on repeating female foursome character typologies.

JS seems to concur with AG, but is more critical of the script writers than the actors. JS writes about the roles of the actors on *Hot in Cleveland* and how they reflect *The Golden Girls* typologies:

> Leeves and Malick are doing great work here. Granted, they are both, more or less, playing the Blanche/Samantha role, but each are working wonders with scripts that would have been rejected on "Golden Girls." Bertinelli is doing great as well, even though she is called upon the be "the nice one."

JS notes that the scripts would not have been good enough to be used on *The Golden Girls*. In this way, JS seems to suggest a backsliding of the writers, who, in her mind, have not written scripts that are equal to those used on *The Golden Girls*. She seems to be concerned specifically that there is not a progressive trajectory and that these types are merely being repackaged and reused without any new material in terms of script writing. This critique by JS reinforces theories of recombination noted in the work of Todd Gitlin (1983) and further explored by Deborah Ann Macey (2008). Macey notes, "This recombination includes characters and/or genre splicing. One example of genre splicing could include the dramedy, which is a combination of a comedy and a drama, as mentioned above. One benefit of recombinant programming is that while the series may very well be a copy, the recombination of characters or formula often passes as novel" (Macey 2008, 13). Hence, what JS's fan post effectively makes the argument that recombining the characters from *The Golden Girls* on *Hot in Cleveland* does not work particularly in the case of Elka Ostrovsky, and JS does not, in fact, find the approach novel. JS ultimately uses a critique of recombination to explain how the show is failing. This fan post demonstrates how closely fans read the shows and the characters and explains how they become sophisticated critics employing media studies approaches to television viewing, reinforcing critical approaches to television that have been documented by scholars in the field.

Similarly, SG is critical of Betty White's character, Elka:

> The reason I started watching this show was to see Betty on it. It is a bonus that Valerie, Jane and Wendie are on it. I don't like Elka being so mean to the girls though. She's not one of their gal pals, yet. Besides, she says things like Joy looks like a hooker, but Elka is more oversexed than any of them. Are the writers trying to make Betty into ALL 4 Golden Girls? She's a mix of Rose (when she colored her hair red and not understanding the "downtown" comments), Sophia (with the meanness), Blanche (she's got a steady guy but wants the other one to fight over her AND she's still going out looking for guys) and Dorothy, who periodically says something to center all of them. Betty's playing everyone making little room for the other actresses to have a clear part.

SG is particularly concerned that Elka's character is tied to all four of the *The Golden Girls* characters, and she points to specific episodes as evidence of this conflation of all four female foursome characters. While it may be argued that the writers are trying to capture what Linda Kaler[7] describes as feminine archetypal patterns of the complete woman, using Jung's four-sided mandala figure, SG's critique, like AG's, points out that this approach does not seem to be working on the show. Perhaps SG and AG actually do feel much more comfortable with each woman representing only one perspective or worldview. They both seem to suggest that having Elka try to embody multiple perspectives muddles the character, thus making it difficult for viewers to identify with her.

Still other fans comment that choosing Betty White to star as a main character purposely elicits comparisons between *The Golden Girls* and *Hot in Cleveland*. AH states:

> Yes, this is kind of a "Golden Girls Lite"—or "Golden Girls Minus 10 (yrs)."
> In that respect, I'm not sure Betty White should have been given a role that
> was sure to elicit comparisons between *Hot in Cleveland* and *The Golden
> Girls*. Better she should have just been a neighbor who constantly comes
> over to borrow sugar, dispense unsolicited advice, or whatever.

Here, AH critiques *Hot in Cleveland* as "Golden Girls Lite" suggesting
that it does not continue to push the boundaries in the same ways that
The Golden Girls did. AH even suggests ways in which the writers could
have used Betty White differently in the storyline. This type of critical
evaluation of the show demonstrates reflection on the part of fans who
really seem to be looking for progression in women's characterizations
on television. Even as fans note that *Hot in Cleveland* does not fulfill
their viewing pleasure by moving the trajectory of television's female
foursome programs forward, they still watch, hoping for more.

In contrast, CT indicates that each of the well-known stars on *Hot
in Cleveland* has been typecast:

> I think I like this because everybody is playing their own stereotype. Valerie
> is always the good girl, Betty is always the old woman with the smart mouth,
> Wendie is always the fashionista with the ex-husbands, and Jane is the quiet
> one.

CT's critique also mirrors longstanding television criticism in which
actors are typecast and do not actually change over time. Taken together,
these fan criticisms of repeating typologies, recombinant characters and
genres, and typecasting reinforce traditional television criticisms available in the fields of media studies, cultural studies and television studies.
What is striking is that these female foursome fans know what they are
watching and they actively critique and negotiate current viewing in
terms of previous viewing experiences, particularly in the case of characterizations of unruly women. What is perhaps disconcerting is that
the trajectory of these unruly women characters seems uncertain, and
viewers' comments suggest that they are looking for more and better
representations of women in contemporary television.

5

Sisterhood in the Global City

Career Women, Working Moms & Golden Girls

As illustrated with the civil rights and women's movements, the results of the Vietnam War, the professional faces of affirmative action, and the beginning of a new deregulatory economic era, America has changed. And television comedy has transformed itself along with it.
—Beretta E. Smith-Shomade, *Shaded Lives: African American Women and Television*

Each of the featured female foursome programs take place in a large, American City: *Designing Women* (Atlanta), *Living Single* (Brooklyn), *Sex and the City* (Manhattan), and *Cashmere Mafia* (also New York), *Girlfriends* (Los Angeles), and *The Golden Girls* (Miami). Throughout the series' runs viewers are told a story of urban women forging alternative communities and carving out woman space in the city. These stories reflect both the value of traditional sisterhood and the need to adapt to the changing demands of postmodern, female subjectivity in the global city. New York, Atlanta, Los Angeles and Miami mark the location for relationships among the characters, but they also serve as catalysts for the emergence of postmodern imagery depicting career women, working moms, and golden girls. The economic, political and social empowerment of these female foursome characters is palpable in their attachment to the global city. Art galleries, live theatre, nightclubs, restaurants, fashion shows—all elements of the cultural life of the city—provide a context for social vitality for these independent working women whose relationships to men, children and extended family become a backdrop for

111

their individual and personal lives as women. The incarnation of the postmodern woman as an autonomous subject living in the landscape of the global city becomes iconic (again after *That Girl*) for a new generation of women who can see themselves living beyond the attachment of traditional family, making homes and lives within a community of women through the bonds of urban sisterhood. These female foursomes live in solidarity with other women, sometimes single and sometimes in partnership, always valuing these female connections at work, at home, and in the city.

While the image of the independent working woman may not be an incarnation of the 21st century, the idea that women are likely to be single more often than partnered during the span of their lives is a new concept. Of these female foursome shows, the twenty-something buppies (black urban professionals) of *Living Single* are the youngest set in this study of upwardly mobile urban women. The characters of *Designing Women* range in age from Charlene Frazier, a naïf in her late twenties at the start of the series, to Julia Sugarbaker, the older of the two Sugarbaker sisters, who is widowed and in her late forties. Both the women of *Girlfriends* and *Sex and the City* are thirty-something except for Samantha, who is the first to be forty in the group, an age that comfortably describes the characters of *Cashmere Mafia* as well. On the other hand, the *Golden Girls* range in age from their late fifties to Sophia's octogenarian status, indicating that at the end of the 20th century and the dawn of the new millennium single status may apply to women in their twenties, thirties, forties, fifties, sixties and beyond.

Reflective of the effects of late capitalism and globalization, many women embark upon their careers before looking for partners. This means women may remain un-partnered through their twenties, thirties or even forties, as is this case for Régine, Khadijah, Max, Samantha, Lynn, Joan, Caitlin and Mia; or they may be divorced as is the case for Maya, Charlotte, Mary Jo, Suzanne, Dorothy, and Juliet; or they may be widowed as is the case for Julia, Blanche, Rose and Sophia. Hence, the depiction of these women as belonging to a sisterhood, and an alternative family in the heart of a global city, transcends the lyrics of *Mary Tyler Moore Show* modernity claiming, "You're gonna make it after all" with the postmodern ideology of a community of women inhabiting the global city as in "my homegirls standing to my left and my right, true blue and tight like glue," and "My girlfriends, there through thick and thin." In fact, it is perhaps the culmination of solidarity through sisterhood and the postmodern bond of shared woman space within the confines of the global city which best defines these female foursome shows. In this way the global city and its public spaces become woman space, a place for women's community and discourse. Through the public spaces of the workplace, art galleries, live theatre, nightclubs, fine restaurants, and fashion shows, we see the lives of these women played out onscreen.

While the workspace in *Designing Women* blurs the lines between the public and private spheres, as it is at once both Julia's home and the main office for Sugarbaker's design firm, it also offers a space for the personal and professional development of each of the *Designing Women*. Ethel Goodstein argues that the internal workspace of Sugarbaker's, as much a home as an office, provides a space for creating familial relationships and a space for women's candid conversations (1992, 175). Mary Jo Shively and Julia Sugarbaker occupy the positionality of both career women and working moms. Midway through season four (episode 14), the arrival of Charlene's daughter, Olivia, redefines Charlene Frazier-Stillfield as wife, mother and office manager. Although white, middle-class privilege defines the careers of Julia and Mary Jo, these characters are also marked by their dual status as career women and working moms. In contrast, Charlene's rural, agrarian roots firmly anchored in the Ozarks of Poplar Bluff, Missouri, reflect the American dream[1] of upward mobility. The series exploits and explores the conflicts and challenges of this dual identity of working mom and career woman: as Mary Jo experiences the guilt of not always being with her children, Julia faces the reality of her son, Payne, going to college, marrying, and becoming a father, and Charlene struggles to take care of an infant, then toddler, in the workplace. Each of these characterizations depicts the friction between the categories of worker and mother[2] while simultaneously building the categories of working mom and career woman. Although the identity marker of working mom may be widely accepted in mainstream American culture, the category remains mired in the backlash against the second wave of feminism and the dueling ideologies of the mommy track and the fast track in the world of work.[3]

However, the set of *Designing Women* operates outside of these institutionalized practices by blurring the lines between the private and public spheres so that Charlene can bring her baby and her nanny to work in Sugarbaker's design firm/Julia's home. Mary Jo can leave to pick-up sick children or attend parent-teacher conferences without fear of reprisal. Julia can work and host her son and his new "girlfriend" without losing a day on the job. In spite of the fact that this workplace offers a refreshing, non-industrialized and decidedly feminine (if not feminist) approach to work, the public/private work and home space of *Designing Women* does not challenge the structure of traditional workplace practices, but rather articulates an alternative workplace environment in which women-owned businesses, particularly informal service sectors, have operated for years.[4] In this case, the characterizations of career moms who operate outside of institutionalized practices do not thwart mainstream dominant culture's perceptions of the role of mothers in society, nor in the world of work. Ethel Goodstein submits, "The Villa Marre [The Little Rock, Arkansas, landmark depicted as the home/office of Sugarbaker's] can be read as an assimilation of women professionals into a larger construct of working girls and ladies of the house, and of the Southern sense of place into a larger American space" (1992, 184). For the characters of *Designing Women* this assimilation depends upon both the blurring of the public and private spheres of their workspace and their engagement in fashion shows, art openings, and design expositions.

Rather than shying away from the public sphere, the women of these female foursome shows engage the public sphere, the city and all it has to offer their lives together. While the city of New York has often been called the fifth lady in the *Sex and the City* series, media studies scholar Tara McPherson argues that Atlanta functions similarly in *Designing Women* as it deploys the image of the new, New South as a kind of character in the series (2003, 282). This desire to refashion the image of the South via the global city of Atlanta surfaces in many of the episodes of *Designing Women*. The series both embraces and troubles this tension between the privileged location of ruling-class, white, Southern femininity signified through the historical icon of the Southern belle and the mature, independent, working women of Atlanta signified by Mary Jo, Charlene, Suzanne and Julia. Perhaps not coincidentally, in episodes about "The Women of Atlanta" (S3 E13) and "Belled," this tension is borne out. In "Belled" (S2 E6) Suzanne Sugarbaker's ex-husband, Dash Goff, a writer (played by Gerald McRaney, Delta Burke's husband), returns depressed to Atlanta after his recent book is rejected by the publisher. He regains his center by visiting with each of the Designing Women, and he describes each one of them as embodying the contradictions of the classic Southern belle. Julia reads aloud from the letter left for them by Dash: "They were sweet-smelling, coy, cunning, voluptuous, voracious, delicious, pernicious, vexing and sexing ... these earth sister/rebel mothers ... these arousers and carousers ... these Southern women. This Suzanne. This Julia. This Mary Jo and Charlene" (S2 E6).

Dash explores the contradictions in Julia, Suzanne, Charlene and Mary Jo by evoking the Old South and imbuing them with the power of what McPherson refers to as the new New South (2003, 282). Certainly the character of Dash Goff works within the frame of the classic virgin/whore dichotomy in his description of them as "earth sisters/rebel mothers." He at once draws upon the situatedness of the Antebellum South and allows McPherson's articulation of the New South. Ethel Goodstein further expands on McPherson's explanation:

> "Being Belled," the title of a novel written by one of Suzanne's ex-husband, drew from this genre of Southern romance, and its concluding frame portrayed the *Designing Women* seated on a country veranda, bathed in impressionistic light and, of course, wearing flowing, Victorian summer dress. Immersed in traditional imagery, the ladies of the Old South and the women of the New South became one [178].

Both McPherson and Goodstein indict the tension, the contradiction and the necessary conflict between what might be described as a virgin-whore dichotomy by feminist cultural critics; however, here the *Designing Women* embody the dichotomy of the Old and New South. McPherson maintains that the sitcom reconstructs Atlanta in the post–civil rights era as both the South of Ted Turner and Newt Gingrich, but most significantly as a global city wherein the identities of the new women of Atlanta are also reconstructed as they challenge the dominant paradigms of the Reagan-Bush era (2003, 174–175). At this point the reconstruction of the global city of Atlanta and the women of Atlanta merge. Of Dash Goff, McPherson declares, "the ladies of Sugarbaker's have 'belled' him, leaving him dazed, wobbly, and squinty eyed.... This is what is known in the South as being belled" (2003, 176). Both Dash

Goff and the viewers of *Designing Women* are "belled" by the women of Atlanta.

However, the women of Atlanta do not maintain a fixed identity throughout the series, and like the cultural flow of globalization, their identities ebb and flow throughout the series. In the episode entitled "The Women of Atlanta," each of the women articulate concerns and questions about the kind of image the photographer, DeWitt Childs, seeks to produce (S3 E13). DeWitt carries with him a portfolio filled with portraits of the stars, and he suggests that each of the *Designing Women* possess certain star-like qualities. Dewitt notes that Julia posses the Greco-Roman profile of Katharine Hepburn, Mary Jo the eyes of Vivien Leigh, and Suzanne reminds him of a young Elizabeth Taylor (S3 E13). DeWitt is photographing a pictorial of "The Women of Atlanta" for a new men's magazine, *Empire*, which according to Charlene is like *GQ* and *Esquire* but more romantic.

Yet, during the photography session, when DeWitt squirts Mary Jo with a spray bottle and asks her to straddle a chair, she responds that she would never wear such an outfit to work, wet or dry, and her mother told her to never sit in that position. As Mary Jo's discomfort grows, Suzanne and Charlene also voice opposition to the outfits and positions into which DeWitt places them. Suzanne says of her own outfit, a pink chiffon costume complete with ruffles and bows, that she looks like Little Bo-Peep. Charlene objects to sitting at her desk with her hands behind her head and her chest thrust forward. When DeWitt asks her how she feels, Charlene smiles and comments about how ridiculous she feels in this pose. In the end, Julia loses control when DeWitt dresses her in a man's suit and hat and drapes a string of pearls through her mouth. Julia intones:

> "If you are looking for somebody to suck pearls, then I suggest you try finding yourself an oyster.... These are not pictures about the Women of Atlanta ... and it doesn't matter if the clothes are on or off, it's just the same old message.... When you start snapping photos of serious, successful businessmen like Donald Trump and Lee Iacocca in unzipped jumpsuits, with wet lips, straddling chairs, then we'll talk!" [S3 E13].

Julia's declaration becomes the battle cry for all of the *Designing Women* as they unilaterally agree that DeWitt has taken advantage of them. Media studies scholar Bonnie Dow argues that Julia's primary role on the show is to politicize the experiences of the *Designing Women* (1992, 134). While Mary Jo indicates her reservations about the kinds of photographs and the title of the pictorial, "The Women of Atlanta"— both before and during the shoot, she lacks the moxie that Julia possesses to rebel and to throw DeWitt out of Sugarbaker's.

Although Julia politicizes the argument against the objectification of women during her diatribe, Mary Jo previously had already articulated the experience of the personal underscoring what is a well known tenet of feminism, that the personal is political (Dow 1992, 135). What Dow deems as a consciousness-raising moment culminates in an act of resistance when Julia describes the *real* women of Atlanta. Julia declares, "The real women of Atlanta are the blue-haired ladies who still play bridge at Merrimac's tearoom. The old bag lady named Ruby who sits out in front of the Capitol building, and Miss Millie Mae Richie who runs a plantation outside of town where her grandfather was once a slave, and the debs who come out every year in their white gowns at the Beaumont Driving Club" (S3 E13).

As the show ends, black and white photos of these women come into focus in homage to the women of Atlanta, but perhaps the greatest act of resistance is that the *Designing Women* themselves have become the *new* women of Atlanta. Their collective action in solidarity with one another and DeWitt's camera assistant, who trades the film of the *Designing Women* in DeWitt's camera bag for some photos of the *real* women of Atlanta depicted at the end of the episode, returns the viewer to the tension between these postmodern *Designing Women* of Atlanta and the nostalgic images of the *real* women of Atlanta.[5]

While the *Designing Women* strive to reimagine the *real* women of Atlanta, the city of New York is personified in an episode of *Sex and the City* where Carrie actually dates the city. In "Anchors Away" (S5 E1), Charlotte, Samantha, Carrie, Miranda (with baby Brady) engage in their ritualistic Saturday brunch and dish session. Communication scholars, Sadler and Haskins, explain the significance of the sense of place created by the New York cityscape in *Sex and the City*. Sadler and Haskins state, "The nodes of New York City become major 'meeting points' for the main characters. The restaurant as a node or public space is an ongoing leitmotif on the show, and it showcases fine New York restaurants. The nodes act as a means of control because they zoom in on one particular aspect of the city image and magnify its significance to the whole picture of New York City" (Sadler & Haskins 2005, 209). In this way the spaces of New York, the nodes of the city, where the women meet, become metonymically linked to the whole of the city thereby expanding the role of the city in the perspectives of viewers and in the lives of the foursome.

At the coffee shop, Charlotte discusses an article she read at the dentist's office, which claims that for each person on the planet there are only two great loves (S5 E1). She blurts out that Carrie's two great loves are Aidan and Big. Carrie retorts, "One, two, and according to you I'm done." Although Charlotte struggles to back-pedal, her words hang in the air like a harbinger of singledom. However, Carrie puts a positive spin on her single life in the city. Carrie comments, "You are never alone in New York. It's the perfect place to be single. The city is your date." Miranda responds, "You're dating the city? How long has this been going on?" Carrie declares, "For about eighteen years. It's getting serious. I think I'm in love" (S5 E1). Later, in Miranda's apartment, Carrie furthers this discussion, juxtaposing her freedom as a single woman dating the city with Miranda's responsibilities as a mother. Shaken by the earlier brunch discussion, Carrie states, "Here lies Carrie. She had two loves and lots of shoes." However, Miranda cannot concentrate on Carrie's concerns, but rather sits frustrated that her child will not latch on for breastfeeding and she cannot participate in a conversation with Carrie. Carrie assures her friend that she understands. Carrie explains that it is okay that Miranda is a mother and that as her best friend, Carrie will keep this secret. Carrie means that Miranda does not have to deny her commitment to motherhood, and, furthermore, Carrie tells Miranda that she can be a good friend and a good mother all at the same time. Miranda asks Carrie if she will go today on her date with the City. Carrie retorts, "Ah, first a trip to the Guggenheim and then lunch, and who knows ... it's New York!" (S5 E1).

Once more Carrie comforts Miranda's motherhood choice, and walks out into the city of possibility only to find that the Guggenheim is closed on Monday's. As she is pelted with rain, Carrie comments, "And a New York museum like a man can sometimes be closed when you wish they were open." So, she runs into a diner where the manager bellows, "Singles at the counter." Carrie sits next to a cheery, gray-haired woman who is crushing lithium tablets and sprinkling them onto her ice cream. The woman quips, "We single girls gotta have a port in a storm." Carrie cringes and after a half hour of crouching under the hand dryer in the ladies room, she intuits, "New York and I didn't have the perfect relationship. It was dismissive and abusive and it made me feel desperate. I was fresh out of great loves." When she runs to get a cab, a young navy sailor, Louis Leroy from Louisiana, holds the cab for her and invites her to the big fleet week party on Staten Island.

That night, Charlotte, Samantha and Carrie, sporting their best runway walks, move along the streets of Staten Island into the heart of a rollicking party that is the toast of fleet week. Within an hour, Charlotte, true to form, hooks up with a naval officer and Samantha dances in the arms of a young sailor. Louis Leroy appears in front of Carrie. Carrie tells him she is going home. Louis argues, "I've come all the way from Louisiana to dance with a New York City girl." Carrie capitulates, and the two engage in a sultry jazz number. Carrie notes, "After the way this city kicked my ass today I needed that dance." Louis proceeds to say he doesn't like the city and all the hustle and bustle. Carrie asks Louis how many great loves he thinks each person is allotted. As she leaves the party she states, "If Louis was right about New York and you only get one great love, New York may just be mine, and I can't have nobody talking shit about my boyfriend." Carrie articulates New York City as her man, a man that can be abusive, and dismissive, but one that is omnipresent in her life, both metaphorically and physically.

In this way, the cityscape itself becomes much more than a location as images of the Chrysler Building, the Brooklyn Bridge, the World Trade Center, Fifth Avenue and even the everyday New York City streets define the lives of the women of *Sex and the City*. American Studies scholar Helen Richards argues that New York City is at once a singles ghetto and a space for women's empowerment and freedom (2003). That these women gain entrée to the public sphere is an understatement. These four women take the city by storm, walking the streets in six-inch Manolos and Jimmy Choos, they are postmodern career women in the global city. Richards asserts that under the terms of modernity the women of *Sex and the City* would be categorized as loose or wanton women; however, via postmodernity and the global city, Samantha, Miranda, Charlotte and Carrie gain access to the public sphere (2003).

As Carrie walks the streets looking for inspiration for her column, "Sex and the City," she takes on the identity of the "sexual anthropologist" or what Richards names as visible flaneuse (2003, 154). Here, the global, postmodern city produces a re-articulation of the male *flaneur* by opening up the practice of *flanerie*/streetwalking to the female subject, Carrie Bradshaw.[6] Bradshaw becomes iconic again, but this time not for fashion, but rather for her capacity to make the city her own ethnographic site vis-à-vis a dash of participant observation along the streets of New York City.

Hence the streets of New York, and in particular the island of Manhattan, become a magical space for the women of *Sex and the City*. Film Studies scholar Fiona Handyside explores the social freedom of the women of *Sex and the City* as "they partake of an elite Manhattan lifestyle of new and exclusive restaurants, designer boutiques, gallery openings, ballet, opera, and museum gala events, all without needing men to escort them" (2007, 413). The global city and its very public sphere proffer social freedom to the privileged, white, single women of *Sex and the City*.

Although Brooklyn is depicted as outside the city in *Sex and the City*, it is revealed as the center of upward mobility and cultural caché in *Living Single*. Maxine Shaw, Régine Hunter, Synclaire and Khadijah James form a cadre of black urban professionals. Brooklyn, and by association New York, signifies hip, trendy, urban culture. This is where bourgeois bohemians, baps, and buppies,[7] make their homes in rent-controlled apartments, brownstones and lofts. Similarly, upward mobility, privileged class signifiers, and elite access to the urban underground thread their way through the backdrop of *Living Single*. Beretta Smith-Shomade says of the women of *Living Single*: "They chilled in art-house cafes, kept up with city-wide cultural occurrences, and knew the latest dances, forms of speech and fashion trends" (2002, 57). This cultural capital is perhaps best demonstrated through *Flavor* magazine and its workplace environment, where Khadijah James is the editor and owner of this urban underground voice of the people. Like the infamous *Village Voice*, *Flavor* amplifies the voice of the populous, the conscience of black urban professionals and promises not to sell out to the mainstream. *Flavor* represents the voice of the people, the black urban counter culture. Although *Flavor* stands as a poignant marker of the social mobility and access to power for the twenty-something buppies of *Living Single*, the term *Flavor* also hints at the commodity fetishism and orientalism of African American culture. In her landmark essay "Eating the Other" bell hooks argues, "The commodification of Otherness has been so successful because it is offered as a new delight, more intense, more satisfying than normal ways of doing and feeling. Within commodity culture, ethnicity becomes spice, seasoning that can liven up the dull dish that is mainstream white culture" (1992, 21). In this way, *Flavor* magazine both represents the rise of black urban professionals in terms of class privilege and commodifies Blackness for the mainstream white culture.

While politics are often couched in social arguments, the identity politics of race, social class, gender and sexuality constantly ebb and flow in the pages of *Flavor* and in the *Living Single* series. Two episodes entitled "Ride the Maverick" (1996 S4, E2) and "Fatal Distraction" (1994 S1, E16), chronicle the struggle of Max and Khadijah not to sell out as they make their way up the ladder of success. In "Ride the Maverick," Maxine Shaw, an attorney, runs for the office of Brooklyn alderman. Khadijah interviews Max for Flavor and tells Max that she wants to hear her positions on the issues. Khadijah begins, "One of the biggest issues is speeding in school zones." Max cuts her off and answers quickly, "Children are not speed bumps." Khadijah moves on and asks a series of questions to which Max responds in sound bites. Finally, Khadijah tells Max, "When you answer the questions, it's okay to actually say something." Max replies, "What you say isn't nearly as important as the rhythm.... Bam Blam Kerblam diggity diggity dong." Then they face off. Khadijah raises the issue of crime, and Max retorts, "Not on my street." Khadijah brings up the topic of education, and Max quips, "Books are silent friends." Khadijah becomes visibly frustrated and counters with the topic of employment, but Max quickly responds, "Work works." Khadijah asks Max to please respond to her questions with complete sentences. To which Max replies, "Complete sentences for every criminal" (S4 E2).

Later, Khadijah admits to Max that she endorsed William Perez, a high school teacher, for alderman. Khadijah argues, "I have responsibility to my readers to endorse the best candidate." Max responds, "Up until now you've been the self-appointed leader of our little foursome. Synclaire needs a job, work for Khadijah. Régine needs a place to live, live with Khadijah. Suddenly, I'm on the verge of winning this election without any help from you and mother cannot stand to share the spotlight." Media Studies scholar, Kristal Brent Zook, argues that Khadijah's role as the self-appointed mother, is enriched by the extratextual appearances, statements and productions of Queen Latifah, the actor who plays Khadijah (1994, 151). As such the character of Khadijah becomes commingled with the cultural capital of Latifah, a strong proponent of black womanism. Zook concludes that "the crosstextual persona of Latifah embodies an implicitly nationalist and feminist sensibility" (151). In this way, Queen Latifah, the actor, inflects Khadijah, the matriarchal character with both an Afrocentric nationalism and womanism.

In contrast, Maxine Shaw often represents a kind of raw second-wave feminist positionality. In this episode, however, the internal conflict between Max and Khadijah becomes secondary to the very real social change at stake in the alderman's race. When Max visits a park to solicit votes for her campaign, she runs into her opponent, William Perez. Perez tells her that his civics class visits the park weekly and cleans the graffiti off of the structures in the park. He explains, "Hey, just because I lose doesn't mean I can't effect a change. A couple of years ago, this park was a vacant lot, fifty drug deals a night. I made cleaning it up an issue of my campaign, so Malaba was forced to make it an issue, too. When he won, he had to clean it up. I may have lost the election, but I won this park for my neighborhood. Why are you running?" (S4 E2) Max decides to drop out of the race and endorses Perez, but Max wins the election as a write-in candidate. Max ends up winning for her altruism, and Khadijah ends up taking the moral high ground without alienating her readers. Khadijah and Max reconcile after Synclaire tells Max that Khadijah voted for her after all. While the ending is trite and unlikely, social justice in the urban jungle becomes the center of the episode. This social justice emerges from a discourse between Black matriarchal empowerment and second-wave feminism as Max and Khadijah approach the problems of urban decay, social stratification and civic engagement from different standpoints. In this way, an ethics of civic engagement and professional integrity undergird the episode as well as the characterizations of Khadijah and Max.

Maintaining professional integrity in the big city, operating a small business against the threat of global media moguls also repeats as a theme on *Living Single*. As editor and owner of *Flavor*, Khadijah occupies a position of social, political and economic authority; however, her authority is challenged by a subordinate in an episode titled "Fatal Distraction" (S1 E16). Khadijah hires a handsome journalist, Xavier, based on his résumé without checking his references. On a shared cab ride home he admits his admiration for Khadijah as a business woman and editor. When she makes a pass at him, he rejects it, and she apologizes in embarrassment. The next day Khadijah reads an article written by Xavier, and she tells him that he will need to revise it. Xavier resolutely stands by his article and threatens to sue Khadijah for sexual harassment if she fires him for non-performance. After worrying all night about the matter, she returns to the office to handle the situation. Khadijah tells Xavier, "Earlier you said you admired me as a good business woman. Well, a good business woman knows when you make a mistake, you have to admit, apologize and correct. Now I've admitted my mistake, and I've apologized. Now all I have to do is correct the situation. I'm letting you go" (S1 E16). Xavier continues to threaten Khadijah with a lawsuit, but Khadijah explains that she will not compromise her values and will not change her business practices because of Xavier's threats. Xavier becomes more entrenched and asks her if she understands what might happen to her business and her professional identity if he files the suit. Khadijah remarks, "Hey, if I'm lucky, it will get me a Supreme Court appointment.[8] And I know if a judge read your article she would sentence you to remedial English" (S1 E16). Although Khadijah initially falters in her own judgment and is embarrassed because of her misreading of the situation with Xavier, she ultimately reverts to the role of professional business woman, entrepreneur and editor to steady herself. In the role of authority figure, she is honest, frank and direct. Khadijah manages to admit her mistake, apologize for it, and correct it. Khadijah holds onto her professional integrity, maintains her position of authority, and illustrates that she belongs to the world of work. Khadijah is not a token female, token African American, token kid from the projects, but rather she is an independent working woman. Her passion, her mission, and her goal as editor and owner of *Flavor* is twofold: (1) to manage a successful magazine and (2) to effect a positive change in the community. This notion of social justice and civic responsibility undergirds many episodes of these female foursome programs. Communication scholar Amanda Lotz argues that Julia Sugarbaker, Khadijah James and Dorothy

TV Female Foursomes and Their Fans

Zbornak occupy the positionality of the voice of reason in each of their respective sitcoms (2006, 100). As such, they function as the mouthpieces for consciousness raising and, in some cases, as the catalysts for social change.

While *The Golden Girls* is perhaps the least political of all the female foursome programs, Dorothy's position as the voice of reason enables her to confront some social problems. In the episode titled "Dorothy's Star Pupil" (S2 E21) Dorothy confronts the social problem of illegal immigration when one of her students, Mario, is deported. She nominates his essay on the subject of what it means to be an American, for which he wins a prize. Dorothy reads the essay aloud to Blanche, "The very first night he was in America his uncle took him to a movie. He felt more excited than he ever had in his whole life watching that movie because of the feeling he got sitting in the theater with all those other people. Laughing together, getting scared together, he felt like those people were his friends. To him that feeling was the feeling of living in America. In America you always felt like you were among friends" (S2 E 21).

To celebrate his winning the contest, Dorothy, Blanche, Rose and Sophia throw him a surprise party, but it is interrupted when an immigration agent appears at the door. Mario runs away and hides in a movie theater, but Dorothy knows where to look for him. There is an Arnold Schwarzenegger film playing in the theater. Dorothy points out that Schwarzenegger is a very successful immigrant who married a Kennedy. She tells Mario that running away will not solve his problems. Mario asks Dorothy to go to see the immigration judge the next day. Dorothy returns home and waits for word from Mario. When he returns, Mario states that he must go back. (We do not know where he is going back to—although Miami maintains large Cuban and Dominican populations.) Dorothy hugs Mario and tells him, "You'll be back here before you know it. This is your home. This is where you belong. You're what this country is all about." While we never know if Mario returns to the United States, the fact that Dorothy confronts this issue, and champions Mario's cause evokes a sense of civic responsibility and historical significance. In short, Dorothy brings legitimacy to a very real problem in American life. Dorothy also stands in as a civic leader and even surrogate family member for Mario, who refers to her warmly as "Teach."

Dorothy's role as voice of reason enables her to operate as a friend, teacher, and mentor. This role carries over into her relationship with the other women as they often use her as a sounding board, emotional support, and life coach. In an episode titled "Diamond in the Rough" (S2 E22), Blanche books the much sought after Versailles room at the Bedford hotel for the Hospital Charity banquet, but she ends up falling for Jake, a working-class guy who owns and operates his own catering company. Although Jake served as an army cook for 25 years, and he parlayed his down-home recipes into a successful catering company, Blanche does not see him as her social class equal. She comments that they come from two different worlds, but when Blanche sees Jake in a tuxedo at the hospital charity benefit, her heart melts. She tells him she made a mistake; however, Jake tells Blanche that she was right, that they are from two different worlds. Blanche sits up late crying on the couch, and Dorothy comes out to comfort her. Blanche declares, "Oh, Dorothy, let's face it. I'm no longer sixteen and there's no longer a line of beaus out on the front porch waiting to ask daddy if they can walk me to town. No more cotillions, no more sorority parties. I just lost the best thing that ever happened to me since I met George [her first husband]. I'm just a stupid, old fool sitting up all night with a broken heart" (S2 E22).

Dorothy lets Blanche know that she is a vital woman in the prime of her life and that she is a beautiful, talented, sexy woman who men adore and actively seek out. Dorothy points out that that Blanche will always be desired and sought out by men for the rest of her life. Blanche thanks Dorothy for the company and her kindness. She hugs Dorothy, and when Blanche is out of earshot, Dorothy looks directly at the camera and says, "Damn, I'm good." Here, Dorothy manages to comfort Blanche and make a real statement about aging beauty, while putting the audience in stitches. As the voice of reason, Dorothy does not chastise Blanche for her snobbery and class privilege, but rather recognizes what is exceptional and special about Blanche. Dorothy's unconventional wisdom comforts Blanche, and Dorothy is able to argue that Blanche's vivaciousness and beauty transcend age. Rose, Sophia, Blanche and Dorothy may be in their golden years, but they still maintain rich and fulfilling lives.

While Dorothy is the voice of reason among *The Golden Girls*, it may be argued that Maya Wilkes is the moral interlocutor among the *Girlfriends*. Maya writes *Oh, Hell Yes!* a self-help book, aimed at black, urban women struggling to move up the ladder of success. In an episode titled "New York Bound," Maya's desperation shows itself in the form of determination. When she cannot find a publisher, Maya decides to self-publish and sell the book herself. She meets Toni and Joan for lunch with copies of the book (S4 E24). Maya tells them they can get first run, autographed, new editions of *Oh, Hell Yes!* And she is charging twenty dollars per copy to her friends. Toni points out that she heard that Maya was selling them for only fifteen dollars in Crenshaw (another part of the greater LA area). Maya states, "I'm getting eighteen on LaBrea, and over here in siddityville[9] it's twenty dollars" (S2 E4). Toni explains that since she is some Fresno, she is only paying five dollars for a copy. Maya quips, "Honey, it's not where you're from, it's where you're at. And you keep messing with me, and I'm going to make it twenty-five" (S2 E4). Joan intervenes, telling Maya that she is happy to pay full price because she is happy for Maya and she wants to purchase two copies because she knows that she will end up paying for one for Lynn eventually, too. Maya remarks, "Well, go ahead and give the other one to your Mama, 'cause Lynn already bought one on the Alvarado off-ramp" (S2 E4). Toni cannot believe that Maya is selling her book on the highway, but Maya replies, "Off-ramp, now get it right" (S2 E4). Through this dialogue, Maya is vividly depicted as a single, divorced mother without a college education. She is struggling to get ahead, to make it, and to grab a piece of the American Dream. When she receives a call from a publishing company, she agrees to fly to New York to sign a book deal with them.

As she walks out of the subway on her way to the publisher's office, she even takes her hat off and throws it in the air à la Mary Richards from *The Mary Tyler Moore Show*. However, when she sits down with the editing, marketing, artwork and advertising staff, Maya cannot believe that they want her to rewrite, re-title and re-design her book, *Oh, Hell Yes!* The primary editor, Julie, tells Maya that she loves the book and that it is amazingly edgy and real while filling a void in a new urban writing market. Maya smiles and thanks her and is caught completely off guard when Julie comments, "But, we want to go in a different direction. The title, *Oh, Hell Yes!* It's a little too around the way" (S4 E22/23). Maya asks Julie what she means when she says that, and Julie replies that the book is "ghet-to" (S4 E22/23). Maya explains that this book realistically portrays who she is and where she comes from, and she feels as if the editorial board is trying to whitewash it, to sanitize her book for consumption by mainstream American white culture.

At this moment, Maya confronts the systems of white supremacy and capitalism through the global media establishment in a move that is reminiscent of Khadijah's fight to keep *Flavor* from corporate takeover. Maya and Khadijah both struggle to make a stand against the homogenization of the mainstream dominant culture. They work to maintain their allegiance to where they come from even as they move through cities that will, as Carrie Bradshaw points out, be abusive and dismissive. Nonetheless, these women make it in the city in a way that Anne Marie (*That Girl*) and Mary Richards could not. They enjoy sisterhood, friendship, and alternative family through postmodernity that make it possible for them to move beyond the idea that a woman would only work until she marries or until she bears children. The global city is the center of their friendship; it provides a space for their woman talk, and their shared community.

However, this shared community and sisterhood is also the site of contestation. In an episode titled "All God's Children," Maya, Lynn, Joan and Toni all weigh in on key issues of race and religion (S6 E11). When Toni's Jewish ex-husband, Todd, tries to gain custody of their daughter, Morgan, Toni decides to allow Morgan to be converted to Judaism in exchange for full custody. However, Maya is relentless in her battle to raise Morgan in the legacy of the Black Church. Maya declares, "I don't want to be flagged and pulled to the side on judgment day because I didn't stand up for Jesus on this day.... I don't understand how you can raise your daughter in a religion that denied the word when it was all fresh and new. Shoot, honey, they heard it straight from His mouth. It wasn't no he said, she said" (S 6 E11).

While Toni argues that this is her decision and that she expects Maya and the others to respect it, Maya cannot let it go. Maya continues her diatribe while Lynn and Joan try to ameliorate the harshness of her message. She states, "Morgan is Black! Black people are Christian—end of story!" Lynn comments, "Actually, Maya, the majority of Black people in the world are Muslim." Maya responds, "I don't know nuthin' about all that." Lynn explains, "Well, I don't know nuthin about that either, but I know there's a lot of them" (S6 E11). Lynn struggles to make sense of

Maya's argument. While Maya argues passionately from a position of faith, Lynn, who is recognized as the most educated member of the sisterhood, argues from a position of scholarship and facts. Maya struggles to respond in more pragmatic terms, citing specific cities with collective Black histories and Black religious traditions, practices and rituals. Maya maintains:

> "I'm talking about Black people in L.A., Atlanta, and Houston. They don't have all those big ole mega churches for nothing. Morgan is part of a proud legacy of Black folk. She needs to know that the church is our rock, our strength. It got us through slavery; it got us through Jim Crow. Girl, I am praying it will get us through George Bush [S6 E11].

There is a collective—Amen. And Joan suggests that Toni and Todd were doing the right thing originally by exposing Morgan to both Christianity and Judaism. Joan ends the scene by asking "Don't all these paths lead to God anyway?" This question hangs in the air and we are forwarded to the next scene of Morgan about to be dunked in the Mikvah.

While Toni does stand up and say that she cannot go through with the ceremony, the audience is left with Joan's question and the arguments presented by Maya and Lynn. In this way, the episode troubles the unity of the sisterhood as it problematizes the conflation of Blackness and Christianity in America. Black culture in America becomes intertwined with the mythologized ideology of a single, monolithic Black Christian church in America. Although Pandora's Box containing the fact that American Slavery institutionalized Christianity vis-à-vis slave missions is not opened, the depth of the relationship between Blackness and Christianity is certainly queried.

However, even as Toni, Maya, Lynn, and Joan contest the historical and material identities of Blackness, Christianity, and sisterhood in America, they reconstitute and reconstruct a postmodern African American female subjectivity predicated on the collective experience of Black upwardly mobile, professional working women in major, global American cities like those articulated by Maya: L.A., Atlanta, and Houston. Although problems exist with this type of monolithic identification, *Girlfriends* and its 1990s predecessor, *Living Single*, incorporate the more traditional ideology of the American Dream[10] with the image of independent, intelligent, African American women who are willing to expose the contradictions that supplant their identifications as privileged

African American women. This is not to say that the complexity of matters of race, class, gender, religion or ethnicity are fully developed and explored in *Girlfriends* or *Living Single*, but rather I argue that Maya, Lynn, Joan and Toni reflect the developmental trajectory of Khadijah, Synclaire, Max and Régine as independent, strong, Black women living out the praxis of sisterhood in the post-modern global city.

6

Having &
Not Having It All

Everywoman, Superwoman
& Strongblackwoman

Superwoman/Strongblackwoman discourse assumes that a black
woman has too many obligations but she is expected to handle
her business. Thus, while postfeminism poses that white women
cannot have it all, racialized postfeminism, at least for black
women, means continuing to be everything for everyone else
and maintaining a sense of self.
—Kimberly Springer, "Divas, Evil Black
Bitches, and Bitter Black Women"

As discussed in previous chapters, the discourses of telefeminism
produce characters who strive to have it all. Binary discourses of having
and not having it all continue to swirl around the epicenter of third-
wave feminist and postfeminist debates where choiceoisie[1] rhetoric
threatens the hard-won battles of second-wave feminism and the
women's movement in the U.S. Although many feminist cultural studies
and media studies scholars critique the easy choiceoisie politics of female
foursome shows that evince liberal feminism as a lifestyle choice, they
also concur that these series produce arguably feminist and/or womanist
discourses.[2] These discourses manifest in the strong, savvy, independent,
professional, working women characters that clearly push the boundaries
of conventional femininity while producing new conceptual models of
contemporary ideal women such as the superwoman, wonderwoman
and strongblackwoman. These new identities, taken up and performed
by the primary female foursome characters through the telefeminist trajectory of *The Golden Girls, Designing Women, Living Single, Sex and*

the City, *Girlfriends*, *Cashmere Mafia*, and *Hot in Cleveland*, expand the female imaginary of viewers and fans to include a more dynamic range of images, identities and roles for women during the post-civil rights era. Communication scholar Kyra Hunting argues that chick-lit series, including the female foursome shows, actively contribute to feminist goals (2012). Hunting notes, "These explicit evocations of previous television programs that featured significant representations of women encourage an understanding of these shows in discursive relationship to the programs that preceded them" (2012, 192). Hence, the discursive engagement articulated and rearticulated through these female foursome series move the feminist project forward in ways that make it accessible and useful to viewers and fans. Fans access the discursive logic of the female foursome series in their own arguments on blogs and fan forums, suggesting that the discursive engagement in these series has moved from the television screen into mainstream society through collective viewership and media critiques of real-world social problems, gender politics, and cultural struggles.[3]

However, this is not to say that these images, identities, and roles run rampant or unchecked as these progressive telefeminist models of female identity and feminine subjectivity are indeed troubled by the structural barriers underpinning the power relations of mainstream, hegemonic culture. In fact, in many ways these characters suffer as they are structurally limited, reduced and confined by interlocking systems of domination, including but not limited to white supremacy, ageism, capitalism, and patriarchy. However, the progressive conceptual models of femininity and feminine subjectivity embodied in female foursome characters remain alive and well in the hearts and minds of fans. Blogs, fan forums, and character surveys asking "Which character are you?"[4] evidence the development of an active female fan imaginary.

The female fan imaginary allows fans to identify with characters and articulate how a particular character's life resonates with personal fan experiences. In message boards, blogs and forums, fans actively access and develop this online imaginary as they articulate how their own lives run parallel to and/or intersect with the issues and concerns faced by characters in the female foursome series. In spite of the fact that fans may chide characters for not living up to fan expectations, fan posts indicate that they genuinely care for these characters, identify with these characters and understand the behaviors and mindsets of these characters. Fans also explain how they might respond in similar situations, and they point out which qualities they admire most in the female foursome characters. Finally, fans frequently post comments about their favorite characters indicating with which characters they most identify and which characters they struggle to understand. SS writes about the wisdom of the women of *The Golden Girls*:

> I loved where Sophia tries to smooth over Kirsten's abrasiveness to Dorothy with "she's scared." Sophia was very wise at times. Rose could also be very wise at times like when Phil died and she helped Sophia and Angela come together. Rose and Sophia just have different styles of how to get to "wise." Dorothy had a lot of "wise" moments and I sort of expect her to since she's a teacher. Dorothy was always stepping back and analyzing things from every angle to define things. Her moments came easier and more frequent. I can't remember any of Blanche's "wise" moments just now. She had to have had some. Just can't think of one.

Here, SS suggests that each of the women of *The Golden Girls* have wisdom to offer, even if it comes in different forms. SS examines Dorothy's role in particular, hinting at Dorothy as a moral interlocutor and connector. SS also compares the wisdom of Sophia and Rose and points out that both characters bring different and necessary viewpoints to the show. SS also indicates (albeit somewhat esoterically) that she knows Blanche demonstrates wisdom on the show, but she just cannot think of an example. Blanche does, of course, provide support and wisdom for the other women on the show as she shares her home and her open and vibrant approach to life. In contrast, RM points out moments when the women of *The Golden Girls* act out of character:

> I love that line too when Dorothy says she's "Crazy-nuts" about him! As another poster brought it up, sometimes the girls behave "out of character," like when Rose gets bitchy or Sophia gets maudlin. Sometimes Dorothy gets giggly/silly/childish and it always makes for good comedy.

LC concurs with RM and points to Dorothy acting out of character when she is around male suitors. LC writes:

> Another example of Dorothy breaking outside her usual "type" was when Sonny Bono and Lyle Waggoner fought over her—but that was just Blanche's (hilarious) dream. People, don't pretend like you don't like "The power, Sonny! The power!"

Each of these fan posts suggests that fans conduct close readings of character behaviors and episodes noting where character behaviors diverge with typical characterizations and identity markers.

In fact, many fan posts mimic the rhetoric of media critics, indicating that fans quickly recognize discrepancies in performances—e.g., how persuasive the acting is in an individual episode or how true to the character the performance is by an actor. L6 writes about how Rue McClanahan's performance of Blanche draws audiences into the show:

> Hands down Blanche is and always will be my favorite! Not to take anything away from the others but, Rue was for sure the strongest actress of the bunch. Even in scenes where she has absolutely no lines at all, she's never not on. Just watch her reaction shots in the background during someone else's line.
> Favorite quote: "When I'm backed in a corner I come out fightin'! Unless of course I've had too much to drink then I just slide down the wall and make mad passionate love on the carpet!"

L6's mention of a favorite quote also points to the role of writers in constructing dialogue that produces the character of Blanche. This quote further reinforces the racy identity of Blanche as a Southern belle, femme fatale and jezebel[5] all rolled into one.

However, fans also document when writers, actors, and scripts mischaracterize their favorite female characters. TT critiques behavior that is out of character for Maya Wilkes on *Girlfriends* when Maya scoffs at Joan flying to New York in coach class instead of business class or first class:

> That display was so ridiculous and out of character for Maya. The same chick who wrote a book called *Oh Hell Yeah!* (that she sold on the streets of LA), has a gay hairdresser cousin named Peaches, complained about the price of mini-bar candy, threw away William's expensive pen, thought Joan was too bougie to appreciate her book, comes in late, leaves early and takes 2 hour lunches. This chick is now looking down on Joan because she's in coach? Not buying it.

LL agrees that Maya has been mischaracterized in several episodes of season five and adds:

> Okay we get it: Maya is the ghetto fabulous girl who got pregnant early but tried to make the best of her situation and her natural abilities by locking down a "good job" as a legal secretary. She is smart enough and hardworking enough to get promoted to Executive Assistant to a partner but we're supposed to believe that she doesn't have better sense than to act a fool with Al Sharpton?

While these mischaracterizations may seem minor, fans notice them immediately, and both LL and TT point out that Maya, who comes from such humble beginnings and works her way up to publishing a book and working as an executive assistant to William, would not act in such a haughty manner. In fact, fans note that it is Maya's street-wise savvy that helps her succeed. As Maya is also deeply religious and reverent, it is difficult to imagine her failing to demonstrate reverence and respect around Al Sharpton (S5 E2) even if she is distracted by her book deal and necessary edits. In short, fans find this behavior and the plotline leading to her consequent firing to be unbelievable, and they write vigorously on this topic.

This snobby and rude behavior contrasts with Maya's identity on the show as the everywoman character and moral interlocutor. However, Maya also shares this role with Joan. Fan posts point out how Joan also occupies the position of the everywoman character, the voice of reason and the moral interlocutor. SS writes:

> Someone as giving and maternal as Joan might befriend all of the women, which in that case, she'd be the only glue that kept the women together. Which seems to be the case on the show. The others don't seem to care about each other too much. The interaction between Maya and Toni was the only time Toni appeared to be human and I was surprised they finally showed emotion and friendship between each other.

Here, SS points to the fact that Joan is the glue person, but Maya cultivates Toni's humanity. SS seems to underscore the shifting roles of Maya and Joan as they share the roles of everywoman, voice of reason and moral interlocutor. This is also the case for Mary Jo Shively and Julia Sugarbaker in *Designing Women*. Joan Clayton, from *Girlfriends*, and Julia Sugarbaker, from *Designing Women*, often operate as the mother and/or matriarch of the female foursome; however, in this role they also protect, govern, and lead the other women in their respective series. Joan and Julia forge together these very different individuals into female foursomes as they operate as voices of reason and moral interlocutors when their sister characters run off the rails. However, both Mary Jo Shively, from *Designing Women*, and Maya Wilkes, from *Girlfriends*, perform the role of the voice of reason and moral interlocutor as well. This happens most often when their respective counterparts, Julia Sugarbaker and Joan Clayton, veer away from their serious and deliberate roles as matriarchal figures holding the foursomes together.[6]

This is perhaps best evidenced on *Girlfriends* when Joan leaves her position at the law firm and begins to drift away from the foursome. This is a critical time when Toni ultimately leaves the show after Joan fails to appear in court as a character reference at Toni's custody hearing. This is a very low point for Joan on the show as the trust between Toni and Joan is ultimately broken, and this time the wrongdoing is on Joan's side. Joan is humiliated, afraid and alone and realizes that she has caused irreparable damage to the foursome (S6 E21/22). The day before the court case, Maya has a housewarming party at her new house in the suburbs, and Joan hands Maya a gift and says she is going to an A-list party in the hills. As she is leaving, Toni asks Joan if she will still show up. Toni says, "I know things haven't been cool between us, but you are still my strongest character witness. And with the whole assault thing, I really need you there" (S6 E21/22). Joan sarcastically says, "Toni, I'm fine. I'm giving you your space" (S6 E21/22). Toni responds with ire, "Whatever, tomorrow is the most important day of my life" (S6 E 21/22). But Joan rolls her eyes, repeats the time and court room number and with a flourish she leaves Maya's house saying that she will be there and that she is well aware what is at stake for Toni. Joan's attitude reflects that she is aware that Toni only cares about Toni and Joan is sick and tired of being Toni's girlfriend.

After Joan and Toni have both left the house, Lynn and Maya discuss how the foursome is drifting apart. Lynn comments, "You moved all the way out here to the boonies. Toni's got a kid, and Joan's gone all A-list and doesn't have any time for us" (S6 E21/22). Maya tells Lynn to forget about Joan, but Lynn is worried that the friendship among their foursome is falling apart and wonders how they came to this place in the sisterhood. That night Joan goes to the A-list party, and is shunned by the A-listers as she over imbibes and dances poolside alone. Later she throws up in the bathroom, and excuses herself from the party after an awkward interruption of a piano sing along (S6 E21/22). Joan spends the night passed out on the grounds of the host's home, and wakes when the sprinklers come on in the morning. She stumbles to her car, and turns the key in the ignition and then runs to vomit again on the side of the road. The car rolls away. After sobbing on the ground, she collects herself. Joan walks down the hill into town to get a cab, but the cabbie won't take her because she has no money. She ends up hitching a ride in the back of a pickup truck. When she finally remembers she is supposed to be in court, she rushes to the courtroom, only to find it vacant. Toni, Maya and Lynn walk out of the courthouse as Joan rushes up and calls to Toni that she is so sorry (S6 E21/22). This is the final scene of the episode involving the friends which prompts a flurry of fan posts vigorously protesting the breakup of the *Girlfriends* female foursome. CN writes: "If it's not the four I will not be watching this really sucks at first it was four black women and it was great and to see—anything different is wrong."

PT comments: "I hope and pray that all the women stay on the show. After six seasons, we need all 5 cast members to keep the comedy going. It isn't 'Girlfriends' if all four women aren't there!!!!!!!!"

JN notes:

> I am really disappointed that Jill Marie Jones (Toni Childs) will not be returning to the show "Girlfriends" for the 7th season. The show will be incomplete without her or without any of the other cast members for that matter. Jill Marie Jones (Toni), Tracee Ellis Ross (Joan), Golden Brooks (Maya), Persia White (Lynn) and Reggie Hayes (William) all make the show what it is. The show is really great but I don't think it will be anymore with one of the cast members missing. I don't think that I will be all that interested in the new season.

These fan posts reflect the fans' deep concerns about the dissolution of the female friendships on *Girlfriends* as each character on the show depicts a worldview and a perspective that balances out the foursome. Fans recognize the critical importance of Toni as the selfish, self-centered, gold digger and her character development into a successful business woman and new mother. That Toni's marriage has failed and that she has become vulnerable in her role as a single mother resonates with viewers. The departure of Toni represents a decline in the popularity and success of the show, and it is not surprising that the show only lasts one more season after this rift occurs between Joan and Toni.

It is important to note that savvy *Girlfriends* fans had already begun to write about the changes that they would like to see in future seasons prior to the departure of Toni from the series. MB writes about the need to strengthen and deepen characterizations:

> I would like to see TPTB do more with the Lynn character next season.
> Because Lynn is quite different from the standard characters on a UPN show, I think the writers have been at a loss for what to do with her. They

stuck her with the Jamaican freeloader and the celibate poet for a while, but mainly they put her in limbo as the mooch.

I used to like the Toni character, until they lost track of her and married her off. It's too early for these people to become caricatures of their former selves. I don't know from what second-rate soap they pulled this season's writers, but they need to remove themselves from this current, melodramatic state of affairs.

This critique by MB suggests just how closely viewers are watching these shows. Fans do not passively accept the depictions of the characters, but rather they actively write about their frustrations when favorite characters are reduced to "caricatures of their former selves." In this way fans actively participate in the construction and constitution of an online female imaginary.[7] These posts also indicate that fans actively engage in negotiated readings of the female foursome shows rather than passive acceptance of preferred readings provided by script writers, producers, and directors. MB demonstrates her engagement in the online fandom by articulating her desire for more nuanced and developed characters and less melodramatic plotlines. Similarly, BJ notes, "Next season I would like to see:

1. Lynn's exploration of her roots covered in more than one episode. Maybe she could start a documentary about adopted biracial children searching for their identity, biological parents, etc.

2. More to Joan's story than falling in love with William. I want to see her truly search for her passion in life, instead of searching for the perfect sandwich or working McJobs.

3. I want to see Toni less crazy and self-absorbed (it's been too over-the-top lately) and really see that she loves Todd. I'd hate for her to be using her pregnancy (real or contrived) as a means to hold on to him. I don't want to see them divorced because I feel we've already had a divorce plotline with Maya and Darnell, and to some extent William and Lynn.

4. I didn't really like the Maya-gets-published storyline but since it's happened, I want to see her be successful. However, she should have some more struggles since I think the whole thing was too easy to begin with.

5. I want to see William with anyone but Joan. Gah!"

Here, BJ actually writes about the changes in plotline and the development in characters that she would like to see on *Girlfriends*. Like MB, she is frustrated with the unsophisticated surface-level drama on the program, and BJ calls for the characters to explore deeper elements of their self-identities—e.g., Lynn's passion for documentary film and her own identity as a bi-racial adoptee might move her toward the creation of a documentary film focused on the lived experience of bi-racial adoptees. Like MB, BJ rejects the shallow plotlines that fail to adequately depict the depth of the women on *Girlfriends*. There is a very real sense of palpable longing, and a belief in the possibility of richer, more vibrant, more robust characterizations for each of these female foursome characters.

However, the loyalty of fans for female foursome shows and their favorite characters still remains prevalent in the fan forums, blogs and message boards in spite of the disappointment and critical reviews posted by many viewers. In this way the forums create a space for the community of online fans to share critical reviews, and praise messages about the shows and their characters. Many fans who post regularly in particular forums still retain their passion for the characters and talk specifically about what they admire most about their favorite characters.

DS writes about loving Régine on *Living Single*:

Kim Fields made LS for me: there are three Régine moments that, to this day, crack me up:

1. Someone (I can't remember who) is getting married and shows off their engagement ring. Régine whips out the microscope (or whatever they call it) to examine the ring. Impressed, she saunters back to her seat and gives this look that made me guffaw.

2. Regine is on a jury—and can't talk about the case. Of course she does. After Max threatens to rat on her, the judge is informed about the leak—and at court, when the judge tells the shocked courtroom that there's been a blabberer, Regine turns around and blurts out, "What the HELL??!!??"

3. The Grant Hill episode. When Regine catches GH and Khadijah kissing, she goes ballistic. I love how she bursts into the living room screaming, "HOW COULD YOU DO THIS TO MEEEE????!!!"

Oh! And during the Regine as a juror episode, Regine is instructing the roommates to not get an actor confused with the character they play. Kyle immediately drops, "Tell that to Tootie." PRICELESS.

SK writes about a favorite *Living Single* episode featuring the Flavorettes:

Did anyone catch the rerun from the last season where Khadijah daydreams that she and her friends are a Supremes-like group called the Flavorettes? It was like a 30 minute version of Dreamgirls. I about died watching Max walk around like a crack addict with that crooked Diana Ross wig.

DD explains how much *LS* means to her: "It's unhealthy how much I miss this show. I have almost every episode on tape and what's even more pathetic is that I'll probably buy every season if/when it comes out on DVD."

DD, SK, and DS demonstrate their connection to *Living Single* through online fandom. They post to the online fan community like they are talking to friends about their favorite episodes, characters, and their shared love of the show. DD, SK, and DS communicate a shared palpable longing and nostalgia for the show that evidences a depth of connection, shared community, collective understanding, along with a desire to relive episodes, characterizations, and storylines again and again.

It is important to note the extent to which the re-watching of the shows on DVD, VHS, and on cable networks is actively engaged by fans as well. The volition of the fandom keeps fans actively seeking new opportunities to re-engage with older episodes and to relive moments on the show. TM writes:

The UPN affiliate in Atlanta shows *Girlfriends* in syndication. Right now, it's back in Season 1, and I'm starting to remember why I fell in like with this show in the first place. The characters are actually *funny*!

I know it's hard to imagine if you haven't seen the first few shows in a long time, but they're really funny. They have great chemistry and they play really well off one another. Each person definitely has a role, but the acting is so authentic (I know, I know) and the dialogue is so fresh that they haven't yet become a caricature of a stereotype.

William is silly and dorky without being too lame. Lynn is moochy and flighty but in a cute way. Maya is ghetto and fiercely devoted to her husband but not harsh. Toni is self-centered but not dismissive of others' feeling. And Joan. Joan is funny and neurotic and confident and excited about dating but not desperate and whiny.

Remember those days?

TM writes nostalgically about re-watching *Girlfriends* and what was original and new about the show in its first season. TM calls upon members of the fandom to remember again their collective experience of watching season one of *Girlfriends*. I argue that this re-watching promotes what Kyra

Hunting refers to as a discursive relationship between female foursome shows (Hunting 2012). This is perhaps no better demonstrated than by blogger Fred Olsen in his *People's Choice Blog* titled "Fabulous Female Foursomes," in which he directly refers to the discursive relationships between *The Golden Girls, Designing Women*, and *Sex and the City*. Olsen writes:

> Bea Arthur (Dorothy), Betty White (Rose), Rue McClanahan (Blanche) and Estelle Getty (Sophia) were sassy senior citizens sharing a home in Miami. Over the course of seven seasons, each one of these actresses would win an Emmy Award for her role in the series. Now they're all gone, save for Betty, our national treasure. But they set the tone for the next wave of shows starring four women. Those old broads certainly knew what they were doing [2012].

Here, Olsen explains that the women of *The Golden Girls* are the originals[8] and that they had paved the way for succeeding fabulous female foursomes. Although the blog post is short and campy, Olsen manages to make the point that, in fact, the discursive relationship that Hunting alludes to is clearly evident in the trajectory of female foursome series. Olsen also lists the run dates for *The Golden Girls, Designing Women* and *Sex and the City* as he identifies the archetypal characters in the foursome: ringleader, sexpot, realist and femme fatale. It is important to note the extent to which Olsen's archetypes dovetail with earlier conceptions of these typologies.[9]

THE ORIGINALS: *The Golden Girls* (NBC 1985–1992)
    Ringleader: Dorothy
    Sexpot: Blanche
    Realist: Sophia
    Innocent: Rose

THE SOUTHERNERS: *Designing Women* (CBS 1986–1993)
    Ringleader: Julia
    Sexpot: Suzanne
    Realist: Mary Jo
    Innocent: Charlene

THE MANHATTANITES: *Sex and the City* (HBO 1998–2004)
    Ringleader: Carrie
    Sexpot: Samantha
    Realist: Miranda
    Innocent: Charlotte

Olsen's reference to *The Golden Girls* as the original "fabulous female foursome" is supported by fans who continue to measure contemporary female foursome shows against the original framework of *The Golden Girls*. JN critiques *Hot in Cleveland* for being too *Sex and the City* and not enough *The Golden Girls*:

> That's a pretty good line to describe the show, it's certainly entertaining, but I was also hoping for a more "Golden Girls" type of sitcom, since this is a little bit too sliding on "Sex and the City." Very much like last episode, they always start off with a good premise to go somewhere and find the funny (and they still get to the funny), but having men problem is becoming a trait of this show.

SS concurs, and notes:

> That's true, but on *The Golden Girls,* there was more closeness between the family members. Even if they fought or had issues, the family relationship always prevailed in the end … for instance, Dorothy and Sophia. Everything we've seen to date on *Hot in Cleveland* seems to imply that the women are fairly estranged from and a bit disconnected from many of their relatives. Remember the episode with all the mothers? Then we've got Emmy, who seems quite angry at her mother and her upbringing, and certainly there's Victoria herself, who has several times forgotten how many children she has (yes, it's played as a joke, but still…). Elka's husband is dead, and certainly her parents, eh, but doesn't she have anyone at all? She has never mentioned it. Of all of them, Melanie is probably the only one who seems to have a healthy relationship with her kids.

MB comments about the improvement of characterizations of *Hot in Cleveland*:

> When this show came on I barely gave it a chance although I love all 4 ladies. I watched a couple episodes and saw nothing but cheap insult humor, and Betty White as the old lady with the semi-smutty insulting one liners. Oh, and Newman and his damned balls (hahahaha yeah). I love VB but Melanie was so over the top chirpy. Then I had it on in the background today—marathon—and actually got caught up in the newer episodes and was very amused. It appears to be "fixed" and toned up and down where it needed to be. The ladies actually exhibited some real friendship and Betty was fabulous. Still a feisty old lady but the nasty mean edge is toned down. Joy is still a bit of a downer most of the time but I like her. I love Victoria Chase in all her delusions. So I've officially changed my mind. I'm pretty sure I like this show. Anyone else who's watched faithfully think it has improved?

MB, SS, and JN all point out the ways in which *Hot in Cleveland* falls short of *The Golden Girls* in terms of their treatment of one another, their relationship with extended family and their plotlines. Although all three fans seem to be committed to the show, it's clear that they feel nostalgia for the women of *The Golden Girls*, and the *Hot in Cleveland* does not fulfill that yet. However, MB points out that *Hot in Cleveland* continues to develop and grow. MB reaches out to the online fandom to see if others share her reading of *Hot in Cleveland*'s improved narrative and characterizations over time. This question to the fandom suggests the connection of fans in this online community and the extent to which fans share a collective understanding of the show and its characters.

The articulation of collective understanding and a shared conceptual map repeats in many fan posts as does an appreciation and valuing of the contributions of each character in the series. KS writes passionately about the value of each member of the *Cashmere Mafia*:

> I actually like something from each character … which is a first for me. I did vote Zoe though…

> Zoe—I love that she's successful, but involved with her family. Her marriage is being sacrificed to that of her relationship and involvement with her children, but I think with the manny there, this could help get her some time with her hubbie. She is strong, and very vocal about the things she sees in life. At the same time though, she never pretends that she can do everything though. I mean, she is willing to fail, or at least trip and stumble a bit, and I love that about her. Yet, she always picks herself up with taste and class. A common thing with all these girls.

> Mia—While, I'm not as fond of her success, just b/c the field doesn't interest me, I do love her insecurities in her relationships. I mean, broken heart from Jack, budding new romance in Jason, and lusty fling with the manny. What is there not to be desired??? Especially with Jack in hot pursuit again.

> Juliet—I love, and admire this woman's strength. By far, the rock of the group, but also, knows when she can let her guard down and just feel the pain a bit. She holds her head high, and doesn't falter when in the midst of negativity. She's comfortable in her skin. She's extremely involved in work, but she makes the time to have this amazing relationship with her daughter, and at one point her husband. Oh, and although he was a cheating S.O.B., her devotion to him, and their marriage, was astonishing … of course before it got just stupid.

> Caitlin—I love that this woman is a hot mess! I mean, her life is chaotic, and there's disorder, and her love life is utterly confusing, and I love it. It shows how realistic these women are, and how easily you can relate to them. They have all the problems any woman would have, but they show the positive way of handling it.

Here, KS explains how each of the women in *Cashmere Mafia* confronts the challenges of careers, marriages, and parenthood amidst the realities of responsibility and achievement. In this way, KS points to *Cashmere Mafia*'s engagement in an ongoing telefeminist dialogue. Feminist communication scholar Kyra Hunting explains that *Cashmere Mafia*, *Lipstick Jungle* and *Sex and the City* continue the trajectory of feminist dialogue between popular images of women in television and second-wave feminist discourses focused on the role of women in American society (Hunting 2012). As KS points out the struggles of the women of *Cashmere Mafia* are very real and resonate with viewers. Kyra Hunting supports KS's perspective and argues that *Cashmere Mafia* and its competitor, *Lipstick Jungle*, focus on the challenges that the female foursomes encounter balancing career, family, and relationships. Hunting notes,

> The more complicated matrixes of responsibility and achievement in these two series may account for the fact that they deal more explicitly with how women's individual lives and choices are constrained and challenged by the expectations of workplaces, spouses, and other members of their communities. Nevertheless, these two series retain *Sex and the City*'s focus on the development of the individual women and their reliance on their social circle [Hunting 2012, 192].

Hunting's analysis confirms KS's reading that each member of the *Cashmere Mafia* plays a valuable role in the foursome, but, perhaps more importantly, the *Cashmere Mafia* itself constitutes a form of female-empowered friendship that makes what Bonnie Dow calls a woman space[10] for the political, social, cultural, and even economic, solidarity of women.

Every Woman and the Strongblackwoman

The "every-woman" character in each of these female foursome programs operates as the moral interlocutor, the voice of reason for the female foursomes. Although this role is sometimes occupied by another character—most often when the everywoman character loses her perspective through some kind of life-changing event—audience members tend to rely on this character to maintain a sense of balance in the series. Dorothy Zbornak of *The Golden Girls*, Julia Sugarbaker of *Designing*

Women, Khadijah James of *Living Single*, Carrie Bradshaw of *Sex and the City*, Maya Wilkes of *Girlfriends*, Zoe Burden of *Cashmere Mafia*, and Melanie Moretti of *Hot in Cleveland* all operate as the primary voice of reason on their respective programs. However, their positions as the voice of reason must sometimes be assumed by another character in times of crisis.

Certainly, a tension exists between each character's dual role as superwoman and moral interlocutor. In an episode titled "In the Black Is Beautiful," Khadijah's Achilles heel is exposed when she realizes that she lacks the capital to print another issue of her magazine, *Flavor* (S1 E5). Khadijah must either run an unsavory ad for a beer company or borrow money from Max to keep the magazine afloat. For Khadijah, this means admitting that she cannot do it all by herself. She must either rely on her friend or compromise her principles to save her business. Khadijah finds both of these options untenable, as her dialogue with Max. Khadijah implies, "I always had to hold things together; I always had to be the strong one; that's who I am" (S1 E5). Max replies, "That's your self-portrait, ain't nobody painting that self-portrait but you" (S1 E5). Here, Khadijah confronts the stereotype of the Strongblackwoman.[11] This stereotype builds on earlier versions of Black womanhood including the matriarch and Black Lady. Sociologist Patricia Collins discusses the damaging effects of the matriarchy thesis:

> These are the women who stayed in school, worked hard, and have achieved much. Yet the image of the Black lady builds upon prior images of Black womanhood in many ways. For one thing, this image seems to be yet another version of the modern mammy, the hardworking Black woman professional who works twice as hard as everyone else. The image of the Black lady also resembles aspects of the matriarchy thesis—Black ladies have jobs that are so all-consuming that they have no time for men or have forgotten how to treat them. Because they so routinely compete with men and are successful at it, they become less feminine. Highly educated Black ladies are deemed to be too assertive—that's why they cannot get men to marry them [2000, 89].

Collins examines and explores the implications of this profoundly damaging stereotype, and although Khadijah fits the stereotype in many ways, her ability to demonstrate heterosexual desire and to be desired by Black men disrupts the asexual elements of the Black lady stereotype and matriarchy thesis.

Similarly, critical race theorist Kimberly Springer's critique of the Strongblackwoman resonates with Collins's description of the Black lady as an extension of the matriarchy thesis. Springer argues succinctly that the strongblackwoman continues to be everything for everyone else and maintains a sense of self (2008, 74). As Khadijah recognizes the cultural power of this mythologized image, it paralyzes her and operates as a structural barrier, denying her access to achieving her dream. Although Khadijah borrows the two thousand dollars she needs from Max to pay the printer, she cannot live with the idea of owing her friend money. Instead, she makes Max a two percent owner of *Flavor*, thus circumventing her feelings of guilt attached to relying on others. On one hand, this tactic might be construed as an exercise in creative problem solving, allowing Khadijah to still see herself as a self-reliant strongblackwoman. On the other, her actions may be read as selling out to the system of capitalism. The preferred reading is likely the first, as Khadijah harnesses the system of capitalism for her own gain. Nonetheless, communication scholar Noelle Sheppard argues, "One of the myths that these characters try to maintain is the notion that Black women are invulnerable and unshakeable. These characters shift to accommodate and distill such myths, depending on the settings" (2007, 99). In this way, Max and Khadijah both reinscribe the power of the myth of the Strongblackwoman.

In spite of the fact that Max critiques Khadijah for painting her own self-portrait as the Strongblackwoman, Max also inhabits this role. In an episode entitled, "Mommy Not Dearest" (S3 E11), Max's mother visits and wants to develop a closer relationship with her. Max and Régine commiserate about their mothers (S3 E11). Régine exclaims, "I know what you mean. It's like they give birth, look at the stretch marks, and they just start trippin'" (S3 E11). Max responds, "Thanks to her I am the woman, the maverick, you see before you" (S3 E11). This is an important moment in the dialogue as Max gives her mother credit for making her stand on her own two feet. Max explains, "Okay, maybe my mom isn't the warmest, most affectionate woman in the world, but she left me the hell alone to go my own way. That taught me independence, self-reliance, initiative" (S3 E11). Here, Max offers her own self-portrait of a Strongblackwoman, eschewing coddling mothers in favor of the ideology of liberal individualism. For Max, independence, self-reliance and initiative replace the traditional patriarchal ideology of raising daughters who grow up to be caregivers and who are dependent on their fathers until they are married when they then care for their husbands and their husbands' children while becoming financially dependent on their husbands who are recognized as the bread winners and the heads of households. In contrast to this ideological construct, Max becomes the embodiment of second-wave feminism. Max's fierce independence, her individuality, her identity as the maverick (a classic western identity reproduced by figures like the Marlboro Man and John Wayne) collide with her mother's desires to share a more traditional mother/daughter relationship. I argue that Max, a strongblackwoman, successfully appropriates the white masculine content of that iconic western image of the maverick and parodies the system of white supremacist capitalist patriarchy as she rides off into the televisual sunset of American television. Certainly, this episode troubles the relationship between mothers and daughters, particularly African-American mothers and daughters, but it also provides a critical lens for viewing Max's self-image as a Strongblackwoman.

Ironically, Max and Khadijah's friendship seems predicated on a mutual appreciation for the other's drive to succeed, passion for perfection, and fight for autonomy and independence. Khadijah and Max are allies against the establishment, the status quo, the imperialist white supremacist patriarchy. As the theme song for *Living Single* states, "My home girls standin' to my left and my right, true blue and tight like glue." The theme song mirrors the kind of relationship shared by Max and Khadijah. However, occasionally their personalities collide and each woman recognizes the other's blind spots and vulnerabilities. In an episode entitled, "I'm Ready for My Close-up" when Khadijah asks Max to write a column about the legal profession for *Flavor*, Max's inability to accept criticism becomes a central issue as Khadijah begins to edit Max's submission (S3 E14). Even Overton and Kyle (Max's love interest with whom she engages in verbal sparring on an ongoing basis) engage in the quarrel. Max pleads with Khadijah, "Please don't use that red pen; it will look like my words are bleeding." (S3 E14). Khadijah points out that Max is unable to handle criticism of any kind and suggests that perhaps Max cannot handle the editorial process. Max responds that she is tough enough to handle criticism and begins to solicit it from the whole group. Kyle chimes in saying, "Please allow me. Maxine, you are as abrasive as sand paper, as caustic as acid and as obnoxious as only you can be" (S3 E14). Max flinches, but she persists in soliciting feedback from Overton. Overton responds slowly, stating, "Well-uh, you're cheap, greedy, shallow, and you have a really foul mouth for a lady, but these are things I have grown to love" (S3 E14). Max sarcastically thanks them for their thoughts, but Khadijah cuts her off and declares, "Wait, wait, my turn. You are stubborn and hard-headed and reject other people's opinions even though you asked for them" (S3 E14). Max's anger and resentment are palpable in her expression and she retorts, "Ah, Khadijah, who asked you?!!!!" (S3 E14) Here, Max's blind spots, her ambition, her directness, her overt struggle for power, mark her as the Strongblackwoman. In spite of the fact that these qualities may be viewed as positive and powerful, in this episode Max's friends expose her inability to take criticism as her tragic flaw. In this way, the episode both deflates the archetype of the Strongblackwoman and underscores the value of the shared friendship between Khadijah and Max. Ultimately, Max and Khadijah both embody and reify the stereotype of the Strongblackwoman even as they deconstruct the myth through the bonds of their female friendship. Viewers come to recognize elements of themselves in these characters, Max, the maverick and Khadijah, the mother.

LL comments : "My favorites are Max 'The Maverick' and Khadijah 'Mother.'"

PM also writes about her favorite *LS* characters:

Maxine "The Maverick" Shaw is the bomb! BUT I identify the most with Khadijah James. I have the same motherly, straight up, independent characteristics as her. PLUS I love Queen Latifah!!! But I am an advocate of each character bringing a certain special something to the show. DAMN I MISS THIS SHOW!!!

DB notes: "I agree with you PM I like every character on the show. There isn't one character I didn't like. But my favorite character is Khadijah James."

Each of these posts points to the fact that the characters of Khadijah James and Maxine Shaw resonate with viewers. Fans identify with these characters, and see them as representations of women they know. However, this everywoman quality is simultaneously overlaid with an exceptional woman quality, a superwoman typology. Khadijah James and Maxine Shaw may seem like just regular folks who work hard, play hard and keep it real with their friends; however, Khadijah builds her own magazine, *Flavor*, from the ground up. She edits, manages, writes, and supervises each issue, and does not go to bed until *Flavor* goes to press. Max graduates at the top of her law school class, and runs for public office and wins. In season two, in an episode entitled "Working Nine to Nine-Fifteen," Max returns to work at the Evans and Bell Law Firm after she is suspended because she advised her wealthy female client to ask her fiancé to sign a prenuptial agreement. However, Max ends up quitting her job in protest of the firm's corrupt Patriarchal values (S2 E4). Max tells her friends that there is no way that she is going back to her previous firm because they will persist in holding her perceived indiscretion over her head in spite of the fact that she made the right choice. Synclaire responds, "Oh, I understand Max. I know what it is like to be trapped in a job you can't stand—trapped like a wolf in a clamp. You just want to chew on your own paw just to be free. Just gnaw ... and then Khadijah hired me. It's good to be free! Let the sun shine in!" (S2 E4). The friends try to convince Max not to quit until she has some other options. They suggest that unemployment is a real risk, and that even if Max hates it, the alternative could be worse. Max retorts, "You are all forgetting that I am Maxine Shaw, the best attorney at law. Now there have been job offers in the past and there will be job offers in the future, and all I have to do is to sit here and wait for your phone to ring" (S2 E4). Although Max risks her career by taking a stand against the good old boys network, she is able to reinvent herself and move forward by building her own law firm. Like Khadijah, Max contributes to the production of the postmodern female imaginary by constructing the iconography of the self-made, exceptional, professional Strongblackwoman.

Having It All Narratives

Reinforcing the iconography of the postmodern exceptional woman, superwoman, and Strongblackwoman, many episodes from theses female foursome shows depict the realities and trials encountered by individual characters bumping up against the cultural power of these images. Like Khadijah they often become paralyzed by their own self-portraits, further reifying the mainstream dominant cultural message that whatever does not kill us makes us stronger. In this way viewers come to recognize that the vulnerabilities shared by the female foursome characters demonstrate not only their weaknesses but their ability to work through these moments of cultural conflict. One such case occurs for Miranda of *Sex and the City* when she decides to purchase her own condominium in an episode entitled "Four Women and a Funeral" (S2 E5). As she meets with the loan officer, Miranda is made painfully aware of her single status, and the source of her purchasing power is questioned. In fact, the loan officer assumes that the down payment must be a gift from her father. Linda Zayer et al. discuss the tensions of gender identity as depicted in the episode: "While Miranda wants to be unapologetic about her independent ways, the contradictions between her success in the traditionally masculine, public world of work as an attorney and her more ambiguous private life leaves her with the perceptions of being short on femininity and long on masculinity" (341). When Miranda talks to Charlotte and Carrie about the discrimination she experiences in the home buying process. Charlotte retorts that she rents because, if she were to own and the man in her life was a renter, the power structure would be imbalanced and emasculating. Men, in her opinion, don't desire independent women. Here, Charlotte's oppositional perspective on the gendered division of property harkens back to early Marxist critiques of capitalism. In his landmark book, *Origin of the Family, Private Property and the State*, Fredrich Engels identifies property as a key component of inequality within the bourgeois marriage in which the wife's economic dependence on her husband constitutes a form of prostitution[12] (Engels 1942). However, Charlotte's worldview and her acceptance of the gendered roles in relationship to property ownership reinscribe the power relations of patriarchal capitalism. In this way, Charlotte challenges the superwoman script. However, many of the female foursome characters actively grapple with the tensions of independent, autonomous self-hood within the context of the traditional parameters of heterosexual partnership, family, friendship and community. Virginia McCarver writes:

> The danger of the Superwoman script comes in the form of largely unattainable examples and the extent to which women uncritically subscribe to the notion that such a path is well within their reach.... Further, the Superwoman script also interacts with the rhetoric of choice and larger cultural

narratives concerning an individual's work ethic and ability to have it all. However, like the You Can't Have It All script, the flip side of individual success is individual failure [McCarver 2011, 32].

McCarver underscores the cultural power that is at work in the superwoman script, and this is perhaps no better demonstrated than through the characterization of Miranda. Miranda operates as a prototypical single-woman, feminist character who struggles against the stigma of being single and alone. However, when she becomes pregnant with Brady, she finds herself sleeping under her desk at her law firm and thereby demonstrating her weakness, a betrayal by her female body that traps her and co-opts her autonomy, forcing her to serve the needs of the parasitic baby growing inside her. Miranda resists the co-optation of her bodily autonomy, but recognizes that she must cede the power of her body to the baby. Even after she gives up her autonomous subjectivity in order to be Brady's mom, she finds herself compromising more and more. Certainly, the episode interrogates the power structures of patriarchal sexism, capitalism, and heterosexism, but it is Miranda's personal struggle as a superwoman that is explored within the episode (S2 E5).

This questioning of self-hood and having it all continues to plague Miranda when, in a later episode titled "Out of the Frying Pan," Miranda makes the ultimate compromise and moves to Brooklyn for her family. Standing in a three-bedroom house in the middle of Brooklyn, Miranda compromises her own identity as a self-proclaimed "Manhattan girl" (S6 E16). Carrie's voiceover explains, "That day Miranda couldn't deny what was best for her family ... and so, she negotiated her way into her future" (S6 E16). Later in the same season, Steve's mom, Mary, who is suffering from Alzheimer's disease, moves in with Miranda and Steve. In a touching finale scene, Miranda bathes Mary in a tub and Magda (longtime house keeper and nanny) kisses Miranda on the forehead, saying, "You love" (S6 E20). In this way the finale of the televised series leaves viewers with a sense that Miranda has finally found out that caring for others is more important than her own needs. However, Miranda's face yields some ambivalence as Magda mothers Miranda.

This plotline is quickly picked up by *Sex and the City: The Movie* (2008) when viewers find out that Mary is now living in an Alzheimer's care facility. However, Miranda remains overworked and exhausted as she struggles to balance her roles as a lawyer, mother, and wife living in

Brooklyn and commuting to Manhattan for work. Early in the film, Miranda and Steve face a crisis in their marriage when Steve cheats on Miranda. He comes to Carrie and Big's wedding rehearsal dinner to try to talk to Miranda. Her reply is abrupt and harsh, and her true feelings erupt. The movie script reads:

Miranda
You broke us! You broke us. What we had is broken!
Three YOUNG SINGLE GIRLS (25) walk past them into the club.
They look back at the scene. Miranda looks down at the
ground. Steve is paralyzed. Miranda turns to leave—looks
back at him with daggers and hurt.
Miranda (cont'd)
I changed who I was for you.
Miranda goes inside. Steve is a stone [King 2008, lines 61–68].

During this scene, the words "I changed who I was for you" hang in the air—unchallenged by Steve. Miranda articulates all of the hurt, the loss, the betrayal that underpins her long, critical perspectives on love and marriage within patriarchal capitalism. Miranda's statement indicates that she allowed her love for him to transform her, and in so doing she privileges the bond of the heterosexual couple[13] within the framework of patriarchal capitalism above her own autonomy and subjectivity. It's clear that Miranda made a choice to be changed within the framework of the couple. However, it is her statement—"You broke us! You broke us. What we had is broken!"—that irrevocably and undeniably confirms that it is the breaking of the bond of the couple that is unforgiveable to Miranda. Miranda values the relationship of the couple above her own self-hood, her own autonomy, and Steve cannot even value the bond above his own sexual desires. This is indeed a pivotal moment when Miranda questions her own choices and what she has given up to be happy and happily married.

All or Nothing Narratives

Later in an episode entitled "All or Nothing" the women of *Sex and the City* struggle with what it means to "have it all" (S3 E10). Carrie's voiceover explains, "Three hours later, I still hadn't found Pete, and I felt as lost as he was. I had a man who loved me and a man who wanted to leave his wife for me. I should have been on top of the world, but I wasn't. I didn't feel like I had it all. I felt like nothing" (S3 E10). Here, Carrie shows the chink in the superwoman armor. Carrie feels the weight of the cultural power of the superwoman script; but, instead of feeling powerful, she feels lost and out of control. This scene in the episode reinscribes the patriarchal power of belonging to a single man. When Carrie is sleeping with both Aidan and Big, she feels powerless and out of control. Rather than boldly occupying the space of the decision maker and either choosing between the two men who claim to love her or continuing to have a relationship with both men, she falls to pieces. Carrie believes she has nothing because she has failed to successfully perform the patriarchal dance of one woman and one man, stepping through life two by two within the safety and comfort of the couple.

Noted feminist philosopher Simone de Beauvoir writes about the cultural significance of the couple within the framework of western society in *The Second Sex*. Beauvoir argues, "The couple is a fundamental unit with the two halves riveted to each other: cleavage of society by sex is not possible. This is the fundamental characteristic of woman: she is the Other at the heart of the whole whose two components are necessary to each other" (1949, 9). Later Beauvoir explains how woman's role as inessential other mirrors that of the Hegelian master/slave dialectic. Beauvoir notes, "And inversely the tyranny wielded by the woman only manifests her dependence: she knows the success of the couple, its future, its happiness and its justification, resides in the hands of the other; if she bitterly seeks to subjugate him to her will, it is because she is alienated in him. She makes a weapon of her weakness, but the fact is she is weak" (1949, 522). Hence, some other possible readings of Carrie's "feeling like nothing" is precisely that she is experiencing her inessential otherness in relation to both Big and Aidan. In this way she is struggling to escape the role of the other within the couple. Another reading is that she is, in fact, making a weapon of weakness because she is weak. Her role as the other situates her within both couplings as the other. She feels she has nothing because she is disempowered through the coupling, and she thinks that one coupling may be better than the other. Instead, both couplings leave her with nothing in the role of the inessential other. Ultimately, the scene leaves the viewer with a variety of reading possibilities and a sense of Carrie's ambivalence. She does seem to be engaging in a superwoman script insofar as her choice of ambivalence potentially situates her outside the couple. In this way, she may be seen as resisting the oppression of monogamous, patriarchal coupling by continuing to keep both relationships going, and by choosing *not* to choose one man or the other.

Choiceoisie and the City

Later in the episode, the discourse of "having it all" repeats as the women go to see Samantha's new apartment in the meat-packing district. Samantha proclaims, "You see us Manhattan, we have it all … let's just say it: we have it all—great apartments, great jobs, great friends, great sex…" (S3 E10). The friends discuss how fortunate they are and how the choices they have made mean that they can be professional women with exciting lives living independently with the world. Samantha points out that by the time her mother was Samantha's age, she had to contend with three children and an alcoholic husband. Although Samantha laments her mother's situation, she also seems to blame her mother for making bad choices. Sam points out that she has the life that she wants by choice. In this way, choice becomes one of the most salient points of the *Sex and the City* series, enough so that we might consider renaming the series "Choices and the City" except that *Sex and the City* sounds so much more provocative. However, the choices that each character makes define her and politicize her. These choices also inform viewers' perspectives and ideas about their own access to choice. During the series, Samantha chooses to live in the meat-packing district and never have a baby, Carrie chooses to leave New York for Paris, Miranda chooses to be a single mom, and Charlotte chooses to divorce Trey and later marry Harry. These choices made during the series define Samantha, Carrie, Miranda, and Charlotte, but they also inflect and influence the politicized perspectives and positionalities of fans and viewers.

This is perhaps no better demonstrated than in the case of Charlotte York who invokes the rhetoric of choice in an episode entitled "Time and Punishment" (S4 E7). Kyra Hunting contends, "Ever since a petulant Charlotte York insisted, '"I choose my choice!"' *Sex and the City* has been cited as an exemplary postfeminist text (2012, 187). Sociologist Beth Montemurro supports Hunting's perspective in an article titled "Charlotte Chooses Her Choice: Liberal Feminism on *Sex and the City*" (2004).

Montemurro argues:

> Furthermore, Charlotte's use of the women's movement as support for her decision co-opts feminist ideas in order to suit her purposes, and liberal feminism's simplistic premise unfortunately lends itself well to such appropriation. When Charlotte says, "the woman's movement is about choice" she implies that any choice—whether it be motherhood, career, or taking a cooking class—should be OK because she claims to be making the decision herself. This is a tactic that has been used by the media and advertisers in order to manipulate women into buying products or ideas about self-improvement under the guise that they deserve to be self-indulgent, that women have put themselves second or last for too long [2004].

Both Montemurro and Hunting focus on the liberal feminist perspectives of Charlotte, and do not fully interrogate the second-wave feminist perspective of Miranda. This is not to say that critique of choiceoisie within the framework of the series is not warranted, but rather I maintain that the choiceoisie rhetoric of choice invoked by Charlotte provides an opportunity for a much stronger articulation of second-wave feminism by Miranda. In fact, I contend that this episode is much less about Charlotte choosing her choice than about exploring the condition of woman in contemporary U.S. society and identifying how this condition is shared by two very different women, Charlotte and Miranda (S4 E7).

Charlotte phones Miranda the morning after Charlotte's announcement in the coffee shop indicating that she is leaving her sought after position at the museum. Charlotte declares, "The women's movement is supposed to be about choice. And if I choose to quit my job, that is my choice" (S4 E7). Miranda is caught off guard and exclaims, "The women's movement? Jesus Christ, I haven't even had coffee yet" (S4 E7). However, Charlotte will not be deterred and engages in the rhetoric of choice pointing out that she has the right to choose what is right for her lifestyle. Charlotte is incensed that Miranda disapproves of her choice to stop working after marriage. Miranda does not want to discuss Charlotte's choice and suggests that she should talk to Trey about her feelings rather than calling Miranda and prattling on about the women's movement. Charlotte cannot believe how judgmental and unsupportive

Miranda seems. Charlotte exclaims "I am quitting my job to make my life better and do something worthwhile like have a baby and cure AIDS" (S4 E7). Miranda retorts, "Oh! You're gonna cure AIDS? Good for you. Just don't be too disappointed if all you wind up with is a pretty ceramic mug with Trey's name on it" (S4 E7). Charlotte crumbles at Miranda's callousness, and she tries to explain that she needs Miranda to support her in making this choice. However, Miranda exclaims, "You get behind your choice" (S4 E7). The end of the scene depicts Miranda trying to get off the phone while Charlotte repeatedly rants, "I am behind my choice. I choose my choice" (S4 E7).

The seemingly superficial statement uttered repeatedly by Charlotte, "I choose my choice" rings empty and hollow in the face of Miranda's more well-defined second-wave feminist politics. However, as Miranda and Charlotte engage on the subject of Charlotte's decision to leave her position at the art gallery to become a wife and mother, Miranda points out that Charlotte should be careful about what she is choosing, why she is choosing it, and what might happen if she makes this choice. Miranda warns that Charlotte might only end up with a coffee mug with Trey's name on it (S4 E7). Miranda carries with her a critical understanding of the importance of autonomous subjectivity and explains precisely how Charlotte's willingness to give this up may very well result in the eclipsing of Charlotte's self-hood, her identity, autonomy, and in the subjugation of herself to that of her husband and child. In this way this Miranda presents a second-wave feminist interpretation of Charlotte's choice while Charlotte argues for a postfeminist interpretation of the same choice (albeit with some significant trepidation). Communication scholar Virginia McCarver argues, "Choice impacts and alters perceptions and understandings of feminism, equating choice—no matter its outcome—with feminist action and thereby reducing feminism to a series of choices uncomplicated by feminist politics or a commitment to larger principles" (2011, 35). McCarver explains that the rhetoric of choice has become synonymous with American feminism. I argue that although Charlotte's choice may not be at the epicenter of feminist debate or women's rights, it is significant in its representation of the choices women make and more importantly feel forced to make every day. Critics will argue that this is a watering down of feminist politics; however, the moves that Miranda makes in responding to Charlotte's choice make it clear that even Charlotte, a bonafide WASP and a proponent of white ruling-class ideal femininity, is not immune to the realities of imperialist, capitalist patriarchy. As Bunny, Trey's mother, states in a later episode, "MacDougal is one of the oldest Highland clans in existence. We have a very proud lineage, one I hope you and Trey will be able to perpetuate. Now, I know some things can't be helped, but I must tell you right now I don't enjoy Mandarin food and I don't enjoy a Mandarin child" (S4 E12). This overtly imperialist, white supremacist, capitalist and patriarchal statement made by the matriarch of the McDougal family, only reifies the structural framework in which well-kept women are complicit. In *The Second Sex*, Simone de Beauvoir articulates the complicity of woman in this relationship and explains how woman may fail to lay claim to her subjectivity both because she lacks economic independence and because she is satisfied with her role[14] (Beauvoir 1949).

Once Charlotte fails to produce a child to carry on the McDougal name, Charlotte's marriage begins to unravel. Even her ruling-class white femininity cannot save Charlotte from her abject failure in the role of McDougal baby maker. As Charlotte grows weary of keeping up appearances of a happy marriage, viewers may be surprised to find that Miranda's second-wave feminist analysis of the risks of Charlotte's choice are quite accurate. Miranda's statement—"Just don't be too disappointed if all you wind up with is a pretty ceramic mug with Trey's name on it"— lays bare the social relations (imperialist, white supremacist, capitalist patriarchy) at play in the marriage of Trey McDougal and Charlotte York McDougal. Miranda underscores what Beauvoir describes as the dangers of Charlotte's willingness to be complicit in this relationship because she is satisfied with her role. Hence, Charlotte's decision to make her choice actively engages the choiceoisie politics of having it all, which is both elegantly proffered by most of the female foursome series, but also roundly undercut by the everywoman, superwoman, and strongblack-woman paradigms.

7

Televised Sisterhood
& Solidarity

Although the four central protagonists of *Sex and the City* did
not overtly label themselves as feminists, they modeled a form
of contemporary feminism for viewers, and a central aspect of
that contemporary feminism was their sisterhood.
—Susan Owen, Sarah R. Stein, and
Leah R. Vande Berg, *Bad Girls*

Perhaps the most elemental tenets of feminism: sisterhood and solidarity, run through the female foursome shows like an I-beam or a central column of support, providing a framework on which to hang
episodes that confront the women of *Hot in Cleveland*, *Sex and the City*,
Girlfriends, *Cashmere Mafia*, *Living Single*, *Designing Women*, and *The
Golden Girls*. This common thread of sisterhood and solidarity often
evidences itself at the conclusion of an episode and/or in a specified
communal space for the foursome. For the women of *Sex and the City*,
this space is often the coffee shop where they meet for a post-mortem
of the previous evening's escapades. On *The Golden Girls*, this is the
kitchen in their communal home where they spend hours talking and
eating cheesecake, ice cream sundaes and other sweet treats. House shar-
ing and eating and drinking remain similarly central to the women of
Hot in Cleveland as it provides a location for woman space, woman talk
and woman culture. For the *Cashmere Mafia*, the language of sisterhood
and solidarity requires cocktails, but the location is flexible. However,
for the women of *Girlfriends*, *Living Single* and *Designing Women*, communal domestic spaces provide the perfect environment for heated
debates, tearful confessions, and collective decision making. At Joan's
home where each of the girlfriends has lived temporarily and sought
refuge, and later at the J-spot (a restaurant/bar that Joan opens after

157

leaving her position at the law firm) the *Girlfriends* hash out their relationships with one another and work together to address both personal and group struggles. The shared apartment of Synclaire, Khadijah and Régine in a Brooklyn brownstone provides the communal meeting space for the women of *Living Single*. *Designing Women* blurs the lines between public and private space of Sugarbaker's design firm as Charlene, Mary Jo, Suzanne and Julia challenge and reconstitute feminist tenets of sisterhood and solidarity. Each of these female foursome programs promotes the mantra that none of these women are ever truly alone. They will always have their sisters. Through collective sisterhood and female solidarity, they will meet the social, cultural, political, and economic challenges that face each woman individually or all women collectively. Although certainly the tools of sisterhood and solidarity point toward a more collective action approach to confronting structural oppressions encountered by women, these female foursome programs address both the structural oppression of women in the United States and the personal conflict of individual female characters. In this way, these series engage the quintessential premise of the American women's movement that the personal is political; however, sisterhood and solidarity through female friendship remain as perhaps the most significant and longest lasting contributions of these female foursome shows.

As conflicts develop in episodes of each of the shows, themes of sisterhood and solidarity resurge as anchors for the principal characters and their friendships during the series. When one sister is in need there is frequently a group response. This is the case in an episode of *Sex and the City* when Miranda's mother dies unexpectedly of a heart attack (S4 E8). Miranda calls Carrie early in the morning to say her mother has died, and Carrie does not know how to comfort her over the phone but tells Miranda that she will come to the funeral. Later that morning, she meets Charlotte and Samantha at the coffee shop and tells them about Miranda's mother, emphasizing how alone Miranda sounded on the phone. The women mobilize and take multiple modes of mass transit to arrive at the funeral in Philadelphia.

When they meet Miranda at the church, she lets them in on the real problem. Miranda explains that she is fine, but certain family members are concerned about how it will look if she were to walk alone down the aisle in back of the coffin. Hence, the need for the collective, for sisterhood and solidarity becomes clearer. As Miranda walks toward them behind the casket at the end of the funeral, Carrie steps out into the aisle and takes Miranda's hand, walking beside her in a visual demonstration of solidarity. Carrie's narration parallels their walk: "There's the kind of support you ask for and the kind of support you don't ask for, and then there's the kind that just shows up" (S4 E8). This theme of just showing up to support one another becomes a cornerstone of sisterhood for the women of *Sex and the City*.

This theme repeats in *Designing Women* when Julia's longtime love interest, Reese Watson, has a heart attack, and Suzanne takes control of the situation (S2 E7). Julia points out how her former husband, Payton, died alone. She worries that they might not come get her if Reese is dying now. She flashes back to the moment when Payton was calling for her, but the medical professionals would not let her go to him. Suzanne explains that she has notified the doctors that they are to come and get Julia if Reese takes a turn for the worse. Furthermore, Suzanne points out that it is a good sign that they have not come to get Julia. Julia is overwhelmed with gratitude for her sister, Suzanne, and Charlene and Mary Jo are awestruck by Suzanne's uncharacteristic careful planning and thoughtfulness. In this case, Suzanne, who is typically characterized as a selfish, vain, femme fatale, draws upon her inner Scarlet O'Hara[1] to demonstrate true sisterhood. Although Suzanne and Julia are sisters on the show, their sisterhood functions as part of the larger group of friends as Julia and Suzanne represent the poles of the spectrum within the foursome. This is significant, both because the sensitivity and empathy demonstrated by Suzanne is rare in the series, and because the other two friends do not fulfill this role of emotional support and advocate. This exchange taking place between the four women in a hospital waiting room underscores the power of the sisterhood as they stand together against the adversity that faces one of their sisters—the possibility of Reese's death.

This story of collective support in the face of personal struggle repeats in each of the female foursome series. The case of Dorothy's diagnosis with Chronic Fatigue Syndrome (S5 E2) is cited as one of the most memorable, according to *The Golden Girls* fans.

JS writes about the Chronic Fatigue Syndrome episode:

It was Susan Harris who had Chronic Fatigue Syndrome and decided they should do a story about it on the show. Bea Arthur mentioned it in a Lifetime TV chat:

Bea: That was Susan Harris, who wrote the show, a great deal of it, did suffer from it, so she wrote something about it, because at that time it was really unknown. I don't know if people even understand it now.

In the second part of the two-part episode Dorothy flies to New York to see a specialist, Dr. Chang, from whom she finally receives a diagnosis of Chronic Fatigue Syndrome (CFS). Dorothy is relieved to finally have a name for this illness. Upon returning to Miami, she celebrates with the girls in a fine dining restaurant where they support her through this diagnosis. Dorothy treats everyone to lunch and Sophia explains to the waiter that this is quite an occasion because Dorothy finally has a diagnosis for her condition. Dorothy declares, "I can't tell you what a relief it is to just be sick—not sick and crazy, and to know what I have and that there are a lot of other people who have the same thing" (S5 E2). The comic relief kicks in and the women argue about renaming the disease from Chronic Fatigue Syndrome to Zbornak's Syndrome, or even Devereaux Disease. The episode builds on the irony that Dorothy is grateful to have a diagnosis for the disease in spite of the fact that the illness is debilitating and incurable. That the women confront the realities of the illness underscores the closeness of the foursome. By renaming the disease, they demonstrate a collective power over the disease. The sisterhood embraces the challenge of this illness and supports Dorothy through this most dreadful ordeal wherein she explains her relief at finally knowing that she is truly sick. As in marriage vows, the female friends are bound together in sickness and in health, and this scene in the restaurant reinforces the extent to which the foursome will hold fast through any crisis.

However, just as the women begin their celebration, Dorothy recognizes Dr. Bud, eating at an adjacent table. It was he who had originally told her that there was nothing wrong with her. Dorothy walks over to the table to confront him. She explains how hurt she was that he had dismissed her, and she points out that he hid behind his medical license rather than tell her the truth, that he did not actually know what was wrong with her. Dorothy's anger is palpable, and she details her journey from sick and afraid to empowered and strong. Dr. Bud is clearly confused that Dorothy is so angry at him, but she persists pointing out his clear bias against women, his dismissive attitude toward patients and his lack of real understanding. Dorothy exclaims, "You'd better start listening to your patients. They need to be heard. They need caring. They need compassion. They need attending to. You know someday Dr. Bud you are going to be on the other side of the table. As angry as I am and as angry as I always will be, I still wish you a better doctor than you were to me" (S5 E2). Here, Dorothy articulates a feminist reading of Dr. Bud's dismissiveness. Dorothy identifies his blatantly sexist remark, his suggestion that she should go to see a hairdresser, and interrogates his poor treatment of her as a patient. Finally, she concludes with a structural argument that all doctors should recognize that patients need to be heard and need compassion and caring and understanding. Through this speech, Dorothy is recognized by fans to be engaging in a feminist soliloquy akin to those of Julia Sugarbaker from *Designing Women*. D8 compares Dorothy and Julia:

> I recall that "Dorothy tells off the doctor" scene vividly, not only because it was so cathartic for Dorothy (and therefore, Susan Harris), but it was as if Dorothy was channeling Julia Sugarbaker of *Designing Women*. But I'd be much more afraid of being beaten up by Dorothy than Julia.

Here, D8 references Julia's frequent feminist diatribes, but suggests that Dorothy is ultimately the more threatening character. However, the feminist discourse that is evidenced in this speech to the doctor by Dorothy positions her as both moral interlocutor and feminist mouthpiece in the foursome, a repeating characterization that is integral to the sisterhood and solidarity in each of the female foursome shows.

This is similarly demonstrated by the role of Miranda when Samantha confesses to the sisterhood that she has breast cancer (S6 E14). Samantha first tells Carrie in a cab on the way to Miranda's wedding, indicating that she does not want to tell Charlotte or Miranda so as not to spoil Miranda's special day. At the wedding reception, Samantha first spills the beans to Charlotte, but when Miranda comes to the table she demands to know what they are talking about. Samantha does not want to ruin Miranda's wedding and tells her so, but Miranda will not hear it. Miranda demands to know what is going on. Samantha comes out with it and announces, "I have breast cancer" (S6 E14). Miranda tears up and Samantha protests, saying that she does not want tears or pity or sadness, and that Miranda should take care of her people. Miranda retorts, "You *are* my people and we'll talk about it now!" (S6 E14). Here, Miranda's statement: "You *are* my people"—underscores the feminist reading of their relationship as sisters and as family, but Carrie's voiceover frames the relationship in terms of a marriage: "For better or for worse, we were all ourselves that day—just the way Miranda wanted it" (S6 E14). Whether sisters or partners in marriage, the power of the collective of shared female friendship repeats in both the message from Carrie and Miranda, the message of sisterhood and solidarity. However, Carrie's role of moral interlocutor and connector remains at the center of the series and this episode, as she is the first person to whom Samantha reveals her diagnosis.

Solidarity versus the Fight for Mr. Right

In fact, Carrie may be seen as the critical link in the sisterhood on *Sex and the City* as she holds the bonds of sisterhood and solidarity together in many episodes of the series. In an episode titled "All or Nothing," Carrie tends to Samantha who is struggling with a bout of the flu in her newly purchased condominium in the up-and-coming neighborhood in the meat-packing district (S3 E10). Samantha's curtain rod has fallen down, and the light from her window keeps her awake. Carrie asks why Samantha has not had the landlord fix the window, but Samantha reminds her that she owns her fabulous meat-packing district condo outright. Samantha tells Carrie that she is alone and has no one to fix her window or care for her when she is sick. Samantha laments that she made a mistake by never marrying. Carrie's voiceover comments, "Three days of sleep deprivation had turned Samantha into a whole new woman—Charlotte. For someone who had it all, she had never felt more alone" (S3 E10). Samantha cannot seem to shake her loneliness and dwells on the absoluteness of female otherness. Samantha states, "I'm gonna tell you something. There's two types of guys out there—the ones that hold your hands, and the ones that fuck you" (S3 E10). Carrie's voiceover responds, "And I'd slept with both of them in the last forty-eight hours" (S3 E10). However, Carrie tells Samantha it will be ok, they are not alone, and they have each other. This exchange between Carrie and Samantha underscores both the stigma of single life for women living in American culture, and the power of sisterhood and solidarity in the face of this stigma. In a moment of personal illness, crisis, or tragedy, each individual woman in the female foursome may feel isolated, alone, and lost; however, the bonds of their alternative family through sisterhood and collective solidarity transcend the cultural pitfalls of singledom, and these independent women actively choose interdependence within the framework of their sustained female friendships. Thus, the bonds of sisterhood operate as a form of resistance to patriarchal capitalism, as the members of the female foursome, the sisterhood, serve to protect, nurture, comfort, encourage, and defend one another against the onslaught of an androcentric world in which women's identities hinge on their relationship to the men in their lives and in which the political economy of the heterosexual couple supersedes the value of the single woman.

However, all of the female foursome shows confront the tension between looking for Mr. Right, engaging female sexual desire and agency, and maintaining female friendships. Cultural critic Meghan Lewit explains that while female friendship stands at the center of these shows, we can envision Samantha, Carrie, Charlotte, and Miranda living similar, albeit more contemporary, retired lives like Blanche, Dorothy, Rose and Sophia in a posh villa or bungalow somewhere in Florida after they have outlived husbands, boyfriends, and raised children and grandchildren (Lewit 2013). Here, Lewit suggests that the women of *The Golden Girls* may well be the future iterations of the women of *Sex and the City*. While this might seem frightening in some ways to imagine the sleek, urban images of Carrie, Charlotte, Samantha, and Miranda as aging grandmothers in single-story bungalows in Miami, it is possible to imagine them aging together and, more importantly, their friendship and sisterhood lasting through divorces, grandchildren, illness, and old age. This is best evidenced by the fact that even as Samantha battles cancer and moves to California to live with Smith Jerrod, her female friends maintain constant contact.

However, fan posts suggest that the blending of the *Sex and the City* and *The Golden Girls'* approaches to relationships in *Hot in Cleveland* is problematic in some ways. Fan posts point out the extent to which the search for Mr. Right threatens to subvert the female friendships on *Hot in Cleveland*. JN comments:

The writers wanted to do a geriatric *Sex and the City* episode. Hey, that line pretty much sums up the whole show, doesn't it? That's a pretty good line to describe the show, it's certainly entertaining, but I was also hoping for a more "Golden Girls" type of sitcom, since this is a little bit too sliding on *Sex and the City*. Very much like last [night's] episode, they always start off with a good premise to go somewhere and find the funny (and they still get to the funny), but having men problems is becoming a trait of this show.

MB contrasts the search for a man on *Hot in Cleveland* and *The Golden Girls*:

My problem, though, is it seems most times when I catch an episode, it seems like everyone is desperate for a man. I much prefer the ones where Victoria is trying to reestablish her career, for example. These ladies could have hilarious plots with jobs, volunteer work, whatever, but other than Victoria they never seem to do anything but talk about wanting men or going to the bar hunting for them. I hesitate to compare this to *Golden Girls* but that said, *The Golden Girls* actually did things, and the only one obsessed with men was Blanche. Hell, even Blanche participated in things and did stuff with the girls now and again.

WP clarifies the tension and argues:

Perhaps I'm just making excuses for the show because I enjoy it, but I don't get the sense that the women are going after men to "complete them" or get married, but that they want to get laid!

Although Elka got [to] the altar last season, she was reluctant, and Joy's whole obsession with men are triggered by her bad experience with being engaged. Victoria lost Huey Lewis because she wouldn't commit to a real relationship. Even Melanie, who seems like your classic homebody, doesn't seem that intent on a long-term relationship after the first season.

I never watched *Sex and the City* (and you can't make me) but I assume getting laid was their objective too, but it just seems like a very different scenario.

WW concurs and points out the distinctions between *Sex and the City* and *Hot in Cleveland*:

In both shows, each character had a slightly different motivation. In *Sex and the City*, I think both Carrie and Charlotte were looking for "Mr. Right," but weren't exactly averse to having a lot of fun along the way. Their *Hot in Cleveland* counterparts would be Joy and Melanie. In *Sex and the City*, Miranda was torn between her career and finding a soul mate, her *Hot in Cleveland* counterpart would be Victoria. On both shows, neither Elka [n]or Samantha seem to be that obsessed in finding a mate (they'd certainly get married if they found the right guy), but are clearly more focused on the short-term goal of getting laid.

The criticism of the search for Mr. Right in these fan posts only builds on existing feminist criticism of female foursome shows. Communication scholar Kristal Brent Zook notes that this struggle between female solidarity and the fight for Mr. Right emerged during Yvette Lee Bowser's pitch for *Living Single*. Zook writes, "Bowser had originally pitched the show as 'My Girls,' but Fox executives feared this would amount to male alienation and shifted the name to *Living Single* and the focus to a 'Fight for Mr. Right' targeting the *Waiting to Exhale* audience" (Zook 1999, 67). In this way, the fan posts criticizing the focus on Mr. Right in *Hot in Cleveland* continues as a thread of the same argument that Bowser encountered during her proposal for *Living Single*. What this means is that the man problem or the heterosexual relationship problem remains in tension with the solidarity of the sisterhood on these female foursome shows. Communication scholar Deborah Macey further complicates this criticism, indicating that the use of insult humor in *Living Single* and *The Golden Girls* further disrupts the notion of female solidarity on these shows (2008, 84). However, Macey also argues that the most progressive outcome of *Sex and the City* is the supportive idea of an alternative family ideal (2008, 84). Here, Macey's arguments contrast with *Hot in Cleveland* fan posts, indicating that the obsession with finding a man is more prevalent in *Sex and the City* than in *The Golden Girls*. Furthermore, Macey explains that the insult humor is more undercutting than the quest for Mr. Right in terms of female solidarity on both *The Golden Girls* and *Living Single*.

However, there can be no doubt that the quest for Mr. Right consumes much of the energy of the women on all of the female foursome shows. In season four of *Designing Women*, Mary Jo fears that her hectic family schedule and career focus will leave her single forever, so after Suzanne dings her car, Mary Jo enlists her help to engage in a manhunt weekend (S4 E10). Julia comments, "Now Mary Jo, I know that you do not believe that a woman has to be married or she's worthless." Suzanne quips, "Maybe it is hard to meet men, I mean for you." Mary Jo boldly states, "I am going to meet a man this weekend or die trying." Suzanne reminds Mary Jo that "You and Julia can poo poo me all you like, but in your hearts you know that I am the one that knows about men." Mary

Jo purchases the book *Power Dating*, with the promise that Suzanne will coach her and they will do everything the book says. Later, Mary Jo is all dressed up in the grocery store. She tries to do her shopping while she waits to meet a man. Suzanne removes items from her cart, indicating that Mary Jo's groceries are not sexy. Suzanne states, "Men do not come up to women who are wheeling around a twenty-five pound sack of dog food and a big box of Kotex!" Monday morning, when none of the plans have come to fruition, Mary Jo laments, "I tried all that tricky stuff, and I just made a big fool of myself. Anyway, the kind of guy that I am looking for is probably a homebody like me. He's sitting in front of the fire, petting his Irish setter—somebody who cares about the same things that I care about, you know, who would appreciate me. That kind of guy is just impossible to meet because he is at home." The end of the episode finds Quinn's teacher coming to Sugarbaker's to drop off a file for the committee that Mary Jo and he will be co-chairing. It turns out that Mr. Berringer is a handsome thirty-something man with an English setter and a fireplace. After he leaves, Suzanne comments, "Well Mary Jo, I guess you were right—you're never going to find someone exactly right." Here, the point seems to be driven home that pairing up is normal, and in spite of the fact that Julia and Suzanne are not married, Mary Jo is lonely because her best friend, Charlene, is married and expecting her first child. Mary Jo feels keenly the absence of her friend and begins to think that she will be just another statistically single woman over thirty. While it may be argued that having the handsome teacher show up at the end of the episode suggests a fairy-tale ending, the series focuses on the communal space of Sugarbaker's and the ups and downs of the lives of these four primary female characters.

However, the competition of looking for Mr. Right is also taken up in an episode entitled "Cruising" (S2 E8), the *Designing Women* sail on a complimentary cruise, tasked with the job of redecorating the ship. However, the rivalry between gentle Mary Jo, and femme fatale Suzanne Sugarbaker erupts in a flurry of feminine wiles as Mary Jo and Suzanne compete for the best-looking man on the cruise. In the end, Mary Jo argues to protect her friend from the ship's Don Johnson lookalike when he indicates that Suzanne is not his type. Mary Jo's defense of her friend underscores her commitment to sisterhood over a relationship with a man who would not value her friend. Her statement also reinforces Mary

Jo's admiration of Suzanne's ideal beauty and femininity and her commitment to their sisterhood in spite of their vast differences.

Clearly, the women of *Designing Women* maintain their sense of sisterhood and solidarity with one another, both when they are single and when they are in committed, loving relationships with men, as in the case of Julia and Reese, Mary Jo and JD, Bill and Charlene and periodically between Suzanne and her ex-husband, Dash Goff (the writer). This is also the case for the women of *Sex and the City* as men float in and out of the lives of Charlotte, Samantha, Carrie and Miranda. This is perhaps best demonstrated in the *Sex and the City* episode titled "The Agony and the Ex-tasy" (S4 E1). As Carrie turns thirty-five years old, she laments the fact that she does not have a man with whom to share her life. Her loneliness is palpable, but Miranda tells her that she is not truly alone. Carrie explains that she thought, by now, she would have found her soulmate even if she does not believe in soulmates. Charlotte suggests that the women of *Sex and the City* are one another's soulmates, and thereby relieves the pressure of idealized patriarchal, heterosexual coupling. In this moment, the female friendship cements the bonds of shared sisterhood and solidarity among the foursome, privileging this relationship over that of the heterosexual couple. In this way, the sisterhood disrupts the power relations of the heterosexual couple within the framework of capitalist patriarchy without arguing against heterosexual partnerships. Instead, the sisterhood operates as a foundation for strong womanhood and community wherein female friendships have the capacity to transcend the full gamut of life changes of its members, including marriage, divorce, sickness, aging, and death.

This theme of sisterhood and solidarity repeats in the one-hundredth episode of *Living Single* titled "Back in the Day," when Khadijah prepares to accept a journalism award for her editorship of the magazine *Flavor* (S4 E15). After a series of transportation mishaps and a stroll down memory lane, Khadijah stands at the podium to accept the award and thanks her friends. Back at the apartment in the Brooklyn brownstone, the women take down their hair, take off their make-up, and get ready for bed when Khadijah's jam comes on the radio. The women sing the 1964 standard "My Girl," using hair brushes and Khadijah's award as microphones. Together they sing to and for one another, demonstrating their commitment to one another as lifelong sisters (S4 E15). This episode epitomizes what communication scholar Samantha Noelle Sheppard refers to as a celebration of female collectivity and sisterhood. Sheppard notes:

> When there are episodes dealing with the notion of female collectivity, the female characters do not disregard relationships that involve men, but they focus more on the importance for a female community and sisterhood. As most episodes end with a re-gathering of the women in the apartment, the series constantly reinstates the thematic notions of female collectivity. The women make it known that men (although sometimes problematic) do serve to enrich their lives, but they should not be the center of their lives. As Khadijah states in the pilot episode, "a world without men would be filled with a bunch of fat, happy women and no crime" [2007, 117].

With the collective sing-along, the one-hundredth episode of *Living Single* reinforces the message that the sisterhood belongs at the center of the foursome and reinscribes the meaning of the lyrics from the *Living Single* theme song, "I'm glad I got my girls" (S4 E15). They gather once again in the apartment in the most intimate of woman spaces, the ladies room, to engage in woman talk and to bask in woman culture. Culminating in the "My Girl" sing-out, the home girls serenade one another with the heterosexual lyrics of the old school Motown jam. They turn the words to appropriate their symbolic value for the sisterhood and harness the mainstream, patriarchal symbolic of "My Girl" to turn it toward the goals of their female friendship. By producing a moment of pure love among the foursome without male intervention, Régine, Khadijah, Max and Synclaire celebrate their collective commitment to sisterhood and solidarity and pay homage to Yvette Lee Bowser's original vision of the show alternately titled "My Girls."[2]

Critical Fandom

This solidarity of the female foursome sisterhood is replicated in fan forums where fans who have never met share intimate details of their lives and experiences with online friends. Self-identified avid fans, lurkers and critics in the fandom express how these female foursome characters resonate with their own lived experiences. Like each member of the female foursome, members on the online fandom find comfort and solace in the words of one another and enjoy the shared conceptual map provided by the female foursome shows. As previously mentioned, fans often ask what would my favorite character do in this situation as in—What would Joan Clayton (*Girlfriends*), Rose Nylund (*The Golden Girls*), Victoria Chase (*Hot in Cleveland*), Maxine Shaw (*Living Single*), Charlotte York (*Sex and the City*), or Mia Mason (*Cashmere Mafia*) do? In this way the characters and their membership in the foursome not only influence and affect individual fans, but also the larger community of online fandom. Collectively, members of the fandom seek connection with other fans and actively participate in dialogic relationships with other fans through shared experience of watching these female foursome shows. However, the shared watching and shared critical analysis of these shows is influenced and affected by the discursive relationships of the shows with one another and, more importantly, the dialogic relationships of the online fandom itself. Hence, the articulation and rearticulation of viewing experiences continues to produce new meaning(s) through the shared community of online fandom, and the solidarity of the sisterhood as viewed through the female foursome becomes a framework for fans to engage in online solidarity and sisterhood.

AW writes: "*Living Single* was my answer to *Friends* where there was no single black person for many years in one of the most diverse places in the world—New York City." For AW, the show itself provides a collective onscreen space to rival other white sitcoms that ignored Blackness and black lives. AW recognizes the power of *Living Single* to move against the white-washed images of American television and to hold in her memory the powerful images of Blackness. Television scholar Herman Gray argues, "Representations of blackness that are produced and that circulate within commercial media and popular culture constitute strategic cultural resources and social spaces where the traces, memories, textures, definitions, and, above all, struggles for and over social and cultural life are lived and waged" (Gray 2004, 55). Resistant readings by fans produce new meanings of agency, autonomy and subjectivity while watching the African American female foursome characters of *Living Single* and *Girlfriends*.

However, some fan criticisms of formulaic patterns indicate dissatisfaction with the characterizations and narratives of *Girlfriends*. MM compares *Girlfriends* to a Black *Sex and the City*:

> I never watched the first season because I think I was just turned off by the whole "Black Sex & the City" thing they were trying to sell. I liked the earlier episodes. Watching it tonight was just terrible. Maya was rude as hell. Toni was just shrill and unlikeable. Joan was just ... why don't you just tell Omarosa that you are not a lesbian and write William a damn letter or something. How old are you? The only one that didn't get on my nerves was Lynn.

MM explains how the characters do not translate into the formula in ways that are satisfying or complete. MM suggests that none of the characters, except for Lynn, offer anything new to viewers. MM argues that a female foursome show focused on four black women should move beyond the narratives of overt competition for men, money, and professional success.

KF concurs, and writes about *Girlfriends* and *Sex and the City*:

> *Girlfriends* was good for awhile, but the obsession with finding a man was killing me and it did hurt a little that it followed *Sex and the City*. Besides shows like EBHC, there are no *Good Times*. Do you think that failure of black dramas (ratings wise) perpetuated these awful black comedies?

Like MM, KF demonstrates her unhappiness with the repeating narrative of finding Mr. Right. However, she also questions the root of the problem asking what perpetuates such lowbrow black comedies. Here, KF suggests that there is a deeper problem concerning the availability of representations of blackness on television, and that *Girlfriends* is part of a larger systemic problem with regard to depictions of Blackness in American television.[3]

A color line is clearly in evidence between these female foursome shows as *Living Single* and *Girlfriends* offer viewers two all-black female casts and none of the female foursome series include a woman of color besides Lucy Liu, appearing in *Cashmere Mafia*. Sheppard argues, "Shows such as *Living Single* make "Blackness" a distinctive product to be consumed" (Sheppard 2007, 56). While I concur with Sheppard's evaluation of *Living Single*, I would add that *Girlfriends*, like *Sex and the City*, relies more heavily on commodified identities to promote and develop the series. However, the proliferation of African American female archetypes[4] under postmodern hip-hop culture remains problematic as they merge with intensified commodification, producing a layering effect of commodified black femininity. Even avid fans of *Girlfriends* point out the difficulties of negotiating these stereotypes.

AJ writes:

I believe Lynn is the only one I wouldn't call a bitch, and maybe Joan as well. Joan has always been there for everybody and their momma, and Maya, Lynn, and Toni have always admitted such. Lynn … she's just there, I suppose. She has definitely taken advantage of her friends and their resources when it comes to food and shelter, but sometimes I think she's the sole voice of reason. She does have 6, 7 degrees in who knows what that she has yet to put to use and barely has held up her odd jobs in the past. I just like her.

While AJ is concerned about the images of all of the *Girlfriends*, she identifies most with Lynn. In this way, AJ resists dismissing the show altogether, but points out her dismay at the negative images of the women and how they treat one another. AJ's comments powerfully demonstrate fan negotiations of negative characterizations and repressive stereotypes. Still AJ strives to look beyond even Lynn's shortcoming as a moocher and a user, but to see that Lynn might still have some greater purpose on the show. AJ explains that she reads Lynn as a dynamic character because Lynn demonstrates her passion for documentary filmmaking.

Through her desire to create social change, Lynn engages with some of the most substantive social issues on the series, including women's sexuality, gay marriage, adoption, sexual education and AIDS research. In an episode titled "The Mommy Returns," Lynn looks beyond her own self-interests in finding her birth father and instead focuses on documentary filmmaking with her birth mother, Sandy (S3 E1). However, the *Girlfriends* have a list of questions for Sandy. Maya wants to know where Sandy has been all of Lynn's life. Toni asks, "And what are you here for, huh? Blood, bone marrow, if it's a kidney, you can forget it because the girlfriends already have a pact on that" (S3 E1). Joan also chimes in, asking about Lynn's father. Lynn recognizes this as a defense mechanism and tells her sister friends that they should give Sandy a chance. Maya, Toni, and Joan work to protect and defend Lynn and to make Sandy accountable for Lynn's abandonment and loss, but Lynn is more focused on the documentary project. Later, Lynn asks Sandy to talk about her plans to produce a documentary about sexuality in America. Sandy declares, "I'm interested in exploring the history of sexual mores in this country" (S3 E1). Lynn responds, "I do hope that you explore the way that we politicize sexuality in this country. When it comes right down to it, I think it's a way for men to control women and maintain the status quo" (S3 E1). In this way, Lynn manages to focus on the larger picture, and to see herself as a documentary filmmaker. For fans, Lynn becomes a three-dimensional character who moves beyond the dramedy of her own adoption and birth parents to find a greater purpose in this breakout moment in the series.[5]

Solidarity in the Fandom

According to fans, the camaraderie and solidarity of the foursomes are the elements that keep viewers watching. CC comments:

> Long time lurker and viewer of *Girlfriends*. I've watched this show since the beginning and probably will until the bitter end. I'll admit that it's gone downhill a lot in the last two and a half seasons, but I guess I'm an optimist. I love the camraderie [sic] between the girlfriends and enjoyed the courtship of Todd and Toni. I remember when he socked a guy to defend Toni. Then I remember storylines like Lynn being painted totally silver and being a mime or some fool thing like that. I wish *Girlfriends* would go back to those days of yore, but it'll probably never happen.

KC also comments female friendships and camaraderie of the *Girlfriends*:

> This show is at its best when they're chasing men. It's not very feminist and/or womanist of me to say but whatever. Give me Joan going on wacky dates and being her usual neurotic self when dealing with men. But also I want the genuine camraderie [sic] and that seemed to be back last night too. I'm tired of seeing them all pout about their various weird predicaments. Last night they seemed to poke fun at each other's crazy situations.

KC and CC both point to the importance of the camaraderie among the *Girlfriends*. Interestingly, KC points to the importance of both the search for Mr. Right and genuine camaraderie and submits that this may not be a particularly womanist or feminist reading of the series. However, it seems clear that KC does not see these pursuits as contradictory or mutually exclusive. CC also points out that she enjoys the courtship of Toni and Todd and loves the camaraderie among the foursome. Here, the critical fandom evinces a more nuanced vision of what is possible and desirable within the framework of the sisterhood. KC and CC articulate a sisterhood predicated on an all for one and one for all approach to female friendship, and they do not imagine that heterosexual coupling undercuts or interferes with the intimacy of the female foursome.

Fans remain at once deeply loyal to the women of *Girlfriends* and yet keen to point out the dynamic strengths and weaknesses of each member of the foursome.

TT 2004 notes:

> Lynn is moochy and flighty but in a cute way. Maya is ghetto and fiercely devoted to her husband but not harsh. Toni is self-centered but not dismissive of others' feelings. Joan is funny and neurotic and confident and excited about dating but not desperate and whiny.

TT 2007 argues that Monica fails as a replacement for Toni.

> This was the underappreciated value add of Jill Marie Jones [Toni]. Her dichotomy of self-centered loyalty tied together Joan's martyrdom, Lynn's flakiness and Maya's bitchiness so nicely. Monica is missing a positive trait to draw the other women in.

Clearly, each member of the foursome contributes to the whole of the sisterhood. TT's critique of Monica underscores the need for dynamic characters to hold the sisterhood together in a meaningful way. TT argues that Monica lacks the intensive loyalty that Jill Marie Jones's character, Toni, brought to the female foursome. However, JP relates the *Girlfriends* friendships to her own and draws a parallel between her own role and Joan's as the nucleus of a foursome. JP explains:

> This is a very true statement. With me, I used to be the nucleus between me and 3 of my friends. They didn't particularly like each other during serious moments but they put up with each other because of me (but we could hang out all day and night—as long as the mood never turned serious) but now they are the best of friends and probably talk to each other more than I talk to them (no particular reason, I tend to be kind of introverted sometimes) and that's cool. Sometimes the most unusual pairings make the best friendships.

JP suggests that each member of the foursome contributes to the whole, and that the characters of *Girlfriends* resonate with the roles she and her friends played in their own female foursome.

Perhaps not surprisingly, fan posts explain how the politics of the female foursome as a whole and the individual characters within the sisterhood resonate with their own experiences. Fan posts often demonstrate empathy with individual characters, circumstances and situations.

This is certainly the case when Toni battles post-partum depression after the birth of her daughter Morgan (S6 E3). JP explains how Toni's onscreen struggle with post-partum mothering brings up with her own.

> Damn, I'm with Star, I felt sorry for Toni too. Maybe it's because I had a tough time adjusting when my daughter was born because all she ever did was cry and cry some more (she had colic). Truthfully, if my mom hadn't been there through it all I can't honestly say what would have happened to both of us. Now, I'll admit that I didn't see the entire episode, but when Toni broke down and cried I teared up because I know what it's like to feel that helpless to feel that broken down and feel like you are giving your all and it's just not good enough. I enjoyed Toni and Maya's talk though and I hope that Toni does learn from her tough battle that lay ahead with Todd.

NL also expresses empathy for Toni's post-partum struggle. NL comments:

> Where's her mother, friends, or anyone? Sheesh. I don't know anyone that has done the process, particularly with their first child alone. I know the show is not realistic, but then they gave her a crying infant? (Perhaps colic?) I have never heard a baby cry that loud and long. I'd feel like throwing myself out the window if I had that baby, too. Newborns usually do not have such developed lungs and they make low whimpering cries, and they sleep more than they cry. Is it any wonder she was about to go crazy?

JP responds:

> As a woman with a child I have to agree with you. Parenting *is* hard and you can read all of the self-help books and "What to Expect When..." books as much as you want but all babies are different and so are their parents. Having help during the first couple of weeks is not unreasonable and, imo, the absolute BEST for the child if their mom is a basketcase because she hasn't adjusted yet.

Although the JP is sympathetic to Toni's post-partum experience, her use of the term "basket case" is pejorative and seems at odds with the sentiment behind her posts. While fan posts often use hyperbolic language and engage in the heightened drama of the episodes, it seems clear that, for JP, this topic hits very close to home. In spite of the seriousness of this topic, the episode does not fully grapple with the long-term effects of post-partum depression, and the next episode largely ignores this issue altogether.

Protest Fandom

Fan posts reveal the extent to which loyal viewers experience the joys and pains, victories and losses of each member of the female foursome shows. As MM reflectively writes about the *Girlfriends* thread on *TWOP*, she relives the whole story of the *Girlfriends* female foursome:

> I sat down and read all 23 pages of this thread (because I have no life tonight...*LOL*) and it's amazing the gauntlet of emotions we've all had about this show Season 3 & 4. It started out with praise of the show (with a few exceptions here and there) and then continued with the highly dramatic wedding finale of Season 3. It's amazing reliving the horror of Season 4 and the relatively few (about 3 I believe) good episodes that became the exception instead of normally the rule. So, now we come to the last few episodes of an overall dreadful season. I guess I'll put on a brave face and watch. But based on the way this season has gone, I'm not holding out much hope.

MM expresses her deep connection to *Girlfriends* and to the TWOP forum where she feels a part of the *Girlfriends* online fan community. MM unites the online fandom through her use of the word "we." Using the word "we," she considers the collective journey of the fandom throughout the series. Through this post MM powerfully expresses her experience of shared viewership, collective critical response, and membership in the online fandom. She also suggests that, as she watches the last few episodes of season 4, she does so with a brave face, relying on the online fandom for support as the season closes out. This is a pivotal moment in the fandom, and it seems clear that MM's trepidation is not only focused on the ending of the season, but the potential ending of the collective experience of the fandom for the season. MM expresses a sense of collective belonging and shared understanding. In spite of the fact that she jokes about not having anything better to do besides re-reading the *Girlfriends* thread in TWOP, she clearly feels compelled to reflect on the shared experience of watching the show, writing about the episodes, responding to community posts, and watching again.

However, the trepidation that MM expresses at the closing of season four is minor compared to the public outcry from fans protests what they deemed a premature cancellation of *Girlfriends*. The official statement from *Girlfriends*' creator, Mara Brock Akil, issued by CBS, appeared in *Variety* in February of 2008.

> Although it's always difficult to say goodbye, I choose to focus my energy on the history that *Girlfriends* has made, the human stories that we told, the beautifully complex images that we projected and the blessings 172 episodes bestowed on us, both personally and professionally. I am immensely thankful to the amazingly talented cast, writers, directors, staff and crew for their endless dedication and hard work for eight seasons, to the network that always wanted us and the studio that always supported us, but mostly to the audience, especially African-American women, who took the time to tune in to us every Monday night at nine to have a dialogue with us and who have been our partner in this journey. I am currently in talks with the studio and network on putting together a retrospective show which will honor and celebrate this landmark series, so please stay tuned [*Girlfriends*: Mara Brock Akil Takes High Road].

Although Brock Akil's official statement is very polished and professional, there is a sense of loss and longing in the way that the cancellation occurred amidst the writers' strike. It is also very clear that Brock Akil believed that the primary audience for the series is African American women and that she wants to continue to create television for this audience. In spite of Brock Akil's poised statement fans' lament a lack of dénouement and conclusion to their beloved *Girlfriends*.

LL writes:

> This is extremely heartbreaking! I love this show and have seen every single episode. After *Soul Food* went off the air, I didn't know what I was going to do, but then there was *Girlfriends*, so that eased my spirit. Now what? These ladies were all strong African-Americans who I was able to relate to. And then for it to go off the air without any final ending. Can Joan just get married after all.... PLEASE! And can Toni come back for a final visit? And can William and Monica have their baby? I need some sort of closure! Can someone have a heart and give us just [one] last show to wrap up the saga of *Girlfriends*?

LL expresses her need for closure and completion to these strong African American women. LL suggests that losing the program will be tantamount to losing good friends but without having a chance to say goodbye. However, DJ blames corporate media for the end of *Girlfriends*:

> If it was such a bad investment to continue what the CW Execs obviously considered to be a subprime show in the 7th season (decision due to the strike my behind) ... why are the box sets over 100 dollars on Amazon? Ahhhh, Corp. America continues to find ways to profit off of their bad behavior.

DJ focuses on the fact that ending the series is a bottom-line decision not one made with the consideration of the fandom. There is a real sense that the fans feel as if their loyalty is being discounted as their beloved *Girlfriends* are sold out. That the fans place a higher value on the personal connections that they feel with the characters and their sister fans seems genuine. Certainly, linkages are made between commodifying Blackness[6] and the end of the series.

LS argues that premature cancellation is tantamount to racism:

> Just like many who posted comments, I am LIVID that the CW would do this to us. I was already upset that Toni left the show 2 years—but I dealt with it. I was also very annoyed when they contemplated not even continuing the show into its 7th and 8th season a couple years before. I thought our voices were truly heard and justice prevailed after so many complaints about it not being on the air. Now it truly IS a slap in the face—to every African American. We only needed 2 more episodes to truly close the show—you mean to tell me that right after the strike concluded, they couldn't write that and give us a proper farewell??!! Many loyal viewers have watched Joan struggle for YEARS trying to get (and keep a man)—she finally has one, they get engaged, he goes away and then just when we THINK we'll see a beautiful black couple exchange vows—they pull the plug on us! This, ladies and gentlemen just goes to show that racism DOES exist!

LS's anger is palpable in this post, as she articulates the sense that the African American viewers of this show have been let down. She explains that this is a Black program made for a Black audience by a Black woman creator, and that canceling the show is evidence of overt racism.

RD voices sorrow at the loss of *Girlfriends*:

> I can't believe they are just going to take *Girlfriends* off the air like that, it's the best show on TV and no matter what they put on tv to take the place of my show it won't be able to stand. *Girlfriends* wasn't just a show, it was encouraging. I mean 4 beautiful black women that were successful. It made you wanta do good. It was like they all was one woman with a lot of personalities. I really hate that i have to say goodbye, and then the network can't even give them a great ending. If any of the *Girlfriends* cast read this just no [sic] that i am a true fan. I never miss one show of *Girlfriends*, and even [if] i got to just watch the repeats its better than nothing. So, goodbye my girls.

VL points out that losing *Girlfriends* is like losing a part of ourselves:

> I have to agree with the words of so many others. I have been a fan of girlfriends since the first show aired 8 years ago. I have watched each character

grow in her/his own ways and become better actors and better persons. At the same time, I have grown with them and shared some of their experiences. It is such a shame to see the show that has come into our homes week after week end without as much as a fair "goodbye." Please reconsider for those of us that feel as if we are saying fairwell [sic] to a part of ourselves.

RD and VL share a similar sense of longing for a show where they agree that four beautiful Black women have shared their life with their African American fans. VL also points out that she has grown alongside the female foursome. In both cases, RD and VL note how they regret that they will not have a chance to say goodbye through a farewell episode.

A similar sense of outrage and loss is expressed by fans of *Cashmere Mafia*. Although the program ran for only one season (as it was also cut short during the writers' strike), fans vehemently opposed the premature cancellation of the series, noting that these empowering female images were an inspiration to working women. GW writes against the cancellation of *Cashmere Mafia*:

Please do not cancel *Cashmere Mafia*. This is my favourite show of 2008! I love this show more than [anything] else and it bothers me that the show has been cancelled! I am signing up with this petition to tell ABC how much this show meant to a lot of people.... Please consider being this show back!! *Cashmere Mafia* was a show to help empower woman. To be honest the 6 or 8 episodes that played, to me is WAY better than the 9 seasons of *Sex and the City*. PLEASE PUT THE SHOW BACK ON!

CW notes the value of having powerful women to watch on *Cashmere Mafia*:

PLEASE bring this show back!!! After *Sex and the City* left the air I thought my friends and I would never find another witty show with powerful women to watch ... and the *Cashmere Mafia* came onto the scene and saved us!! this show is sooooooooooooo much better than *Lipstick Jungle* from the cast to the writing and production. PLEASE bring this show back we NEED it!!!!!!!!!!!!!!!!!!!!!!!

Having powerful images of women to watch after *Sex and the City* is cited as a critical rationale for the series, further highlighting the need *Cashmere Mafia* fulfills in moving feminist discourse further vis-à-vis telefeminism. That these shows remain in discursive relationship to one another is underscored by the CW's references to previous *Sex and the City* viewership and the need the show filled in their viewing lineup. XX also points out the relevance of *Sex and the City* in discursive relationship to *Cashmere Mafia*:

> Please bring *Cashmere Mafia* back! The writers strike threw everything off! *Lipstick Jungle* got more buzz and therefore more viewers—but there shouldn't be a competition. They may be the same genre (just like there are MANY crime/law/reality shows out there!)—but that doesn't mean they are the same! I personally watch both and would be sad to see either go. There has never been a serious women in business genre before (*Sex & the City* was great—but was not about women in the business world), and it would be a shame for ABC not to keep their status as one of the forerunners.

XX explains the role of the writers' strike and its negative impact on *Cashmere Mafia*. XX compares *Cashmere Mafia* to *Lipstick Jungle* and is concerned that they are in competition as if there is only room for one program that is focused on strong, professional business women. XX argues that *Cashmere Mafia* is the logical next step in the trajectory of female foursome programs as it focuses on women in the business world, unlike *Sex and the City*. Fans of the show actively point to the contributions of *Cashmere Mafia* to the female imaginary where women feel forced to choose between work and family.

GL comments:

> I would definitely like to put in my bid to un-cancel *Cashmere Mafia*. As a Stanford graduate who is currently dealing with the business or family dichotomy, I found the characters insanely relatable. I personally think I'd fit Zoe. It was something that I honestly looked forward to every week, recorded and watched. I enjoyed these characters and wanted to see where they went. It's not just about "girly tv" or "sisterhood," it's much more than that, and I think *Cashmere Mafia* hit it dead on. Please bring it back! It didn't deserve to be cancelled!

OG writes:

> Please don't cancel this show!!! It's good for working moms to see that you can work and have a family or just be a working woman and be happy about it. For once, women are cast in roles other than just housewives!! Keep the show going! Women Unite. We need this!

Both GL and OG explain that the women of *Cashmere Mafia* provide a visual for understanding what it might be like to balance work and family. GL and OG call on women to unite in support of *Cashmere Mafia* because it is a show that offers a vision of real sisterhood among working women. That *Cashmere Mafia* fans feel so impassioned about a show that was only on the air for seven episodes is truly amazing. While it is sad to imagine that fan posts did not prevent the termination of the series, it is powerful to see an online fandom so focused on the need for more, better, and stronger images of women on television. That the fans of *Girlfriends* fought so passionately for a real farewell episode for the series does not seem surprising in light of the *Cashmere Mafia* fan posts. The loyalty of *Girlfriends* fans who watched through eight long seasons demonstrates the need for more, better and stronger images of African American women.

This study of online fandom reveals that fans are not passive, but rather that they engage in the development of resistant, oppositional and negotiated readings and the construction of an online fan imaginary that has the capacity to empower members of the fandom and to support re-visioning of historical and contemporary female foursome shows. That I, as a scholar fan, have the opportunity to engage as a participant observer in the community of online fandom, has been inspiring. I have learned much from fan posts and from their productive epistemologies. Even as I write new episodes, new characters and new situations continue to be developed. The continued discursive relationship between female foursome shows and their fans cannot be denied.

I would just like to submit for the record that the critiques which argue that these female foursome programs are pro-woman but antifeminist, racist and homophobic, and that they are representative of commodified white, ruling-class, dominant culture kind of feminism do not adequately address the very challenging cultural work that these TV female foursomes and their fans are doing. They indicate that we are moving in a direction toward female empowerment. Is it a straight path? No. Is it a bumpy road? Yes. Are there wrong turns and missteps? Certainly, but we are going, and the proliferation of these female foursome programs should not just be critiqued until all of the pleasure of women's solidarity, dialogue, community, and negotiated feminisms and femininities have been poured down the drain. There are episodes of these programs that make me wince, and there are episodes that make me laugh and make me cry, but I never felt like my feminist membership card would be revoked for viewing. On the contrary, I tell my students that I never watch without my feminist cultural studies reading glasses. Like many of my friends, colleagues and feminist sisters, wearing these critical lenses I scan media productions, hoping and wishing for a glimpse of something good for women, good for working-class women, good for women of color, good for women who are looking for change, for alternative ways of depicting gender, relationships, sex, aging, fashion, friendship, birth, death, motherhood, bill paying, laundry, leisure, work and life.

Appendix A

Which of
The Golden Girls
Are You?

1. **Do you carry a purse?**
   - ☐ Everywhere I go. Ever!
   - ☐ Only to carry the must haves: keys, condoms...
   - ☐ Do I carry a purse where?
   - ☐ I carry a wallet in my back pocket.

2. **Are you currently seeing anyone special?**
   - ☐ The young man who gives me my dialysis is cute!
   - ☐ A few special gentlemen...
   - ☐ My husband ... sniffle ... is dead.
   - ☐ My high school boyfriend who got me knocked up.

3. **Sum up your personality in a word or a few.**
   - ☐ Smarter than you.
   - ☐ Spunky, Southern and Sexy!
   - ☐ I've always done poorly on tests.
   - ☐ Hardcore, nobody likes me, bitch.

4. **Which of the *Sex and the City* girls do you most closely identify with?**
   - ☐ Carrie
   - ☐ Samantha
   - ☐ Charlotte
   - ☐ Miranda

5. **Confirm the suspicion... Are you the *Sex and the City* girls ... just OLD?**
   - ☐ Shoes are my life. Yes. Shoes are everything.
   - ☐ Next to me, that Samantha is kid stuff!
   - ☐ I like Charlotte; she's nice!
   - ☐ You're an idiot. That doesn't even make sense.

6. **Would my prior question make more sense if I told you that I have discovered that Dorothy is actually 3 months older than Sophia! The lies!**
   - ☐ I told you! I love shoes. Dorothy is a hag.
   - ☐ Samantha does remind my of myself at her age.
   - ☐ What are we talking about?
   - ☐ Shady Pines, Ma!

7. **So are you or aren't you the *Sex and the City* girls just OLD?**
   - ☐ No. Never. Not at all. I hate shoes.
   - ☐ Aww, I guess not.
   - ☐ Why do you keep capitalizing?
   - ☐ Very good, Ma.

8. **What is the worst thing that has ever happened to you?**
   - ☐ Picture this: Sicily, 1928...
   - ☐ Once, Daddy said we were gonna play dress up...
   - ☐ Back in St. Olaf, my cousin Huckleberry fell...
   - ☐ Stanley

9. **Favorite fabric?**
   - ☐ Polyester
   - ☐ Polyester
   - ☐ Polyester
   - ☐ Polyester

10. **And, finally, would you ever move in with your 3 best girlfriends when you're OLD?**
    - ☐ It's better than ... you know ... that place...
    - ☐ As long as they hate the game and not the playa.
    - ☐ Why do you keep doing that?
    - ☐ Only if I'm too poor to live alone.

Appendix B

Which *Designing Women* Character Are You?

Created by happybunnies15 on 05/12/2008

What are you most likely to have on your desk?
- ☐ picture of n'sync
- ☐ planner and important papers clipboard and pencils
- ☐ plastic mini ostrich with bright blue feathers and a matching hat
- ☐ i have a desk?
- ☐ keys and picture frames

In a crisis you...
- ☐ totally fall apart
- ☐ take control and sort everything out
- ☐ give lots of hugs
- ☐ try to make a joke
- ☐ bring food stare at the wall

What do you look for in a mate?
- ☐ will snuggle up by the fire
- ☐ wealth
- ☐ family oriented
- ☐ still breathing
- ☐ sexy
- ☐ distinguished

What do you think of Pamela Anderson?
- ☐ hubba hubba
- ☐ those are NOT real
- ☐ how does she stand up with those?
- ☐ she's like a Macy's balloon, are you kidding me?
- ☐ did i miss something?

Which of these describe you? (select 4)
- ☐ trusting
- ☐ loud
- ☐ cautious
- ☐ outspoken
- ☐ naive
- ☐ creative
- ☐ paranoid
- ☐ oblivious
- ☐ bubbly
- ☐ caring
- ☐ a little bit crazy
- ☐ strong willed
- ☐ you hear voices
- ☐ you're a diva
- ☐ like to look in the mirror

Appendix B

What is your preferred mode of transportation?

☐ station wagon ☐ Volvo
☐ limo ☐ van
☐ Lincoln Town Car ☐ golf cart

Pick a quote

☐ "Oh, oh! I've got one. This just makes me furious. You know when men use women's liberation as an excuse not to kill bugs for them. Oh I just hate that! I don't care what anybody says, I think the man should have to kill the bug!"

☐ "I probably wouldn't have fallen except that I'd put my pantyhose on so twisted this morning I've been walking like John Wayne all day."

☐ "Just so you know, Allison. I did not appreciate waking up this morning and finding my wardrobe on the front lawn."

☐ "I keep a list of people who touch my behind without permission. Some of them have died unnatural and untimely deaths."

☐ "I want a movie where a woman with a gun knows how to use it, and doesn't let some man wrench it out of her wimpy little wrist."

☐ "Do you know that if the Avon lady falls down on your property you have to pay for it?"

Pick another quote

☐ "Like I'm gonna go over to the clerk and yell, 'Hey! I'm a desperate, single woman lookin' for a copy of "How to Trap Myself a Man."'"

☐ "Well, I'm sorry Julia, but I don't think it's in good taste to have that many children. Unless of course, you're Mormon."

☐ "They didn't say anything about a tape at the store! I thought you just sent the whole camera in. Oh, darn! Another beautiful Kodak Moment down the toilet!"

☐ "The question should be, "Where have I been all night?" I'll tell you where I've been. I was locked in the basement!"

☐ "I can't believe it. Did you see this? Droves of vicious killer bees are headed toward the United States. They're from South America and are expected to arrive in three to four years. That is terrible; can you imagine? I'll bet our bees are scared to death."

☐ "And I don't care how many pictures you've taken of movie stars—when you start snapping photos of serious, successful businessmen like Donald Trump and Lee Iacocca in unzipped jumpsuits with wet lips, straddling chairs, then we'll talk."

Appendix C

Which *Living Single* Character Are You?

Created by KitanaJ056 on 05/12/2008

1. What is your gender?
- ☐ I'm a Male
- ☐ I'm Female
- ☐ I'm a female but have that male personality.
- ☐ *chuckle* This is all man!
- ☐ I'm a female! What do you think!?
- ☐ Oh, I'm a female. ^_^

2. Which phrase describes you?
- ☐ "Freak, freak, freakity, freak!"
- ☐ "Oh, oh... Woo, woo, woo!"
- ☐ "Yeah well as my Uncle says..."
- ☐ "What is childhood without the Stock Market Exchange?"
- ☐ "What's the name of your magazine?"
- ☐ "It's all about me."

3. What do you like to do during the day?
- ☐ Eat, but I never get fat. ^_^
- ☐ Work, but I have to, what I'm doing it my dream after all.
- ☐ Go to Acting school, and spending time with my life mate.
- ☐ Dressing good and looking nice so I could find a good man.
- ☐ Fixing things.
- ☐ Singing & dancing to jazz.

4. What type of clothes do you like to wear?
- ☐ Something expensive.
- ☐ Some old jeans, shirt and my work belt.
- ☐ Oh, something just casual that I like.
- ☐ Something that suits my style.
- ☐ Dress jeans, something professional.
- ☐ I'm a professional—insert profession here—, what do you think?

5. How do you wear your hair?
- ☐ I don't, I'm bald.
- ☐ I got my exclusive lines of wigs honey.
- ☐ It's all nice and permed, and usually up.
- ☐ Sometimes down, or up in some fashion.
- ☐ Whatever suits this handsome man/beautiful woman, *chuckles*
- ☐ It's just short ... meh. Now give me some food.

Appendix D

Which *Girlfriends* Character Are You?

http://quizfarm.com/run.php/QuizRunner

1. You're big on family.   eww no ☐ ☐ ☐ hell ya
2. You can be lost in your thoughts and confused sometimes.   eww no ☐ ☐ ☐ hell ya
3. You would do anything to look good.   eww no ☐ ☐ ☐ hell ya
4. Do you want to become big and successful one day?   eww no ☐ ☐ ☐ hell ya
5. You don't need high priced items to make you happy, you're fine with what you have.   eww no ☐ ☐ ☐ hell ya
6. You love shopping.   eww no ☐ ☐ ☐ hell ya
7. You want a man that can satisfy your every need.   eww no ☐ ☐ ☐ hell ya
8. Do you put others' needs before your own? eww no ☐ ☐ ☐ hell ya
9. Do you stay true to what you believe in? eww no ☐ ☐ ☐ hell ya
10. It's all about the sex, baby.   eww no ☐ ☐ ☐ hell ya
11. You try your hardest at everything you do. eww no ☐ ☐ ☐ hell ya
12. You're somewhat disconnected from your. family and friends are all you have left. eww no ☐ ☐ ☐ hell ya
13. You're not ashamed to be who you really are.   eww no ☐ ☐ ☐ hell ya
14. You can be selfish and greedy at times.   eww no ☐ ☐ ☐ hell ya
15. You believe in true romance rather than one night stands.   eww no ☐ ☐ ☐ hell ya
16. You're a real "deep" person.   eww no ☐ ☐ ☐ hell ya

Appendix E

Which *Sex and the City* Girl Are You?

http://quizfarm.com/run.php/QuizRunner

1. People would describe you as a princess. Disagree ☐ ☐ ☐ ☐ ☐ Agree
2. People would describe you as curious. Disagree ☐ ☐ ☐ ☐ ☐ Agree
3. You're smart. Disagree ☐ ☐ ☐ ☐ ☐ Agree
4. Anything a man can do, a woman can do better. Disagree ☐ ☐ ☐ ☐ ☐ Agree
5. A successful career is very important to you. Disagree ☐ ☐ ☐ ☐ ☐ Agree
6. You have remarkable style. Disagree ☐ ☐ ☐ ☐ ☐ Agree
7. You love art. Disagree ☐ ☐ ☐ ☐ ☐ Agree
8. People would say you're quite a flirt. Disagree ☐ ☐ ☐ ☐ ☐ Agree
9. You don't have too much faith in your looks. Disagree ☐ ☐ ☐ ☐ ☐ Agree
10. You like to be pampered. Disagree ☐ ☐ ☐ ☐ ☐ Agree
11. You ask a lot of questions. Disagree ☐ ☐ ☐ ☐ ☐ Agree
12. You believe in true love. Disagree ☐ ☐ ☐ ☐ ☐ Agree
13. You are fiercely independent. Disagree ☐ ☐ ☐ ☐ ☐ Agree
14. More often than not, you're a bit cynical. Disagree ☐ ☐ ☐ ☐ ☐ Agree
15. You like bold accessories. Disagree ☐ ☐ ☐ ☐ ☐ Agree
16. You are, or would like to be, a writer. Disagree ☐ ☐ ☐ ☐ ☐ Agree
17. You're a city girl. Disagree ☐ ☐ ☐ ☐ ☐ Agree
18. If you were a drink, you'd be a dirty martini or strawberry daiquiri. Disagree ☐ ☐ ☐ ☐ ☐ Agree
19. You're an optimist. Disagree ☐ ☐ ☐ ☐ ☐ Agree
20. You're not much of a relationship person. Disagree ☐ ☐ ☐ ☐ ☐ Agree
21. If you were a drink, you'd be a strong red wine. Disagree ☐ ☐ ☐ ☐ ☐ Agree

22. You're very feminine. Disagree ☐ ☐ ☐ ☐ ☐ Agree
23. You recognize yourself as a strong Disagree ☐ ☐ ☐ ☐ ☐ Agree
    woman.
24. Shoes are your one true love. Disagree ☐ ☐ ☐ ☐ ☐ Agree

Chapter Notes

Introduction

1. For a complete description of the category of woman, see Beauvoir 1989 [1949].

2. Which [*The Golden Girls, Designing Women, LS, Girlfriends, Sex and the City*) Character Are You? (see appendix A–E).

3. Fan postings continue on all of these shows on tvwop.com under "Sitcoms and Other Yucky Stuff."

4. For a full discussion of fan-scholar audience reception studies, see Monaco 2010; Lotz and Ross 2004; and Hills 2002.

5. The decision to incorporate fan postings with textual analysis came with my first conception of the project at the Popular Cultural Association Annual Conference in Boston in the spring of 2006. However, I continued to struggle with merging online audience reception data with textual analysis throughout the writing process.

6. Recombinant is defined by Gitlin 1983 as a recombination of elements to produce something new.

7. Lotz indicates that the redesign of the Lifetime website in March of 2000 ended the usage of the term Lifetime Lounge, and it is now listed only as Bulletin Boards (2000).

Chapter 1

1. See Japp 1991 and Byars and Meehan 1994 for a discussion of television's working women.

2. See Vavrus 2000 for a discussion of the 1996 media articulation of the soccer mom trope.

3. See Brown 1990; Fiske 1990; Press 1991; Douglas 1994; Feuer 1995; Dow 1996; Bobo & Seiter 1997; Brunsdon, D'Acci & Spigel 1997; Means Coleman 1998; Harlovich & Rabinovitz 1999; Hollows 2000; Smith-Shomade 2002; Arthurs 2003; Spangler 2003; McRobbie 2004; Lotz 2006; and Johnson 2007.

4. *The Tom Joyner Morning Show*, a nationally syndicated radio program, launched a campaign to save *Living Single.* See the 1997 article "The 9 Lives of *Living Single*" in *Ebony* 53.1. A letter-writing campaign (50,000 letters) organized by Viewers for Quality Television saved *Designing Women.* See Rabinovitz 1999.

5. See Stephens and Phillips 2003; McDonald 1995, 118–119; Kirby 1978, 72; Butler 1993, 14–16; Bogle 1973 & 2001; and Hill Collins 2000.

6. For a complete discussion of the racialized, exotic other, see Burns-Ardolino 2009.

Chapter 2

1. Simone de Beauvoir explains the enculturation of young girls into the cult of femininity by mothers, aunts, older sisters, and teachers. Beauvoir explains how becoming woman necessarily calls for a performance of acceptable femininity including an understanding of the virgin/whore dichotomy. See Beauvoir 1989 [1949].

2. Bell refers to ethnographic participants as co-researchers.

3. For a fuller discussion of the Strongblackwoman, see also chapter 6, Morgan 1999 and Springer 2008.

4. For a full discussion of bell hooks' terminology: white supremacist, capitalist, patriarchy, see hooks 1992a and 1992b.

5. For a more complete discussion of the New Negro during the Harlem Renaissance, see Levine 1993.

6. See Wollstonecraft 1996 [1792] for further discussion of the role of mother in the private sphere particularly in relationship to the role of educating future citizens through mothering.

7. See bell hooks 1993 for a fuller discussion of interlocking systems of oppression and domination models of power.

Chapter 3

1. See Butler 1990 for a complete argument regarding the decoupling of sex and gender.

2. See Rabinovitz 1999 for a more thorough examination of this critique of lesbian desire in female friendships on television.

3. White, ruling-class, male privilege is frequently interrogated on *Designing Women* as seen through the lens of second wave feminism; however, race is rarely addressed on *Designing Women* except in terms of class privilege. Anthony's Blackness is addressed mainly in terms of his imprisonment, poverty, and his social mobility. However, when he is arrested by a mall cop, racial profiling becomes a topic on the show. Also, in a later episode focusing on the nostalgia for the old south, slavery is referenced as a negative product of the old south.

Chapter 4

1. Like Régine Hunter of *Living Single*, Suzanne Sugarbaker is known for wearing wigs and hair pieces.

2. See Jonathan Swift's "A Beautiful Young Nymph Going to Bed" 1731.

3. For a full discussion of black feminist positionalities and standpoint theory, see Collins 2000.

4. For a full discussion of the Eurocentric, slender ideal body, see Burns-Ardolino 2007, and Bordo 1993.

5. See Smith-Shomade 2002, 62–64.

6. This quotation comes from *Designing Women* Season 2, Episode 7. For more detailed description of this episode, see chapter 7.

7. See Chapter 1, "Beyond the Binary: Femininity and Feminism on Television" and Kaler 1990.

Chapter 5

1. For a discussion of the American Dream, social mobility, and Blackness on television, see Haggins 1999.

2. See McRobbie 1991 for a Marxist feminist reading of female reproduction as an improper coding for the category of worker within the system of industrial production.

3. For a contemporary discussion of career women, working mothers and public engagement in feminist choice rhetoric, see McCarver 2011.

4. For a full discussion of homemaking and the domestic sphere, see Harlovich 1989.

5. Interestingly, there is one image that is not mentioned by Julia that appears, that of a woman sitting outside a building with a sun reflector shield held up to her face. This image is perhaps indicative of Mary Jo, Charlene, Julia and Suzanne who might be candidly caught on their lunch hours sunning themselves.

6. See also Anne Friedberg 1993 for a complete discussion of postmodern woman, shopping and flanerie.

7. See George 1992 for analysis of buppies, baps and bohos.

8. This is a poignant reference to the 1991 confirmation hearings for Clarence Thomas as Supreme Court judge. Anita Hill, a university law professor, accused him of sexually harassing her years earlier. The Clarence Thomas hearings are also referenced in an episode of *Designing Women*. See Spangler 1996.

9. Maya is referring to this section of town as siddityville. Siddity is a colloquialism meaning uppity, bourgeois, and privileged.

10. See Haggins 1999.

Chapter 6

1. For a fuller discussion of choiceoisie in terms of commodity fetishism, female consumerism, the American Dream and upward mobility, see chapter 1 and Arthurs 2003, Lotz 2006, and Haggins 1999.

2. See Dow 1992 and 1996, Rabinovitz 1999, Arthurs 2003, Lotz 2006, McCarver 2011, and Hunting 2012.

3. For a fuller discussion of negotiated meanings of African American sitcoms, see Means Coleman 2000, and for a detailed comparison of negotiated characterizations by fans, see Lewit 2013.

4. See appendices A–E for sample character analysis surveys.

5. See chapter 4 for a fuller discussion of Blanche's characterization as femme fatale and southern belle, and see chapter 2 for a fuller discussion of Blanche's characterization as modern day jezebel.

6. See chapter 1 for a discussion of Julia Sugarbaker veering away from her typical characterizations when she begins moonlighting as a nightclub singer named Jazelle and becomes obsessed with jogging.

7. See Irigaray 1985 for a discussion of the male imaginary and male symbolic.

8. Olsen references *The Golden Girls*, *Designing Women*, and *Sex and the City* as precursors to the new show *Girls*. *Girls* is not taken up by this study, but may be arguably part of the continuing trajectory for female foursome shows.

9. For a comparison see Bogle 1973 and 2001, Kirby 1978, Meehan 1983, Kaler 1990, Butler 1993, McDonald 1995, Hill Collins 2000, Stephens and Phillips 2003, and Macey 2008.

10. See Dow 1992 and 1996 for a more complete discussion of woman space, woman talk, and feminist consciousness raising.

11. For a fuller discussion of the Strongblackwoman see Morgan 1999 and Springer 2008.

12. Engels also argues that working class marriages are more egalitarian because both husband and wife are wage earners. While contemporary Marxist feminists dispute Engel's notion of the working class marriage as egalitarian, they agree with Engels that unremunerated domestic labor, child care, and elder care are key issues in the condition of exploitation under the gender division of labor (Stabile 1995, Gordon 1990, and MacKinnon 1988 and 1989).

13. See Beauvoir's discussion of the couple in *The Second Sex* 1989 [1949].

14. Beauvoir also contends that economic independence is not enough to release her from the bonds of oppression. See Beauvoir 1989 [1949] xxvii and 725. See also Burns-Ardolino 2007, 141–142, for a more detailed discussion of complicity and economic independence of woman.

Chapter 7

1. For complete discussion of the archetype of Dixie Bitch and Scarlett O'Hara as classic typology of southern woman, see chapter 4 and Kirby 1978.

2. See Zook 1999, 67 for details regarding the original title of the *LS* pitched by Yvette Lee Bowser, "My Girls."

3. For a fuller discussion of the commodification of Blackness on television, see Haggins 1999; Bogle 2001; Means Coleman 2000; Smith-Shomade 2002; and Gray 2004 and 2005.

4. For a more complete discussion of the proliferation of archetypal roles of the matriarch, jezebel, mammy and welfare mother proliferate under postmodern hip-hop culture to produce contemporary images of African American women as divas, gold-diggers, freaks, dykes, gangster bitches, sister saviors, Earth mothers, and baby mamas See Stephens and Phillips 2003.

5. Fan posts in chapter 6 point to the groundbreaking elements of Lynn's documentary filmmaking and indicate that fans hoped to see further character development from Lynn in future episodes.

6. See bell hooks 1992a for a complete discussion of commodified otherness and eating the other.

Bibliography

Anderson, Karin Vasby, and Jesse Stewart. 2005. "Politics and the Single Woman: The 'Sex and the City Voter' in Campaign 2004." *Rhetoric & Public Affairs* 8.4: 595–616.

Arnold, Alyson Chace. 2003. "Supporting Patriarchy and Consumerism through Sex Rhetoric: Power, Foucault and *Sex and the City*." M.A. Thesis, University of Rhode Island.

Arthurs, Jane. 2003. "*Sex and the City* and Consumer Culture: Remediating Postfeminist Drama." *Feminist Media Studies* 3.1: 83–98.

Atkin, David J., Jay Moorman, and Carolyn Lin. 1991. "Ready for Prime Time: Network Series Devoted to Working Women in the 1980s." *Sex Roles* 25.11/12: 677–685.

Avril, Chloe. 2010. "More for the Fit: Gender and Class in the Representation of Designated Adoption in a Selection of U.S. *Television Series*" *Nordic Journal of English Studies* 9.3 (Nov.): 173–195.

Bartky, Sandra. 1988. "Foucault, Femininity, and the Modernization of Patriarchal Power." In *Feminism and Foucault: Reflections on Resistance*, edited by Irene Diamond and Lee Quinby. Boston: Northeastern University Press.

Baym, Nancy K. 1992. *Tune In, Log On: Soaps, Fandom, and Online Community*. Thousand Oaks, CA: Sage.

Bell, Katrina E. 1999. "The More They Change, the More They Remain the Same: Representations of African-American Womanhood on *Living Single*." In Trevy McDonald and T. Ford-Ahmed, eds., *Nature of a Sistuh: Black Women's Lived Experiences in Contemporary Culture*. Durham: Carolina Academic Press.

Beauvoir, Simone de. 1989 [1949]. *The Second Sex*. New York: Vantage.

Bobo, Jacqueline. 1995. *Black Women as Cultural Readers*. New York: Columbia University Press.

Bobo, Jacqueline, and Ellen Seiter. 1997. "Black Feminism and Media Criticism: The Women of Brewster Place." In Charlotte Brunsdon, Julie D'Acci and Lynn Spigel, eds., *Feminist Television Criticism: A Reader*. New York: Oxford University Press.

Bogle, Donald. 2001. *Primetime Blues: African Americans on Network Television*. New York: Farrar, Straus and Giroux.

Bordo, Susan. 1993. *Unbearable Weight: Feminism, Western Culture, and the Body*. Berkeley: University of California Press.

Brasfield, Rebecca. 2006. "Rereading: *Sex and the City*: Exposing the Hegemonic Feminist Narrative." *Journal of Popular Film & Television* 34.3: 130–139.

Brown, Malaika. 1995. "Sisterhood Televised." *American Visions* 10.2: 42. Academic Search Premier. Web. 20 Dec. 2013.

Brown, Mary Ellen, ed. 1990. *Television and Women's Culture: The Politics of the Popular*. London: Sage.

Brunsdon, Charlotte, Julie D'Acci, and

Lynn Spigel, eds. 1997. *Feminist Television Criticism: A Reader*. New York: Oxford University Press.

Brunsdon, Charlotte, and Lynn Spigel, eds. 2008. *Feminist Television Criticism: A Reader*. 2nd Edition. New York: Open University Press.

Bryant-Davis, Thelma. 2005. "African American Women in Search of Scripts." In Ellen Cole and Jessica Henderson Daniel, eds., *Featuring Females: Feminist Analyses of Media*. Washington: American Psychological Association.

Burns-Ardolino, Wendy. 2007. *Jiggle: (Re)Shaping American Women*. Lanham, MD: Lexington.

Burns-Ardolino, Wendy. 2009. "Jiggle in My Walk: The Iconic Power of the Big Butt in American Popular Culture." In Esther Rothblum and Sondra Solovay, eds., *The Fat Studies Reader*. Berkeley: University of California Press.

Busselle, Rick, and Heather Crandall. 2002. "Television Viewing and Perceptions about Race Differences in Socioeconomic Success." *Journal of Broadcasting & Electronic Media* 46.2: 265–282.

Butler, Jeremy G. 1993. "Redesigning Discourse: Feminism, the Sitcom, and *Designing Women*." *The Journal of Film and Video* 45.1 (Spring): 13–26.

Byars, Jackie, and Eileen R. Meehan. 1994. "Once in a Lifetime: Constructing 'The Working Woman' through Cable Narrowcasting." *Camera Obscura* Special Issue 33–34: 12–41.

Cato, Mackenzie, and Francesca Renee Dillman Carpenter. 2010. "Conceptualizations of Female Empowerment and Enjoyment of Sexualized Characters in Reality Television." *Mass Communication and Society* 13: 270–288.

Childs, Chito. 2005. "Looking behind the Stereotypes of the 'Angry Black Woman': An Exploration of Black Women's Responses to Interracial Relationships." *Gender & Society* 19.4: 544–561.

Cicciu, Wendy M. 2005. "Stereotypes of Women in the Media: A Content Analysis of *Sex and the City* and *Desperate Housewives*." M.S. Thesis, University of Louisiana at Lafayette.

Cole, Ellen, and Jessica Henderson Daniel, eds. 2005. *Featuring Females: Feminist Analyses of Media*. Washington: American Psychological Association.

Collins, Patricia Hill. 2005. *Black Sexual Politics: African Americans, Gender and the New Racism*. New York: Routledge.

Collins, Patricia Hill. 2006. *From Black Power to Hip Hop: Racism, Nationalism and Feminism*. Philadelphia: Temple University Press.

Collins, Patricia Hill. 2009 [2000]. *Black Feminist Thought*. New York: Routledge.

Cooper, Brenda. 2000. "'Chick Flicks' as Feminist Texts: The Appropriation of the Male Gaze in *Thelma & Louise*." *Women's Studies in Communication* 23.3: 277–306.

Cosby, Camille O. 1994. *Television's Imageable Influences: The Self-Perception of Young African Americans*. Lanham, MD: University Press of America.

Cramer, Janet. 2007. "Discourses of Sexual Morality in *Sex and the City* and *Queer as Folk*." *The Journal of Popular Culture* 40.3: 409–432.

Curtin, Michael, and Thomas Streeter. 2001. "Media." In Richard Maxwell, ed., *Culture Works: The Political Economy of Culture*. Minneapolis: University of Minnesota.

Date, Jannette. 2005. "Black Women Decision Makers in Entertainment Television." *Journal of Popular Film & Television*. 33.2 (Summer) 68–79.

Doty, Alexander. 1993. *Making Things Perfectly Queer: Interpreting Mass Culture*. Minneapolis: University of Minnesota Press.

Doty, Alexander. 2012. "*Flow* Remembers the Work of Alexander Doty: Hot in Cleveland: Everything Old Is New Again." *Flow* 16: 1–4.

Douglas, Susan J. 1995. *Where the Girls*

Are: Growing Up Female with the Mass Media. NY: Three Rivers Press.

Dow, Bonnie J. 1992. "Performance of Feminine Discourse in Designing Women." *Text & Performance Quarterly* 12.2: 125–145.

Dow, Bonnie J. 1996. *Prime-Time Feminism: Television, Media Culture, and the Women's Movement since 1970*. Philadelphia: University of Pennsylvania Press.

Elasmar, Michael, Kazumi Hasegawa, and Mary Brain. 1999. "The Portrayal of Women in U.S. Prime Time Television." *Journal of Broadcasting & Electronic Media* 44.1: 20–34.

Engels, Frederich. 1942 [1884]. *Origin of the Family, Private Property and the State*. New York: International.

Ensler, Eve. 2001. *The Vagina Monologues*, rev. ed. New York: Villard.

Feuer, Jane. 1995. *Seeing through the Eighties: Television and Reaganism*. Durham: Duke University Press.

Feuer, Jane. 1999. "Averting the Male Gaze: Visual Pleasure and Images of Fat Women." In Mary Beth Harlovich and Lauren Rabinovitz, eds., *Television, History, and American Culture: Feminist Critical Essays*. Durham: Duke University Press.

Field, Syd. 2005. *Screenplay: The Foundations of Screenwriting*. New York: Bantam Dell.

Fiske, John. 1990. "Women and Quiz Shows: Consumerism, Patriarchy and Resisting Pleasures." *Television and Women's Culture: The Politics of the Popular*. London: Sage.

Gerhard, Jane. 2005. "Sex and the City: Carrie Bradshaw's Queer Postfeminism." *Feminist Media Studies* 5.1: 37–49.

Gillis, Stacy, and Joanne Hollows. 2009. *Feminism, Domesticity and Popular Culture*. New York: Routledge.

"*Girlfriends*: Mara Brock Akil Takes the High Road." 2008. *Variety*. February 14. Online.

Gitlin, Todd. 1983. *Inside Prime-time*. New York: Pantheon Books.

Glascock, Jack. 2001. "Gender Roles on Prime-Time Network Television: Demographics and Behaviors." *Journal of Broadcasting & Electronic Media* 45.4: 656–669.

Goodstein, Ethel S. 1992. "Southern Belles and Southern Buildings: The Built Environment as Text and Context in Designing Women." *Critical Studies in Mass Communication* 9.2: 170–185.

Gordon, Linda, ed. 1990. *Women, the State and Welfare*. Madison: University of Wisconsin Press.

Gray, Herman. 2004. *Watching Race: Television and the Struggle for Blackness*. Minneapolis: University of Minnesota Press.

Gray, Herman. 2005. *Cultural Moves: African Americans and the Politics of Representation*. Berkeley: University of California Press.

Gray, Jonathan, Cornell Sandvoss, and Lee Harrington, eds. 2007. *Fandom: Identities and Communities in a Mediated World*. New York: New York University Press.

Gregory, Mollie. 2005. "Galloping in Slow Motion: Women's Influence on Film and Television. In Gayle Kimball, ed., *Women's Culture in a New Era: A Feminist Revolution?* Lanham, MD: Scarecrow Press.

Gripsrud, Jostein, ed. 2010. *Relocating Television: Television in the Digital Context*. New York: Routledge.

Haggins, Bambi. 1999. "There's No Place Like Home: The American Dream, African American Identity, and the Situation Comedy." *The Velvet Light Trap* 43: 23–36.

Hall, Stuart. 1980. "Encoding/Decoding." In S. Hall, D. Hobson, A. Lowe and P. Willis, eds., *Culture, Media, Language*. London: Hutchinson. 128–138.

Harlovich, Mary Beth, and Lauren Rabinovitz. 1999. *Television, History, and American Culture: Feminist Critical Essays*. Durham: Duke University Press.

Harris, Tina M., and Patricia S. Hill. 1998. "'Waiting to Exhale' or 'Breath(ing) Again': A Search for Identity, Empowerment, and Love in the 1990's." *Women and Language* 21.2 (fall): 9–20.

Harwood, Jake, and Howard Giles. 1992. "Don't Make Me Laugh: Age Representations in a Humorous Context." *Discourse Society* 3: 403–436.

Henderson, Felicia D. 2009. "Successful, Single, and 'Othered': The Media and the 'Plight' of Single Black Women." In Rhonda Hammer and Douglas Kellner, eds., *Media/Cultural Studies: Critical Approaches*. New York: Peter Lang.

Hills, Matt. 2002. *Fan Cultures*. New York: Routledge.

Hollows, Joanne. 2000. *Feminism, Femininity and Popular Culture*. Manchester: Manchester University Press.

hooks, bell. 1992a. "Eating the Other: Desire and Resistance." In *Black Looks: Race and Representation*, ed. b. hooks, Boston: South End Press.

hooks, bell. 1992b. "Selling Hot Pussy: Representations of Black Female Sexuality in the Cultural Marketplace." In *Black Looks: Race and Representation*, ed. b. hooks. Boston: South End Press.

hooks, bell. 1993. *Cultural Criticism and Transformation*, dir. Sut Jhally. Media Education Foundation.

Hunting, Kyra. 2012. "Women Talk: 'Chick Lit' TV and the Dialogues of Feminism." *The Communication Review* 15.3: 187–203.

Imre, Anikó. 2009. "Gender and Quality Television: A Transcultural Feminist Project." *Feminist Media Studies* 9.4: 391–407.

Irigaray, Luce. 1985. *This Sex Which Is Not One*. Trans. Gillian C. Gill. Ithaca: Cornell University Press.

Japp, Phyllis M. 1991. "Gender and Work in the 1980s: Television's Working Women as Displaced Persons." *Women's Studies in Communication* 14.1: 49–74.

Johnson, Merri Lisa, ed. 2007. *Third Wave Feminism and Television: Jane Puts It in a Box*. New York: I.B. Tauris.

Kaler, Anne K. 1990. "Golden Girls: Feminine Archetypal Patterns of the Complete Woman." *Journal of Popular Culture* 24.3: 49–60.

Kim, L.S. 2001. "Sex and the Single Girl" in Post Feminism." *Television & New Media* 2.4 (Nov): 319–334.

Kirby, James T. 1978. *Media-made Dixie: The South in the American Imagination*. Baton Rouge: Louisiana State University Press.

Klein, Allison. 2006. *What Would Murphy Brown Do? How the Women of Prime Time Changed Our Lives*. Emeryville, CA: Seal.

Lauzen, Martha, David Dozier, and Nora Horan. 2008. "Constructing Gender Stereotypes through Social Roles in Prime-Time Television." *Journal of Broadcasting & Electronic Media* 52.2 (June): 200–214.

Lentz, Kirsten Marthe. 2000. "Quality versus Relevance: Feminism, Race and the Politics of the Sign in 1970s Television." *Camera Obscura* 15.43 (January): 44–93.

Levine, Lawrence W. 1993. "The Concept of the New Negro and the Realities of Black Culture." In *The Unpredictable Past: Explorations in American Cultural History*. Cambridge: Oxford University Press.

Lewit, Meghan. 2013. "Thank You for Being a Friend Hannah Horvath." *Salon* (February 13): http://www.salon.com/2013/02/18/thank_you_for_being_a_friend_hannah_horvath/

Lotz, Amanda D. 2002. "Televising Feminism: Postfeminist Discourse in the Post-Network Era." Diss., University of Texas.

Lotz, Amanda D. 2006. *Redesigning Women: Television After the Network Era*. Urbana: University of Illinois Press.

Lotz, Amanda D., and Sharon Marie Ross. 2004. "Toward Ethical Cyberspace Audience Research: Strategies for Using the Internet for Television Audience Studies." *Journal of Broadcasting & Electronic Media* 48.3: 501–512.

Macey, Deborah Ann. 2008. "Ancient Archetypes in Modern Media: A Comparative Analysis of *The Golden Girls*, *Living Single*, and *Sex and the City*." Diss., University of Oregon.

MacKinnon, Catharine A. 1989. *Toward a Feminist Theory of the State*. Cambridge: Harvard University Press.

MacKinnon, Catharine A. 1988. "Desire and Power: A Feminist Perspective." In Cary Nelson and Lawrence Grossberg, eds., *Marxism and the Interpretation of Culture*. Urbana: University of Illinois Press.

Markham, Annette N., and Nancy K. Baym. 2009. *Internet Inquiry: Conversations About Method*. Thousand Oaks, CA: Sage.

Maxwell, Richard, ed. 2001. *Culture Works: The Political Economy of Culture*. Minneapolis: University of Minnesota.

McCarver, Virginia. 2011. "The Rhetoric of Choice and 21st Century Feminism: Online Conversations about Work, Family and Sarah Palin." *Women's Studies in Communication* 34.1: 20–41.

McDonald, Myra. 1995. *Representing Women: Myths of Femininity in the Popular Media*. London: Edward Arnold.

McKee, Robert. 1997. *Story: Substance, Structure, Style, and the Principles of Screenwriting*. New York: HarperCollins.

McPherson, Tara. 1993/94. "Disregarding Romance and Refashioning Femininity: Getting Down and Dirty with the *Designing Women*." *Camera Obscura* 32: 102–123.

McPherson, Tara. 2003. *Reconstructing Dixie: Race, Gender, and Nostalgia in the Imagined South*. Durham: Duke University Press.

McRobbie, Angela. 2004. "Post-Feminism and Popular Culture." *Feminist Media Studies* 4.3: 255–264.

Means Coleman, Robin. 1998. *African American Viewers and the Black Situation Comedy: Situating Racial Humor*. New York: Garland.

Meehan, Diana M. 1983. *Ladies of the Evening: Women Characters of Prime-Time Television*. Metuchen, NJ: Scarecrow Press.

Meehan, Eileen R., and Jackie Byars. 2000. "Telefeminism: How Lifetime Got Its Groove, 1984–1997." *Television & New Media* 1.1: 33–51.

"Memories of Rue McClanahan and *The Golden Girls* as Gay Icons." 2010. *TV Squad*, June 6. Online.

Monaco, Jeanette. 2010. "Memory Work, Auto ethnography and the Construction of Fan-Ethnography." *Participations: Journal of Audience & Reception Studies*. 7.1 (May): 102–142.

Montemurro, Beth. 2004. "Charlotte Chooses Her Choice: Liberal Feminism on Sex and the City." *The Scholar & Feminist Online*. 3.1. (Fall). Online.

Morgan, Joan. 1999. *When Chickenheads Come Home to Roost: My Life as a Hip Hop Feminist*. New York: Touchstone.

Nelson, Fred O. 1999. "Fabulous Female Foursomes." People's Choice, April 13. http://blog.peopleschoice.com/2012/04/13/fabulous-female-foursomes/

Negra, Diane, and Yvonne Tasker. 2005. "In Focus: Postfeminism and Contemporary Media Studies." *Cinema Journal* 44:107–110.

NIV. n.d. *Holy Bible*. New International Version. Colorado Springs: Biblica. Online. https://www.biblegateway.com/

Owen, Susan, Sarah R. Stein, and Leah R. Vande Berg. 2007. *Bad Girls: Cultural Politics and Media Representations of Transgressive Women*. New York: Peler Long International Academic Publishers.

Penn, Ray. 1990. "What Designing Women Do Ordain: The Women's Ordination Movement Comes to Prime-

Time." *Studies in Popular Culture*. 13.1: 89–102.

Press, Andrea. 1991. *Women Watching Television: Gender, Class, and Generation in the American Television Experience*. Philadelphia: University of Pennsylvania Press.

Press, Andrea, and Terry Strathman. 1993. "Work, Family and Social Class in Television Images of Women: Prime-Time Television and the Construction of Postfeminism." *Women and Language* 16.2: 7–27.

Rabinovitz, Lauren. 1999. "Ms.-Representation: The Politics of Feminist Sitcoms." In Mary Beth Harlovich and Lauren Rabinovitz, eds., *Television, History, and American Culture: Feminist Critical Essays*. Durham: Duke University Press.

Radway, Janet. 1991. *Reading the Romance: Women, Patriarchy and Popular Literature*. Chapel Hill: University of North Carolina Press.

Reid-Brinkley, Shanara R. 2008. "The Essence of Res(ex)pectability: Black Women's Negotiation of Black Femininity in Rap Music and Music Video." *Meridians: Feminism, Race, Transnationalism* 8.1: 236–260.

Richards, Helen. 2003. "Sex and the City: A Visible Flaneuse for the Postmodern Era?" *Continnum: Journal of Media & Cultural Studies* 17.2: 147–157.

Rose, Tricia. 1997. "Never Trust a Big Butt and a Smile." In Charlotte Brunsdon, Julie D'Acci, and Lynn Spigel, eds., *Feminist Television Criticism: A Reader*. New York: Oxford University Press.

Ross, S. M. 2005. "Talking Sex: Comparison Shopping Through Female Conversation in HBO's Sex and the City." In M. M. Dalton and L. R. Linder, eds., *The Sitcom Reader*. New York: State University of New York Press. 111–125.

Rowe, Kathleen K. 1997. "Roseanne: Unruly Woman as Domestic Goddess."

In Charlotte Brunsdon, Julie D'Acci and Lynn Spigel, eds., *Feminist Television Criticism: A Reader*. New York: Oxford University Press.

Sadler, William J., and Ekaterina V. Haskins. 2005. "Metonymy and the Metropolis: Television Show Settings and the Image of New York City." *Journal of Communication Inquiry* 29.3 (July): 195–216.

Sedgwick, Eve. 1990. *Epistemology of the Closet*. Oakland: University of California.

Sheppard, Samantha Noelle. 2007. "In a '90s Kind of World, I'm Glad I Got My Girls: African American Representation and Shifting Ideological Narratives in *Living Single*." Thesis, Dartmouth.

Sigel, Paul, ed. 1996. *Outsiders Looking In: A Communication Perspective on the Hill/Thomas Hearings*. Cresskill, NJ: Hampton Press.

Smith-Shomade, Beretta E. 2002. *Shaded Lives: African-American Women and Television*. New Brunswick, NJ: Rutgers.

Smith-Shomade, Beretta E. 2008. *Pimpin' Ain't Easy: Selling Black Entertainment Television*. New York: Routledge.

Spangler, Lynn. 1996. "Designing the Hearings on Designing Women: Creative and Business Influences on Content." In Paul Siegel, ed., *Outsiders Looking In: A Communication Perspective on the Hill/Thomas Hearings*. Cresskill, NJ: Hampton Press.

Spangler, Lynn. 2003. *Television Women from Lucy to Friends: Fifty Years of Sitcoms and Feminism*. Westport, CT: Praeger.

Spigel, Lynn. 2009. *TV by Design: Modern Art and the Rise of Network Television*. Chicago: University of Chicago.

Springer, Jennifer Thorington. 2008. "'Roll It Gall': Alison Hinds, Female Empowerment, and Calypso." *Meridians: Feminism, Race, Transnationalism* 8.1: 93–129.

Springer, Kimberly. 2008. "Divas, Evil Black Bitches, and Bitter Black Women: African American Women in Postfeminist and Post-Civil-Rights Popular Culture." In Charlotte Brunsdon and Lynn Spigel, eds., *Feminist Television Criticism: A Reader*, 2d ed. New York: Open University Press.

Stabile, Carol. 1995. "Feminism Without Guarantees: The Misalliances and Missed Alliances of Postmodernist Social Theory." In Antonio Callari, Stephen Cullenberg and Carole Biewener, eds., *Marxism in the Postmodern Age: Confronting the New World Order*. New York: Guilford Press.

Stephens, Dionne, and April Few. 2007. "Hip Hop Honey or Video Ho: African Preadolescents' Understanding of Female Sexual Scripts in Hip Hop Culture." *Sex Cult* 11.4: 48–69.

Stephens, Dionne, and Layli Phillips. 2003. "Freaks, Gold Diggers, Divas, and Dykes: The Sociohistorical Development of Adolescent African American Women's Sexual Scripts." *Sexuality and Culture* 7.1: 3–47.

Stillion Southard, Belinda A. 2008. "Beyond the Backlash: Sex and the City and Three Feminist Struggles." *Communication Quarterly* 56.2 (May): 149–167.

Sullivan, Patricia A. and Steven R. Goldzwig. 1996. "'Women's Reality' and the Untold Story: Designing Women and the Revisioning of the Thomas/Hill Hearings." In Paul Siegel, ed. *Outsiders Looking In: A Communication Perspective on the Hill/Thomas Hearings*. Cresskill, NJ: Hampton Press.

Swartz-Karuaihe, Umbiroo A. 1997. "Is Light Still Right? The Perception of Light-Skinned Black Women versus Dark-Skinned women in the 1990s Situation Comedies *Living Single* and *Family Matters*." M.S. Thesis, University of Tennessee.

Swift, Jonathan. 1731. "A Beautiful Young Nymph Going to Bed." *The Literature Network*. http://www.online-literature.com/swift/3507/. Online. Accessed September 23, 2014.

Tropp, Laura. 2006. "'Faking a Sonogram': Representations of Motherhood on Sex and the City." *Journal of Popular Culture* 39.5: 861–877.

Vavrus, Mary D. 2000. "From Women of the Year to 'Soccer Moms': The Case of the Incredible Shrinking Women." *Political Communication* 17.2: 193–213.

Wee, Valerie. 2008. "Teen Television and the WB Television Network." In Sharon Marie Ross and Louisa Ellen Stein, eds., *Teen Television: Essays on Programming and Fandom*. Jefferson, NC: McFarland.

Williams, Linda. 2004. "Why I Did Not Want to Write This Essay. *Signs: Journal of Women in Culture and Society* 30.1: 1264–1271.

Winch, Alison. 2012. "We Can Have It All: The Girlfriend Flick." *Feminist Media Studies* 12.1: 69–82

Wollstonecraft, Mary. 1996 [1792]. *A Vindication of the Rights of Women*, 2d ed. Mineola, NY: Dover.

York, Ashley Elaine. 2010. "From Chick Flicks to Millennial Blockbusters: Spinning Female-Driven Narratives into Franchises." *The Journal of Popular Culture* 43.1: 3–25.

Zayer, Linda Tuncay, et. al. 2012. "Consumption and Gender Identity in Popular Media: Discourses of Domesticity, Authenticity, and Sexuality." *Consumption Markets & Culture* 4.15: 333–357.

Zook, Kristal Brent. 1994. "How I Became Prince of a Town Called Bel Air: Nationalist Desire in Black Television." Diss., University of California.

Zook, Kristal Brent. 1999. *Color by FOX: The FOX Network and the Revolution in Black Television*. Oxford: Oxford University Press.

Television Series, Films, and Scripts

Akil, Mara Brock, exec. prod. 2000–2008. *Girlfriends*. Hollywood: CBS and Paramount.

Bloodworth-Thomason, Linda, creator. 1986–1993. *Designing Women*. New York: Sony Home Entertainment.

Bowser, Yvette Lee, exec. prod. 1993–1998. *Living Single*. Burbank, CA: Warner Bros.

Harris, Susan. (Creator). (1995–1992). *The Golden Girls*. [TV Series] Burbank: Buena Vista Home Entertainment, Inc., and Touchstone Television.

King, Michael. *Sex and the City: The Movie*. Script. http://www.imsdb.com/scripts/Sex-and-the-City.html. Online 2008.

Martin, Suzanne, creator. 2010–present. *Hot in Cleveland*. New York: TV Land.

Sex and the City Transcripts. http://www.satctranscripts.com/. Online. 2008.

Star, Darren, exec. prod. 1998–2004. *Sex and the City*. New York: HBO.

Wade, Kevin, exec. prod. 2008. *Cashmere Mafia*. New York: Sony Home Entertainment.

Blogs and Message Boards

designingwomenonline.com.

ew.com.

imdb.com.

racialicious.com.

"Sitcoms and Other Yucky Stuff," tvwop.com.

topix.com.

tv.com.

Index

Index